THE
SELECTED
POETRY
OF

RAINER MARIA
RILKE

THE
SELECTED
POETRY
OF

RAINER MARIA
RILKE

EDITED
AND TRANSLATED
BY STEPHEN MITCHELL

WITH AN
INTRODUCTION BY
ROBERT HASS

VINTAGE BOOKS
A DIVISION OF RANDOM HOUSE
NEW YORK

To Robert L. Mitchell

First Vintage Books Edition, January 1984

Introduction copyright © 1982 by Robert Hass.

Some of these translations first appeared in the following
periodicals: *American Poetry Review, Kenyon Review, New York
Review of Books, Occident, Paris Review, The Ten Directions,
Threepenny Review, Zero.*

*Grateful acknowledgment is made to the following for permission to
reprint previously published material:*

Bechtle Verlag (Munich): Excerpts from Rainer Maria Rilke's
Briefwechsel mit Benvenuta, edited by Magda von Hattingberg

Harper & Row, Publishers, Inc.: "Sometimes a man stands up"
(p. 49) from *Selected Poems of Rainer Maria Rilke*. A Translation
from the German and Commentary by Robert Bly. Copyright ©
1981 by Robert Bly. Reprinted by permission of the publisher.

Library of Congress Cataloging in Publication Data
Rilke, Rainer Maria, 1875-1926.
The selected poetry of Rainer Maria Rilke. Reprint. Originally
published: New York:
Random House, 1982.
English and German.
Includes bibliographical references and index.
I. Mitchell, Stephen. II. Title.
[PT2635.165A2525 1984]   831'.912   83-47799
ISBN 0-394-71636-1

CONTENTS

LOOKING FOR RILKE

Last fall, in Paris, a friend promised to take me to the café, not far from Rue Monsieur-le-Prince, where Rilke was said to have breakfasted in the early years of the century when he was working as Rodin's secretary. I was glad for the pilgrimage because, of all poets, Rilke is the hardest to locate in a place. He was born a year after Robert Frost, in 1875, a little too soon to be a young modernist, and the dissimilarity between his work and Frost's is so great that the fact does not help to anchor for me a sense of his life. The house where he had lived in Prague as a child cannot be seen; it was destroyed during the war. Besides, Prague—"that, God forgive me, miserable city of subordinate exist-ences," he had written—seemed to explain very little. In his childhood, it was the capital of Bohemia. Rilke's family belonged to the German-speaking minor-ity that formed the city's professional class in those years. He was insulted once to be called a German, and, when the speaker corrected himself, "I meant, Austrian," Rilke said, "Not at all. In 1866, when the Austrians entered Prague, my parents shut their windows." He had a lifelong sense of his own homeless-ness.

Anyway, Rilke came to hate his native city. His father was a failed army officer who became a petty clerk for the railroad. His mother, a complicated woman, cold and fervent, driven alternately by a hunger for good society and by pious Roman Catholicism, was an affliction to him. There was probably nothing more suffocating than the life of a genteel, aspiring European house-hold of the late nineteenth century in which failure brooded like a boarder who had to be appeased, or like the giant cockroach which was to appear in another Prague apartment in 1915. All his life Rilke carried that suffocation inside him; and it was very much on my mind because I had just been reading Stephen Mitchell's fresh, startlingly Rilkean translations of the poems. Here, finally, was a Rilke in English that would last for many generations. Walking through European cities with Mitchell's Rilke in my ear, trying to see with Rilke's eyes, I could begin to feel in the new downtowns, in the old city squares like stage sets with their baroque churches by the rivers and restored fortresses on the hills, the geography of that suffocation; it flares in the bril-liant anger of the *Duino Elegies*—in the Fourth, for example, where the im-ages that the world presents to him seem so much like a bad play that he swears he'd prefer a real puppet theater and imagines himself as a kind of demented critic who refuses to leave the theater until *something* happens:

Who has not sat, afraid, before his heart's
curtain? It rose: the scenery of farewell.
Easy to recognize. The well-known garden,
which swayed a little. Then the dancer came.
Not *him*. Enough! However lightly he moves,
he's costumed, made up—an ordinary man
who hurries home and walks in through the kitchen.
　　I won't endure these half-filled human masks;
better, the puppet. It at least is full.
I'll put up with the stuffed skin, the wire, the face
that is nothing but appearance. Here. I'm waiting.
Even if the lights go out; even if someone
tells me, "That's all"; even if emptiness
floats toward me in a gray draft from the stage;
even if not one of my silent ancestors
stays seated with me, not one woman, not
the boy with the immovable brown eye—
I'll sit here anyway. One can always watch.

Or the Tenth, which envisions adult life as an especially tawdry carnival:

And the shooting-gallery's targets of prettified happiness,
which jump and kick back with a tinny sound
when hit by some better marksman. From cheers to chance
he goes staggering on, as booths with all sorts of attractions
are wooing, drumming, and bawling. For adults only
there is something special to see: how money multiplies, naked,
right there on stage, money's genitals, nothing concealed,
the whole action—educational, and guaranteed
to increase your potency . . .

This anger is probably part of the reason why the Elegies took ten years to complete. Rilke seems to have needed, desperately, the feeling of freedom which he found only in open, windy spaces—Duino, Muzot.

　　Wandering the empty Sunday-morning warren of streets off Boulevard St.-Michel, remembering how passionately Rilke had argued that the life we live every day is not life, I began to feel that looking for him in this way was actively stupid. There was another friend with us, a Dutch journalist named Fred, who was hungry and could not have cared less where Rilke ate breakfast. It was Fred who asked me if I knew the name of the woman who had loaned Rilke a room in Duino Castle. I did. She was Princess Marie von Thurn und Taxis-Hohenlohe. Trying to imagine what it would mean to have a name like that discouraged me from thinking I would ever understand Rilke's social milieu. It signified a whole class of people, seen at a distance like brilliantly colored birds, which had been wiped out by the First World War. Fred was in Paris to interview the Rumanian writer E. M. Cioran, who has been called "the last philosopher in Europe," about the new European peace movement. He pointed out to us the little garret, tucked like a pigeon coop under the roof of a building just off the Place de l'Odéon, where Cioran lives and works, as if he hoped that it would serve as a reasonable substitute, or would at least drag us back to the present. For it was clear that my friend Richard was also looking for something that the memory of his student days in Paris had stirred in him. He had lost some map in his head and felt personally anxious to retrieve it.

And it was clear that he wasn't going to find it. The transience of our most vivid experience is the burden of another of Rilke's complaints, the one in the Second Elegy where he compares humans with angels:

But we, when moved by deep feeling, evaporate; we
breathe ourselves out and away; from moment to moment
our emotion grows fainter, like a perfume. Though someone may tell us:
"Yes, you've entered my bloodstream, the room, the whole springtime
is filled with you . . ."—what does it matter? he can't contain us,
we vanish inside him and around him. And those who are beautiful,
oh who can retain them? Appearance ceaselessly rises
in their face, and is gone. Like dew from the morning grass,
what is ours floats into the air, like steam from a dish
of hot food. O smile, where are you going? O upturned glance:
new warm receding wave on the sea of the heart . . .
alas, but that is what we *are*. Does the infinite space
we dissolve into, taste of us then?

We abandoned the search, standing in front of a bar called King Kong, where Richard may have had breakfast in a former life of the establishment twenty years before and Rilke fifty years before that. The morning had begun to warm up, and the streets filled with people. Like many other young artists at the turn of the century, Rilke was drawn to Paris, and there, under the tutelage of Rodin, he began to be a great writer in the poems of *Neue Gedichte,* but he didn't altogether like the city, either its poverty or its glamour, both of which shocked him at first and saddened him later. It was hard, watching the street come alive with shopkeepers, students in long scarves, professors in sleek jackets solemnly lecturing companions of the previous night who walked shivering beside them, shoppers already out and armed with that French look of fanatic skepticism, not to set beside the scene the annihilating glimpse of the city in the Fifth Elegy:

> Squares, oh square in Paris, infinite showplace
> where the milliner Madame Lamort
> twists and winds the restless paths of the earth,
> those endless ribbons, and, from them, designs
> new bows, frills, flowers, ruffles, artificial fruits—, all
> falsely colored, —for the cheap
> winter bonnets of Fate.

The *Duino Elegies* are an argument against our lived, ordinary lives. And it is not surprising that they are. Rilke's special gift as a poet is that he does not seem to speak from the middle of life, that he is always calling us away from it. His poems have the feeling of being written from a great depth in himself. What makes them so seductive is that they also speak to the reader so intimately. They seem whispered or crooned into our inmost ear, insinuating us toward the same depth in ourselves. The effect can be hypnotic. When Rilke was dying in 1926—of a rare and particularly agonizing blood disease—he received a letter from the young Russian poet Marina Tsvetayeva. "You are not the poet I love most," she wrote to him. " 'Most' already implies comparison. You are poetry itself." And one knows that this is not hyperbole. That voice of Rilke's poems, calling us out of ourselves, or calling us into the deepest places in ourselves, is very near to what people mean by poetry. It is also what makes him difficult to read thoughtfully. He induces a kind of trance, as soon as the whispering begins:

> Yes—the springtimes needed you. Often a star
> was waiting for you to notice it. A wave rolled toward you
> out of the distant past, or as you walked

under an open window, a violin
yielded itself to your hearing. All this was mission.
But could you accomplish it? Weren't you always
distracted by expectation, as if every event
announced a beloved? (Where can you find a place
to keep her, with all the huge strange thoughts inside you
going and coming and often staying all night.)

Look at how he bores into us. That caressing voice seems to be speaking to the solitary walker in each of us who is moved by springtimes, stars, oceans, the sound of music. And then he reminds us that those things touch off in us a deeper longing. First, there is the surprising statement that the world is a mission, and the more surprising question about our fitness for it. Then, with another question, he brings us to his intimacy with our deeper hunger. And then he goes below that, to the still more solitary self with its huge strange thoughts. It is as if he were peeling off layers of the apparent richness of the self, arguing us back to the poverty of a great, raw, objectless longing.

This is why the argument of the Elegies is against ordinary life. Nor does it admit, as comfort, any easy idea of transcendence. "Who, if I cried out," the poems begin, "would hear me among the angels' hierarchies?" And the implicit answer is "No one." The great, stormy movements of those poems that seem to open out and open out really aim to close in, to narrow, to limit: to bring us up against the huge nakedness and poverty of human longing. He himself did not necessarily see this project of his art clearly. The Elegies were begun in 1912 and he did not complete them until 1922. The last of them, the Fifth, Seventh, Eighth, Ninth and Tenth, were not composed until after he was visited, suddenly, by the early *Sonnets to Orpheus*. In the first of them, he speaks of the mythic project of Orpheus:

And where there had been
just a makeshift hut to receive the music,

a shelter nailed up out of their darkest longing,
with an entryway that shuddered in the wind—
you built a temple deep inside their hearing.

It is that hut I want to call attention to. It is how Rilke saw our unformed inner lives—what he is always telling us about ourselves. He was not, in the end, interested in Paris. There is very little evidence that he was interested in breakfasts (except for one occasion when he first discovered in 1901 a California health food—Quaker Oats—and enthusiastically sent a packet to his future wife, with the recipe—Boil water, add oats.) He is always arguing against the world of days and habits, our blurred and blurring desires, "a makeshift hut to receive the music, / a shelter nailed up out of our darkest longing, / with an entryway that shuddered in the wind." This hut is the place one means when one says that Rilke wrote from a great depth in himself, and it is, I believe, what Marina Tsvetayeva meant when she said that Rilke *was* poetry. His work begins and ends with this conviction of an inner emptiness. It is what he says at the very beginning of the Elegies:

> Don't you know *yet*? Fling the emptiness out of your arms
> into the spaces we breathe; perhaps the birds
> will feel the expanded air with more passionate flying.

It even provides a clue to the odd fact that Rilke started writing in French just before his death. The only explanation for it he ever offered was to say that he found the language useful, since there was "in German no exact equivalent for the French word *absence,* in the great positive sense with which Paul Valéry used it." For what Orpheus has done is to turn the hut of our emptiness into something positive, into a temple, and that is also apparently what Rilke felt Valéry had done. The project of his poetry, then, was to find, in art, a way to transform the emptiness, the radical deficiency, of human longing into something else.

    This project was, to some extent, an inheritance—it recapitulates many currents in European poetry in the nineteenth century. The romantic poets at the beginning of it opened up the territory. Hölderlin spoke of a new poetry, almost overwhelmed by the discovery of an infinite human inwardness. And Wordsworth had said that poets had to give that inwardness a local habitation and a name. It is important to remember that when he said this he was still a political radical, sympathetic to the French revolution, who believed that the social and artistic projects were parallel, because after the failed European revolutions of 1848, those two projects were divorced. For Baudelaire, nature had become a temple where one only read symbolic meanings, and the poet, like an albatross, was understood to be hopelessly ungainly on the ground of social life and graceful only in the air. Poets trafficked with the infinite. In the work of Mallarmé, this led to a changed notion of poetry itself. As the poet pulled away from the social world the words in a poem pulled away from referential meaning. Poetry was an art near to music. It did not reach down to the mere world of objects. It made a music which lifted the traces of objects where they half survived in the referential meaning of words—street, apple, tree —toward a place where they lived a little in the eternal stillness of the poem. Something like this idea—it went by the name of symbolism—was inherited by the last, decadent or Parnassian, generation of nineteenth-century poets. The poem was to have as little commerce as possible with the middle-class world, and the poet, in his isolation, served only his art, which was itself in the service of beauty.

If there is any doubt that this ambience was felt by the young Rilke, it is dispelled by a description of him in provincial Prague at the age of twenty-one. "He went about," one of his contemporaries wrote, "wearing an old-world frock coat, black cravat, and broad-brimmed black hat, clasping a long-stemmed iris and smiling, oblivious of the passersby, a forlorn smile into ineffable horizons." His attachment to the role of decadent and aesthete was qualified, however, by his interest in Nietzsche, particularly Nietzsche's Zarathustra, who had given a name to the yearning place that the young poet had already hollowed out in himself: the death of God. And it was Nietzsche who had defined the task of art: God-making. This interest of Rilke's was intensified by one of the important events in his life; he met a remarkable older writer, Lou Andreas-Salomé. She was thirty-four at the time. When she was eighteen, Nietzsche had fallen in love with her and proposed marriage. It was already part of her legend that her refusal of him was responsible for the philosopher's derangement. Later, she would become an associate of Sigmund Freud's. In 1913 she brought Rilke, who was terrified by the idea of mental health, to a Psycho-analytic Congress and introduced him to Freud, an experience which issued in Rilke's own descent into what he called "the mother experience" in the Third Duino Elegy. But in 1899, she took the young poet for a lover and, in that year and the next, accompanied him on a pair of trips to Russia.

His first readable work, the prose Tales of God and The Book of Hours, comes out of his experience of Russia and Nietzsche and Lou. The poems are written, appropriately enough, in the persona of a young Russian monk. A young monk because that could stand for Rilke's sense of his own apprenticeship and for the God who he felt was only just coming into being. Russian because it was on this trip, in the immense open spaces of the Russian countryside and in the bell-ringing churches of old Moscow, that Rilke first discovered a landscape which he felt corresponded to the size and terror and hushed stillnesses of his own inner life. The poems themselves are a beginning—they already have the qualities of Rilke's mind and imagination, but formally they belong to the dreamy, musical mold of the symbolist lyric. This is a reason why, I think, they sometimes seem more interesting in English translation than they really are. Here is an example. To understand the point I'm trying to make, the reader without German has to attend to it anyway and try reading the poem out loud, noticing the tinkling regularity of the meter and the neat finality of the rhymes, *Abendbrot* and *tot, geht* and *steht.*

> Manchmal steht einer auf beim Abendbrot
> und geht hinaus und geht und geht und geht,—
> weil eine Kirche wo im Osten steht.
>
> Und seine Kinder segnen ihn wie tot.
>
> Und einer, welcher stirbt in seinem Haus,
> bleibt drinnen wohnen, bleibt in Tisch und Glas,
> so dass die Kinder in die Welt hinaus
> zu jener Kirche ziehn, die er vergass.

Here is the poem in the vigorous, unrhymed, unmetered translation of Robert Bly:

> Sometimes a man stands up during supper
> and walks outdoors, and keeps on walking,
> because of a church that stands somewhere in the East.
>
> And his children say blessings on him as if he were dead.
>
> And another man, who remains inside his own house,
> stays there, inside the dishes and in the glasses,
> so that his children have to go far out into the world
> toward that same church, which he forgot.

Rilke's theme is already present, the abandonment of ordinary life for the sake of a spiritual quest. And so is his intensity. Robert Bly has muted it, by having the father *stay* rather than *die* in the house, but in either case the poem insists that the spirit will have no rest until the quest is undertaken, which is probably Rilke's understanding of his relationship to his own father. But the poem has a feeling of being too neat, too pat, which disappears, I think, in the English translation. A way to hear this might be to look at an English poem on a similar theme. Yeats's "Lake Isle of Innisfree" is a little more luxuriant, but it has the same end-of-the-century music and the same desire to escape:

> I will arise and go now, and go to Innisfree,
> And a small cabin build there, of clay and wattles made:
> Nine bean-rows will I have there, a hive for the honeybee,
> And live alone in the bee-loud glade.

Imagine if you can a translation of this stanza into twentieth-century free verse:

> I'm going to get up now, and go west to Innisfree,
> and I'll build a small cabin there out of reeds and clay.
> I'll make nine rows of beans and a hive for honeybees
> and I'll live by myself in that bee-loud valley.

What goes are the wistfulness and the music. They are replaced by a sense of active will and specificity, which aren't really in the original poem.

There is something else to notice in this comparison. In both Yeats and Rilke, the spiritual search or the aim of art does not occur inside life, but somewhere else. For Yeats and his readers, Innisfree could stand for the wild naturalness of the west of Ireland and for Irish nationalism and for the elsewhere of symbolist art. In Rilke's poem, a comfortably symbolic "church in the East" does similar work. It is easy to see, biographically, how potent a symbol it was for him. It combined the experience of Russia, his Nietzschean spiritual strivings, his artistic vocation, and his first serious love affair. Heady stuff. But a church in the East is a long way from that tattered hut in the first Sonnet to Orpheus. In order to get there, Rilke had to descend into the terrible and painful sense of his own emptiness, which lay behind the hunger for the ideal. That, finally, is why *The Book of Hours* seems like apprentice work and why it seems so limited by the dexterity and gracefulness of its writing.

Rilke needed to think less about art as visionary recital and more about it as a practice. The next phase of his development gave him a chance to do that. It took him, almost directly upon his return from Russia, to Worpswede, an artists' colony in the fen country near Bremen. The atmosphere combined fresh air, the sensibility of the English arts-and-crafts movement, and landscape painting—it was here that Rilke developed his enthusiasm for Quaker Oats. The place brought him into contact with the plastic arts and with two women who played a large part in his life, the sculptor Clara Westhoff, whom he married, and the painter Paula Modersohn-Becker. The prose that grew out of these associations—"On Landscape," *Worpswede, Auguste Rodin*—deal with the visual arts and lent him both the title and the spirit of his next volume of poems, *The Book of Pictures.* It contains the poems through which many readers of Rilke first discover him. The religious tonality of *The Book of Hours* is gone, replaced by solitude and majestic sadness. These are the poems of invitation, of seductive intimacy, calling us away from ordinary life. *Wer du auch seist,* whoever you are, one of them begins, *am Abend tritt hinaus,* in the evening go outside, *aus deiner Stube,* out of your room, *drin du alles weisst,* where you know everything. The language is clear, calm, only slightly poetic. (The room, for example, is *Stube,* whereas Gregor Samsa suffers his domestic embarrassment in a more modern and neutral *Zimmer.*) Many of them are gorgeous, especially "Autumn Day," with the sad, rich cadence of its final lines:

> Whoever has no house now, will never have one.
> Whoever is alone will stay alone,
> will sit, read, write long letters through the evening,
> and wander on the boulevards, up and down,
> restlessly, while the dry leaves are blowing.

But it is possible to make an argument against these poems, to say that they are the first pleasant face of everything that is terrible and painful about human loneliness. Later, in the First Elegy, Rilke will say it: "Beauty is nothing but the beginning of terror . . ." Here, though, the poems—just slightly—tend to congratulate the poet and his reader for having feelings and experiencing beauty. Partly this was a matter of Rilke's temperament, but it is also partly a matter of symbolist aesthetics.

Let us locate the moment. Rilke arrived in Paris in 1902. His wife had been a student of Rodin's and through her he came to know the sculptor, then at the height of his fame, and eventually became his secretary. During this time, from 1902 to 1906, he worked on *The Book of Pictures,* but as early as 1903, another project, inspired by Rodin, was forming in his mind. What impressed him about Rodin was how hard he worked. Rilke's ideas of art had been based on the symbolist myth of solitary inspiration, in which the artist was a passive receptor of intimations of large spiritual realities. But Rodin *made things,* working hard for long hours with a great concentration of energy. And Rilke, following his example, began to think about a different kind of poem. He wanted to write poems, he said, "not about feelings, but about things he had felt." *Ding-Gedichte,* thing-poems, he called them, poems about looking at animals, people, sculptures, paintings, in which the focus was thrown off the lyrical speaker of the poem and onto the thing seen. From this experiment came *New Poems,* work done between 1903 and 1908.

And it is poetry of a different order. Phenomenal changes were in the air in the decade before the First World War. Apollinaire was also in Paris, writing the poems of *Alcools.* "Zone," in fact, with its twentieth-century freshness, seemed to be inventing the new age:

After all you are weary of this ancient world.

Shepherdess O Eiffel Tower your flock of bridges is bleating this morning.

You have had enough of living in a Greek and Roman antiquity.

In London, Ezra Pound was on the verge of writing the first imagist poem, a vision of the Paris Métro. Osip Mandelstam was also in Paris in 1906, an awkward high school boy with funny ears. He would return to Russia and write a manifesto in 1910, "The Morning of Acmeism," which declared that symbolism with its theurgy and its Gothic yearning had come to an end. Pablo Picasso had startled the world, though the world didn't know it yet, with his *Demoiselles d'Avignon. New Poems* marks Rilke's participation in this great shift in sensibility. But, in fact, he never made himself over into a modernist poet. His work came to have, through Rodin, a feeling of being actively made, but it does not have that modernist sense of the active and refreshing presence of the world. He was not deeply touched by the explosion of German expressionism in 1911. His Picasso is the painter of the pink and blue periods, as the Fifth of the Elegies shows, the painter of melancholy and isolated saltimbanques. It is possible to see him, for all these reasons, as the last symbolist. He takes a great deal from the eyes and the working methods of Rodin, but he takes it on his own terms. For all their objectivity, *Neue Gedichte* are profoundly inward poems.

Inward and almost savage. When Rilke began to look at things, the first thing he looked at was a caged animal. "The Panther" is a much celebrated poem. It is also a terrifying one. In it Rilke says something to himself that he hasn't quite said before; he discovers, looking at the big cat pacing behind the bars in the Paris zoo, that the world is not for him a series of symbols of the infinite but a cage. The shock of that discovery initiates the poem, which is half a self-portrait, half the recognition of some profound otherness, difference, emptiness, power in the animal he might have liked, ideally and comfortably, to become:

> His vision, from the constantly passing bars,
> has grown so weary that it cannot hold
> anything else. It seems to him there are
> a thousand bars; and behind the bars, no world.
>
> As he paces in cramped circles, over and over,
> the movement of his powerful soft strides
> is like a ritual dance around a center
> in which a mighty will stands paralyzed.
>
> Only at times, the curtain of the pupils
> lifts, quietly—. An image enters in,
> rushes down through the tensed, arrested muscles,
> plunges into the heart and is gone.

There is a second shock for me in those last lines—after all the concentration and furious accuracy in the articulation of the poem: nothing. The question is, Where does that image go? Or, to put it another way, What is in that animal's heart? The answer seems to be "Nowhere, nothing." Is that good or bad? Does the image disappear because the animal is so magnificently self-contained that he doesn't need it? Or does it die because he is encaged and can't use it? The answer seems to be "Both and neither." The poem doesn't answer a philosophical question, it presents or enacts a moment at which a will pacing around a center sees at the center nothing, and renders in that recognition a sudden, not at all pleasant, sense of liberation. Analogous poems may be helpful. The ones that occur to me are Buddhist. Basho, walking in the mountains in a storm, wrote: "Hailstones / on the rocks / at Stony Pass." Hard things striking hard things in a hard place: it is a poem about nothingness. Again, famously, he wrote the poem that invented haiku: "An old pond; / frog jumps in, / plop." Where did the frog go? Where the image taken in by the panther went. Rilke, deciding to write poems about really seeing, wrote immediately a poem about the exhaustion of seeing. It took him to a much deeper place, and stripped away entirely the lyrical ego of his early poems.

That ego did not, of course, disappear. "Archaic Torso of Apollo" is an agonizingly personal poem. Like "The Panther," it begins from a sense of shock. In this case, the feeling occurs because, looking at a mutilated piece of old Greek sculpture, he suddenly realizes that it is more real than he is—not more perfect but more real. It is even, as he sees it, sexually more alive than he is:

> We cannot know his legendary head
> with eyes like ripening fruit. And yet his torso
> is still suffused with brilliance from inside,
> like a lamp, in which his gaze, now turned to low,
>
> gleams in all its power. Otherwise
> the curved breast could not dazzle you so, nor could
> a smile run through the placid hips and thighs
> to that dark center where procreation flared.
>
> Otherwise this stone would seem defaced
> beneath the translucent cascade of the shoulders
> and would not glisten like a wild beast's fur:
>
> would not, from all the borders of itself,
> burst like a star: for here there is no place
> that does not see you. You must change your life.

Stephen Mitchell's translation, here as elsewhere, renders exactly Rilke's own sculptural articulation, so that it becomes possible for English readers to sense his inner, stylistic development. Formally, the main difference between *New Poems* and Rilke's earlier work lies in the way he uses the poetic line. In the earlier poems, the line and the image or idea contained in the sentence tend to coincide, as they do in this English version:

> Whoever has no house now, will never have one.
> Whoever is alone will stay alone.

There is a pause at the line-end, and this pause is emphasized by the rhyme. In other words, the ideal paradigm of the poetic form is always emphasized. This physical fact about a poem can express many different things, but in Rilke it tends to say, beneath whatever is actually being said, Look at how the movement of my thought, this flow of tender and melancholy images, is attuned to an ideal shape. There is a sense that the poet, making the poem, is loyal to the ideal rather than the actual. But in "Archaic Torso," the thought tends to muscle past the line-end to complete itself in a restless pause at mid-line, and then plunge onward. Sculpture provides an analogy. The sculpture of a human body is made up of certain clearly separate parts—the head, the tapering mass of the torso, etc. The delight of looking at it, the presence in it of the energy of its making, comes from the way the parts are seen to be related to one another, which is the sculptor's particular energy of seeing and creating. In this poem, the rhymes are still present *(Bug/trug, Drehen/gehen)*, but they are de-emphasized by the sinuous movement of the lines. The poem, as a result, seems absolutely given over to the moment of its making. That is why the torso in the poem, luminous, animal, radiantly sexual, feels so present and alive. It is also why, throughout *New Poems,* one feels that Rilke has made himself over into a twentieth-century poet.

And yet this is what would seem to be a classic nineteenth-century poem: a sonnet about the ideal perfection of a statue. The mere description would have induced nausea in Apollinaire, or the impulse to hang a FOR RENT sign on the sculpture. What makes it more than its subject is partly the furious concentration with which the poem is made, but also the persistent strangeness of Rilke's imagination. Characteristically, he begins with what is absent. "We cannot know his legendary head . . ." Absence, more mysterious and hopeful to Rilke than any presence, introduces immediately the idea of growth. *"Darin die Augenäpfel reiften"*—in which the eye-apples ripened—is the rather startling phrase in German. The ripening that he has imagined passes like light into the body of the Apollo where it becomes both animal and star, animal because it is at home in the world in a way that human beings are not, star because it also belongs to what is distant from us and perfected. In this poem the speaker stands at a midpoint between them, neither one thing nor the other. That is when the eyes come back into the poem. "For here there is no place that does not see you." It is an odd thing to say. What is seeing him is not there, and yet has passed everywhere into the torso, so that it makes the speaker visible—in the absence of those qualities in himself. That is what, for me, has always made the shock of the poem's last, imperative sentence almost sickening in its impact. There is a pause in that last line: *"die dich nicht sieht. Du musst . . ."* It is as if the brief silence—the heart-pause, Rilke calls it elsewhere—between *sieht* and *Du* were a well that filled suddenly with a tormented sense of our human incompleteness, from which leaps the demand for transformation: "You must change your life." The difference between this and other similar poems is that Rilke does not praise the perfection of art, he suffers it.

But there is also a counter-emotion in the poem, just because the poet is being seen. Rilke had already spoken of this in a little essay, "Concerning Landscape," that he wrote in 1902:

> To see landscape thus, as something distant and foreign, something remote and unloving, something entirely self-contained, was necessary, if it was ever to be a medium and an occasion for an autonomous art; for it had to be distant and very different from us, if it was to be capable of becoming a redemptive symbol for our fate. It had to be almost hostile in its sublime indifference, if it was to give a new meaning to our existence . . . For we began to understand Nature only when we no longer understood it; when we felt that it was the Other, indifferent toward men, which has no wish to let us enter, then for the first time we stepped outside of Nature, alone, out of the lonely world.

He takes up this theme again, more forcibly and strangely, in a wonderful essay about dolls (*Puppe,* in German—the noun is feminine) written in 1914:

> . . . in a world in which fate and even God himself have become famous above all because they answer us with silence . . . the doll was the first to inflict on us that tremendous silence (larger than life) which later kept breathing on us out of space, whenever we came to the limits of our existence. It was facing the doll, as it stared at us, that we experienced for the first time (or am I mistaken?) that emptiness of feeling, that heart-pause, in which we could have vanished . . .

"Archaic Torso" reflects the attitude of the essay on landscape, whereas the fury and dark comedy of "Some Reflections on Dolls" is the tone of the early Elegies. Taken together they suggest the underlying rhythm of the thing-poems.

Looking at things, he saw nothing—or, to paraphrase Wallace Stevens, "the nothing"—that arose from his hunger for a more vivid and permanent world. He had a wonderful eye for almost anything he really looked at, dogs, children, qualities of light, works of art; but in the end he looked at them in order to take them inside himself and transform them: to soak them in his homelessness and spiritual hunger so that when he returned them to the world, they were no more at home in it than he was, and gave off unearthly light. In this dialectic, everything out there only drives him deeper inside himself, into the huge raw wound of his longing and the emptiness that fueled it. It is true that the Apollo answers him. Art answers him, but only by intensifying his desire to pass over into the country it represents. This explains to me why I have always thought that Rilke's attitude toward art seemed slightly mortuary, Poe-esque. There is something vaguely necrophiliac about it. "Archaic Torso" is primarily, stunningly, a poem about the hunger for life, but its last, darkest echoes carry the suspicion that its true provenance is death.

I think I should report that when I first recognized this impulse in these poems, I had a very strong, divided response. It made me feel, on the one hand, that Rilke was a very great poet, that he had gone deeper than almost any poet of his age and stayed there longer, and I felt, on the other hand, a sudden restless revulsion from the whole tradition of nineteenth- and early-twentieth-century poetry, or maybe from lyric poetry as such, because it seemed, finally, to have only one subject, the self, and the self—which is not life; we know this because it is what in us humans stands outside natural processes and says, "That's life over there"—had one subject, the fact that it was not life and must, therefore, be death, or if not death, death's bride, or if not death's bride, its lover and secret. It is not only that this portrait of the self's true dialectic has terrifying implications for our age—implications which the reader can conjure by imagining my friend Fred in his battered journalist's trenchcoat patiently interviewing the last philosopher in Europe on the prospects for our imminent and total extermination while the young on Boulevard St.-Michel dye their hair turquoise, dress in black, and wear buttons that say, "No Future" (so much for finding the Rilke of 1908)—but that it also has the effect of making my own self seem like a disease to me. This is very much a case of blaming the messenger. Rilke has clearly not abandoned the symbolist quest for the absolute in *New Poems,* he has dragged it, like a sick animal, into the twentieth century and brought it alive before us.

What about human relationships? They are more or less what we mean by life, once nature and art have been disposed of. Rilke had marked views on the subject. The short version is that he thought they were distraction and evasion. The purest creatures of his imagination, the angels of the Elegies, don't need relationship because they are complete as they are. They are *"mirrors,* which scoop up the beauty that has streamed from their face / and gather it back, into themselves, entire." In a late poem about childhood, he pictures a child at home by himself, beginning to feel his strange solitariness in the world. Then his parents come home and ruin everything. And in his version of the story of the prodigal son, the young man leaves home because he couldn't stand the fact that people loved him there, because what that really meant was that they wanted him to be their mirrors. "In their eyes he could see observation and sympathy, expectation, concern; in their presence he couldn't do anything without giving pleasure or pain. But what he wanted in those days was that profound indifference of heart which sometimes, early in the morning, in the fields, seized him with such purity . . ." And there is his version of the story of Orpheus and Eurydice. As he tells it, Eurydice is lucky to be in the underworld, where she is finally complete. She is not full of that hungry emptiness that made her open to love. "Her sex had closed / like a young flower at nightfall." And, in Rilke's version, Orpheus wants to ruin that, out of his need for her, and bring her back into the transitory world. But she is "no longer that man's property," and when Orpheus turns around to look at her, she is saved. The poem is stranger and more beautiful than this summary conveys, and the translation is one of Stephen Mitchell's triumphs.

The most extraordinary poem Rilke ever wrote on this theme is the "Requiem" of 1908. Its occasion was the death of his friend, one of the great German painters of the early part of the century, Paula Modersohn-Becker. Rilke met her, as we have seen, with Clara Westhoff at Worpswede, and he seems to have fallen in love with them both. Shortly after Paula became engaged to the painter Otto Modersohn, Rilke proposed marriage to Clara. They lived together only for a year or so, long enough to have a child and for Rilke to discover his unsuitability for domestic life. After that, they decided to give themselves the freedom they felt they needed as artists. Paula's life with Otto Modersohn had a different outcome. He was the director of Worpswede, a much more famous painter than she, and her life in his shadow became filled with domestic tasks. Eventually, she took a year off and went to Paris to be by herself and paint. During that year she was importuned with letters from her husband and her parents, urging her to return to Germany and take up the duties of a wife. Almost as soon as she did so, she became pregnant, and in the winter of 1907 she gave birth to a child and died shortly afterward. She is a very moving and original painter. Rilke, though he loved her company in the year at Worpswede and talked to her long hours about the idea of art (he wrote letters to Clara, one biographer observed, and poems to Paula), seems not to have understood her work while she was alive. It was apparently in the summer after her death, when he attended the Cézanne retrospective in Paris, that he realized, looking at Cézanne's late work, what a great painter she had been. Her death was a profound shock to him. "It stood in front of me," he wrote to a friend, "so huge and close that I could not shut my eyes." "Requiem" was written in the fall of that year. It was begun, appropriately enough, on the eve of All Hallows.

Part of its appeal is that it is so raw and personal a poem. It is not Rilke onstage, not the great necromancer of the Elegies with the seductive voice and the breathtaking shifts of argument which leap from image to surprising image. This poem, written in blank-verse paragraphs, proceeds in bursts: it has the awkwardness of grief, which seems to exhaust itself and then breaks out again. It is also full of awkward ideas, contrary emotions. For all these reasons, it is a poem that is probably more revealing and less self-preoccupied than anything else Rilke ever wrote. The opening lines address Paula's ghost. The anxiety that they express is not feigned.

> I have my dead, and I have let them go,
> and was amazed to see them so contented,
> so soon at home in being dead, so cheerful,
> so unlike their reputation. Only you
> return; brush past me, loiter, try to knock
> against something, so that the sound reveals
> your presence. Oh don't take from me what I
> am slowly learning. I'm sure you have gone astray
> if you are moved to homesickness for anything
> in this dimension. We transform these Things;
> they aren't real, they are only the reflections
> upon the polished surface of our being.

The fascination of these opening lines is the depth of Rilke's identification of art with death. I should confess that it is what put me off reading the poem for many years. It seemed like the poet at his most morbid and talky. It was not until this brilliant translation by Stephen Mitchell taught me to hear the nakedness of the voice in which the poem is spoken that I could even get through it. And when I did, it stunned me. Still, it is very peculiar: this is an Orpheus talking Eurydice *back down* into the underworld, telling her how wonderful it is to be dead:

> . . . that you too were frightened, and even now
> pulse with your fear, where fear can have no meaning;
> that you have lost even the smallest fragment

of your eternity, Paula, and have entered
here, where nothing yet exists; that out there,
bewildered for the first time, inattentive,
you didn't grasp the splendor of the infinite
forces, as on earth you grasped each Thing . . .

The key to this is the idea of mirroring. He imagines the artist as a polished surface, disinterested (and, in that, unlike the face of a parent or a lover), which mirrors the world back to itself and, by wanting nothing of it, makes it real. This is how he sees Paula Becker's calm self-portraits:

And at last, you saw yourself as a fruit, you stepped
out of your clothes and brought your naked body
before the mirror, you let yourself inside
down to your gaze; which stayed in front, immense,
and didn't say: I am that; no: this is.
So free of curiosity your gaze
had become, so unpossessive, of such true
poverty, it had no desire even
for you yourself; it wanted nothing: holy.

I don't think Rilke ever made a plainer statement of what he wanted art to be: cessation of desire; a place where our inner emptiness stops generating that need for things which mutilates the world and turns it into badly handled objects, where it becomes instead a pure, active, becalmed absence:

And that is how I have cherished you—deep inside
the mirror, where you put yourself, far away
from all the world. Why have you come like this
and so denied yourself?

The stubbornness of Rilke's conviction—and the wholeness of his imagination—only dawns on us when we see, later in the poem, how he takes up the idea of Paula's pregnancy. Flawed, somehow, by her own desire or by her husband's possessiveness, she has, he imagines, broken the perfect circuit of mirroring energy in her painting:

Let us lament together that someone pulled you
out of your mirror's depths. Can you still cry?

> No: I see you can't. You turned your tears'
> strength and pressure into your ripe gaze,
> and were transforming every fluid inside you
> into a strong reality, which would rise
> and circulate, in equilibrium, blindly.
> Then, for the last time, chance came in and tore you
> back, from the last step forward on your path,
> into a world where bodies have their will.

This distrust of birth seems so strange in the twentieth century, so literal, that it is as if it were drawn from an ancient text, the Tibetan or Egyptian Book of the Dead; as if Paula were Pandora opening the box, initiating, through desire, the whole endless natural cycle of birth and death:

> Ah let us lament. Do you know how hesitantly,
> how reluctantly your blood, when you called it back,
> returned from its incomparable circuit?
> How confused it was to take up once again
> the body's narrow circulation; how,
> full of mistrust and astonishment, it came
> flowing into the placenta . . .

There is a personal subtext here, of course: Rilke's jealousy of Otto Modersohn. (How could you have married that man?) And a deeper and more troubling one than that. He has tried to imagine himself inside a woman's body because of his own identification with what is female.

This needs looking at. It is a famous fact of Rilke's childhood in that apartment in Prague that his mother, having lost a baby girl in the year before his birth, raised her baby son as a girl. She gave him a first name, René, which was sexually ambiguous (he changed it to Rainer after meeting Lou Andreas-Salomé), dressed him in beautifully feminine clothes, and called him, in coy games they played, "Miss." These practices ended when he went to school—the latter part of his schooling occurred at a particularly brutal military academy of his father's choosing. Far back in Rilke's childhood—and farther back than that, in his mother's unconscious wishes—there is a perfect little girl, brought into this world to replace a dead one.

This fact requires a second detour. The occasion of *The Sonnets to Orpheus* was the death of a young girl, Vera Knoop. She was the daughter of an

acquaintance of Rilke's. A gifted dancer as a young child, she developed a
glandular disease, which caused her to grow fat. She abandoned dance and turned
to the piano, which she also played beautifully, while becoming more and more
deformed, until her death at the age of nineteen. Orpheus, as we have seen, is
the figure in the First Sonnet. Vera is the figure in the Second:

> And it was almost a girl who, stepping from
> this single harmony of song and lyre,
> appeared to me through her diaphanous form
> and made herself a bed inside my ear.
>
> And slept in me. Her sleep was everything:
> the awesome trees, the distances I had felt
> so deeply that I could touch them, meadows in spring:
> all wonders that had ever seized my heart.
>
> She slept the world. Singing god, how was that first
> sleep so perfect that she had no desire
> ever to wake? See: she arose and slept.
>
> Where is her death now? Ah, will you discover
> this theme before your song consumes itself?—
> Where is she vanishing? . . . A girl, almost. . . .

The connection of this poem to "Requiem" seems clear enough. Rilke was
moved by the idea of young women artists because they represented his own
deepest psychic sources. And, as girls practicing an art, they are emblems of eros
in a kind of undifferentiated contact with being, before it has become sexuality
and located itself in the world. Paula, unlike Vera Knoop, lived to be a woman.
Almost all of Rilke's close friends were women. He was deeply sympathetic to
the conflict which the claims of art and family caused in a woman's life. When
those social claims seemed to kill Paula Becker, it confirmed his belief that life
was the enemy of art, that sexuality and the world were the enemies of eros
and eternity. It is for this reason that, in one of the strongest passages in the
poem, he lashes out against her marriage:

> For *this* is wrong, if anything is wrong:
> not to enlarge the freedom of a love

> with all the inner freedom one can summon.
> We need, in love, to practice only this:
> letting each other go. For holding on
> comes easily; we do not need to learn it.

This is very striking; and I don't think we deny its power by noticing that, as is so often the case in Rilke, he is teaching his readers something they probably need to know more than he does. All the evidence of his own life is that he fled relationships, that he was always attracted by the first flaring of eros and terrified of its taking root. What was hard for *him,* as Louise Glück has observed, was holding on; and she believes that there is a certain amount of bad faith in his pretending otherwise. It is certainly the case that he was not possessive, or tempted to be. He chose solitude, and took the grief of his own loneliness as his teacher.

This solitude sends him back, in the first Orpheus poem and in the dialectic of the *New Poems,* always to the ragged hut of his own inner emptiness. He did not trust relationships, but the truth was that he did not have much capacity for them either. Psychoanalysis is not to the point here; we all know enough about choosing solitude and then suffering loneliness not to imagine that because the details of Rilke's life are different from ours, his situation is aberrant and local. He has seen to it in his art that he can't be regarded as a case history. What one of his lovers said about him is what any reader of his poems would have guessed:

> His outcries of astonishment and admiration interrupted his partner's words. At the same time, I could not fend off the impression that basically they resolved themselves into monologues, or dialogues with an absent one—was it perhaps the angel? . . . In truth, he fulfilled himself with his own. Did he ever take pains, even in love, to see the partner as she was? Did he not usurp both roles?

It would be wrong to conclude from this, as some readers have, that Rilke was simply narcissistic, if we mean by that a person who looks lovingly into the shallow pool of himself. He was, if anything, androgynous. The term has come to stand for our earliest bi- or pan-sexuality, and this is not quite what I mean. Androgyny is the pull inward, the erotic pull of the other we sense buried in the self. Psychoanalysis speaks of the primary narcissism of infants, but in the sense in which we usually use that term, only an adult can be narcissistic. Rilke

—partly because of that girl his mother had located at the center of his psychic life—was always drawn, first of all and finally, to the mysterious fact of his own existence. His own being was otherness to him. It compelled him in the way that sexual otherness compels lovers.

I think this is why, in "Requiem" and in the Elegies, he has a (for me tiresome) reverence for unrequited love and writes about sexual love as if those given over to it were saints of a mistaken religion:

Lovers, gratified in each other, I am asking *you*
about us. You hold each other. Where is your proof?

When the Elegies were nearly complete in 1922, when the whole labor of bringing them into being was finally over, he added a passage at the end of the Fifth. It reads like a final, petulant, and funny exclamation point:

Angel!: If there were a place that we didn't know of, and there,
on some unsayable carpet, lovers displayed
what they never could bring to mastery here—the bold
exploits of their high-flying hearts,
their towers of pleasure, their ladders
that have long since been standing where there was no ground, leaning
just on each other, trembling,—and could *master* all this,
before the surrounding spectators, the innumerable soundless dead:
Would these, then, throw down their final, forever saved-up,
forever hidden, unknown to us, eternally valid
coins of happiness before the at last
genuinely smiling pair on the gratified
carpet?

I love the energy, the comic desperation of the writing. No one has ever composed a more eloquent indictment of fucking: if it is so great, why hasn't it catapulted all the dead directly into heaven, why is the world still haunted by the ghosts of so much unsatisfied desire? But I would guess that most people have known what it meant to be one of that "genuinely smiling pair." They have felt the dead go pouring into heaven. "Copulation," Baudelaire said, accurately but with a great deal of disdain, "is the lyric of the mob." Walt Whitman would have cheerfully agreed, would have added that it was, there-fore, what made the lyric—and politics—possible. Mostly, people experience the possibility of union with the other in their bodies, with other people. But it would seem that for Rilke this was not so. He defined love once as two solitudes that protect and border and greet each other. And though it is a moving statement, it leaves out the fury of that greeting. It makes people sound as if they were soap bubbles bouncing off one another, whereas each of those two solitudes is a charged field of its own energy, and when they meet, they give off brilliant sparks.

In any case, this is the answer to the question of Rilke's attitude toward human relationships. It is not that he was not involved, intensely and intimately, with other people. He was, all his life. But he always drew back from those relationships because, for him, the final confrontation was always with himself, and it is partly because he was such a peculiarly solitary being that his poems have so much to teach us. There are pleasures, forms of nourishment perhaps, that most people know and that he did not. What he knew about was the place that the need for that nourishment came from. And he knew how immensely difficult it is for us to inhabit that place, to be anything other than strangers to our own existence. To learn not to be a stranger is the burden of the *Duino Elegies*. It is what causes him, at the end of "Requiem," to take Paula's death inside in the way that she took the world and a child inside herself. It is an incredibly strange and moving moment, because he is asking her, almost, to impregnate him with her absence. Here is the prayer with which that poem ends:

> Do not return. If you can bear to, stay
> dead with the dead. The dead have their own tasks.
> But help me, if you can without distraction,
> as what is farthest sometimes helps: in me.

All of this wandering through Rilke's life should help a reader to hear clearly the many resonances of the cry that opens the *Duino Elegies*:

> Who, if I cried out, would hear me among the angels'
> hierarchies? and even if one of them pressed me
> suddenly against his heart: I would be consumed
> in that overwhelming existence. For beauty is nothing
> but the beginning of terror, which we still are just able to endure,
> and we are so awed because it serenely disdains
> to annihilate us. Every angel is terrifying.

> And so I hold myself back and swallow the call-note
> of my dark sobbing. . . .

Even when it has become familiar to us, this intensity of grief registers its shock. Not the world, the young man in Prague had vowed sixteen years before, an iris in his fist, but the infinite. Now he calls that vow back. In a stroke, he has leapt to the center of his imagination and cut out from under himself the ground of his own art. It is hard to know what is most breathtaking about the moment, the shock of self-understanding or the stifled cry.

The angels embody the sense of absence which had been at the center of Rilke's willed and difficult life. They are absolute fulfillment. Or rather, absolute fulfillment if it existed, without any diminishment of intensity, completely outside us. You feel a sunset open up an emptiness inside you which keeps growing and growing and you want to hold on to that feeling forever; only, you want it to be a feeling of power, of completeness and repose: that is longing for the angel. You feel a passion for someone so intense that the memory of their smell makes you dizzy and you would gladly throw yourself down the well of that other person, if the long hurtle in the darkness would then be perfect inside you: that is the same longing. The angel is desire, if it were not desire, if it were pure being. Lived close to long enough, it turns every experience into desolation, because beauty is not what we want at those moments, death is what we want, an end to limit, an end to time. And—it is hard to think of Rilke as ironic, as anything but passionately earnest, but the Elegies glint with dark, comic irony—death doesn't even want us; it doesn't want us or not want us. All of this has come clear suddenly in Rilke's immensely supple syntax. He has defined and relinquished the source of a longing and regret so pure, it has sickened the roots of his life. It seems to me an act of great courage. And it enacts a spiritual loneliness so deep, so lacking in consolation, that there is nothing in modern writing that can touch it. The company it belongs to is the third act of *King Lear* and certain passages in Dostoevsky's novels.

Only the first two poems came to him at Duino in the winter of 1912. But the conception of them—that there would be ten, that they would arrive somewhere—came in a flash with these first few lines. He wrote down the beginning of the last Elegy, "Someday, emerging at last from the violent insight, / let me sing out jubilation and praise to assenting angels," and made a start on several others, then the impulse died away. It is not surprising that it did. He had committed himself to taking all of his yearning inside himself, its beauty and destructive contradictions, everything he had seen—thrust of tower and cathedral, the watercolor sadness of the city embankments of European rivers, night, spring, dogs, plaintiveness of violins, as if he were swallowing *Malte*—and to integrate it somehow so that he could emerge praising. The project needed to gestate and he needed to live with his desolation. The record of the last years before the war is restless traveling, inability to write, makework, a little real work, discontent. Even his letters echo the decision of the First Elegy:

> I am sick to death of Paris, it is a city of the damned. I always knew that; but in the old days an angel interpreted their torments to me. Now I have to explain them to myself and I can find no decent elucidation.

It was going to cost him a great deal, but the gains were already great. The main one is the incredible fluidity of the early Elegies. It is as if, not having a place to stand, the author of these poems is everywhere. Really, they are the nearest thing in the writing of the twentieth century to the flight of birds. They dive, soar, swoop, belly up, loop over. Look again at a passage that I quoted earlier:

> But we, when moved by deep feeling, evaporate; we
> breathe ourselves out and away; from moment to moment
> our emotion grows fainter, like a perfume. Though someone may tell us:
> "Yes, you've entered my bloodstream, the room, the whole springtime
> is filled with you . . ."—what does it matter? he can't contain us,
> we vanish inside and around him. And those who are beautiful,
> oh who can retain them? Appearance ceaselessly rises
> in their face, and is gone. Like dew from the morning grass,
> what is ours floats into the air, like steam from a dish
> of hot food. O smile, where are you going? O upturned glance:
> new warm receding wave on the sea of the heart . . .
> alas, but that is what we *are*. Does the infinite space
> we dissolve into, taste of us then? . . .

The subject is the volatility of emotion; what is extraordinary is the volatility of the writing itself. Beginning with a communal *we,* it becomes a young woman addressing her lover, the lover she addresses, a man gazing at beautiful women, and then, moving from the expression of faces to dew on the grass to steam coming off food to waves receding from shore, leaps to a metaphor of space. This energy and freedom of movement become, in the long run, not just how the poem is written but what it is about. But it was ten years before that recognition was accomplished.

The narrative here becomes complicated. The facts are that Rilke moved from place to place before the war broke out. He was in Germany at the time and so was detained there, for the most part bored, passive, and unhappy. Then he wandered for three more years, from 1919 to 1922, before he settled in Switzerland. The Third Elegy—the Freud Elegy, if you will, or the one in which he uses what he had seen of psychoanalysis to construct an argument against sexuality as a home for desire—had been finished in Paris in 1913. Most of the Sixth, which he called the Hero Elegy, was written in the same year in Spain. It is an attempt to pursue the questions that end the Third, I think, and sits rather uneasily in its position in the final text. The Fourth was written in Germany during the war. It came in a burst of creative energy which ended very quickly because Rilke was drafted, a grim enough event for a man whose only permanent hatred was for the military academy of his adolescence. The poem seems almost to anticipate the event. It is one of his darkest, full of the atmosphere of the war years, though it is about other things—the father he could not please, the women he could not live with, the self he had chosen to inhabit which seemed to have no meaning but its own death. It is full of disgust with the obsessive scenery and the repetitive melodrama of his own heart, but it is also stubborn:

> am I not right
> to feel as if I *must* stay seated, must
> wait before the puppet stage, or, rather,
> gaze at it so intensely that at last,
> to balance my gaze, an angel has to come and
> make the stuffed skins startle into life.
> Angel and puppet: a real play, finally.

He can't get rid of the wish for the angel, but the puppet, one remembers from the essay on dolls, is akin to those wooden, wide-eyed creatures that teach us the indifference of the angels by receiving impassively the pure ardor of our childish affections. There is a glimpse of reconciliation here. At the end of the poem, with a glance at the war, he redefines his task:

> Murderers are easy
> to understand. But this: that one can contain
> death, the whole of death, even before

> life has begun, can hold it to one's heart
> gently, and not refuse to go on living,
> is inexpressible.

This brings us to Muzot and the winter of 1922. Rilke was forty-seven years old, settled in a small house in the Valais region. Suddenly, in less than a month, he finished the Elegies and wrote the fifty-nine *Sonnets to Orpheus.* It is fairly astonishing, not just because of the quantity and quality of work produced in so short a time, but because it represents a transformation of the terms of his art. Simply—as simply as he himself announces it in the First Sonnet —Orpheus replaces the angel:

> A tree ascended there. Oh pure transcendence!
> Oh Orpheus sings! Oh tall tree in the ear!
> And all things hushed. Yet even in that silence
> a new beginning, beckoning, change appeared.

This is a shudder of hearing and seeing. It is also almost giddy with pleasure —how that tall tree in the ear has offended literal-minded critics! Rilke had not written a poem that mattered to him in four years, he had written very little for almost twice that long. And now the inner music has begun again. What is happening in this poem is that he recognizes it and greets it.

It is possible to say something about what this means. If the angel is the personal demon of Rilke's inner life, it is also a figure for a very old habit of human spirituality, as old, at least, as the Vedic hymns. All dualisms spring from it, and all cult religions of death and resurrection. For Rilke, however, the angels were never hermetic knowledge. They were the ordinary idea, the one that belongs to children at home by themselves looking in the mirror, to lovers bewildered by the intensity of their feelings, to solitaries out walking after dinner: whenever our souls make us strangers to the world. Everyone knows that impulse—and the one that follows from it, the impulse to imagine that we were meant to be the citizens of some other place. It is from this sensation that the angels come into existence, creating in this world their ambience of pure loss. It is the ambience in which Rilke had moved and the one that Orpheus sweeps away.

He is, of course, a figure for poetry, as an energy that moves inside this world, not outside it. He is that emotion or imagination of estrangement as it returns to the world, moving among things, touching them with the knowledge of death which they acquire when they acquire their names in human language.

Through Orpheus, Rilke has suddenly seen a way to hack at the taproot of yearning and projection that produced the angels. It is a phenomenal moment, for announcing, as Nietzsche did, that God is dead is one thing—this was, after all, a relief, no more patriarch, no more ultimate explanation, which never made any sense in the first place, of human suffering—but to take the sense of abandonment which follows from that announcement, and the whole European spiritual tradition on which it was based, inside oneself and transform it there, is another. For once the angel is gone, once it ceases to exist as a primary term of comparison by which all human life is found wanting, then life itself becomes the measure and source of value, and the task of poetry is not god-making, but the creation and affirmation of the world.

The death of a young girl prompted this discovery, but it was the experience of hearing the music rise in himself to greet Vera Knoop's death and all of his own unassuageable grief, I think, that finally jarred Rilke loose. He *felt* the energy of life starting up out of death in this most profound and ordinary way. That is why Orpheus also represents more than poetry. He stands where human beings stand, in the middle of life and death, coming and going. And so Rilke is also able not only to greet his presence, but to accept his absence:

> Erect no gravestone to his memory; just
> let the rose blossom each year for his sake.
> For it *is* Orpheus. Wherever he has passed
> through this or that. We do not need to look
>
> for other names. When there is poetry,
> it is Orpheus singing. He lightly comes and goes.

From here, it is not far to the completed Elegies. The final breakthrough, I think, occurs in the Third Sonnet. Creature of habit, Rilke compares us with Orpheus and is again dismayed:

> A god can do it. But will you tell me how
> a man can penetrate through the lyre's strings?
> Our mind is split. And at the shadowed crossing
> of heart-roads, there is no temple for Apollo.

You can almost hear the music of the beauty of what we are not, cranking up again. But he resists, or leaps across. The last thing he had to give up was this seductive presentation in his poems of beautifully unsatisfied desire. And when that goes, as it does for a moment in the seventh line of this poem, we come to the untranslatable heart of Rilke's late poetry: *Gesang ist Dasein,* singing is being, or song is reality, the moment when the pure activity of being consciously alive is sufficient to itself:

> Song, as you have taught it, is not desire,
> not wooing any grace that can be achieved;
> song is reality. Simple, for a god.
> But when can *we* be real? When does he pour
>
> the earth, the stars, into us? Young man,
> it is not your loving, even if your mouth
> was forced wide open by your own voice—learn
>
> to forget that passionate music. It will end.
> True singing is a different breath, about
> nothing. A gust inside the god. A wind.

I love the way this moves. There is that second stutter after the discovery, "But when can *we* be real?" and then he lectures himself; and then he is simply taken up into the singing, an embrace altogether unlike the annihilating arms of the angel.

Rilke wrote the twenty-six poems of the first half of the *Sonnets* in less than four days. Then he turned to the Elegies and the change is immediately apparent. He began with the Seventh:

> Not wooing, no longer shall wooing, voice that has outgrown it,
> be the nature of your cry; but instead, you would cry out as purely as a
> > bird
> when the quickly ascending season lifts him up, nearly forgetting
> that he is a suffering creature and not just a single heart
> being flung into brightness, into the intimate skies. . . .

They culminate, for me, in the Ninth which, though it proceeds by self-questioning, is, like the First Sonnet, almost crazy with happiness. Listen:

> . . . when the traveler returns from the mountain-slopes into the valley,
> he brings, not a handful of earth, unsayable to others, but instead
> some word he has gained, some pure word, the yellow and blue

gentian. Perhaps we are *here* in order to say: house,
bridge, fountain, gate, pitcher, fruit-tree, window . . .
. . . .
Here is the time for the *sayable, here* is its homeland.
Speak and bear witness.
. . . .
Praise this world to the angel, not the unsayable one,
you can't impress *him* with glorious emotion; in the universe
where he feels more powerfully, you are a novice. So show him
something simple which, formed over generations,
lives as our own, near our hand and within our gaze
Tell him of Things. He will stand astonished; . . .
. . . .
Look, I am living. On what? Neither childhood nor future
grows any smaller . . .

The transformation here is complete. It is wonderful just to be able to watch
the world come flooding in on this poet, who had held it off for so long. Human
feeling is not so problematical here. It does not just evaporate; it flows through
things and constitutes them. And, in the deepest sense, it is not even to the point.
Feeling, after all, belongs to the angels. They are the masters of intensity. The
point is to show, to praise. Being human, the poem says, being in the world
is to be constantly making one's place in language, in consciousness, in imagination. The work, *"steige zurück in den reinen Bezug,"* is "to rise again into pure
relation." Singing *is* being. It creates our presence. This echoes his description
of Paula Becker painting, so absorbed that she was able to say *This is,* and it
foreshadows the last of the *Sonnets to Orpheus:*

whisper to the silent earth: I'm flowing.
To the flashing water say: I am.

The second part of the Sonnets, twenty-nine of them, came on the heels
of the Elegies. They are a sort of long suite of gratitude at having finished the
larger, darker poem. And though there are a few really terrible poems among
them—imprecations against the machine age in Kiplingesque meters—they are,
for the most part, very strange and subtle work, full of calm, like light circulating in water. Orpheus has mostly disappeared from them, as the angel disappeared from the Elegies. Vera Knoop is the central figure. She is also Eurydice
and, I would guess, that young girl who was Rilke's dream of his earliest self,

pure art, perfect attention, death. The Thirteenth Sonnet is central. He begins it by reminding himself again that the way to be here is to have already let go:

> Be ahead of all parting, as though it already were
> behind you, like the winter that has just gone by.
> For among these winters there is one so endlessly winter
> that only by wintering through it will your heart survive.

The next line is the remarkable one. It echoes and revises the common Christian prayer for the dead: *Wohn im Gott,* dwell in God:

> Be forever dead in Eurydice—more gladly arise
> into the seamless life proclaimed in your song.
> Here, in the realm of decline, among momentary days,
> be the crystal cup that shattered even as it rang.

I think that readers, to have the full force of this, must also hold in mind the Second Sonnet, where that young girl first appeared, making a bed inside his ear:

> And slept in me. Her sleep was everything:
> the awesome trees, the distances I had felt
> so deeply that I could touch them, meadows in spring:
> all wonders that had ever seized my heart.

> She slept the world. . . .

Earlier, I said that Rilke's project was the transformation of human longing into something else. Eurydice is that something else. She is Koré, Persephone, the ancient figure from vegetation myth, and she is also a figure for Rilke's own, peculiar psychology and the unfolding drama of his poems: mirror, dancer, flower, cup. She is the calm at the center of immense contradiction. Most of all, and most surprisingly, she is the Buddha of his "Buddha in Glory," the sweet kernel of the world, a positive emptiness from which death flows back into life. That is why the end of this poem so much resembles and contrasts with the stony moment at the end of "The Panther." Through Eurydice, it would seem (in the Thirteenth Sonnet), he is able to experience his own death, to add it to hers, and disappear with perfect equanimity:

Be—and yet know the great void where all things begin,
the infinite source of our inmost vibration,
so that, this once, you may give it your perfect assent.

To all that is used-up, and to all the muffled and dumb
creatures in the world's full reserve, the unsayable sums,
joyfully add your*self,* and cancel the count.

Sei—the German says—*und wisse zugleich des Nicht-Seins Bedingung.* It is
difficult to render those meanings created by adding one noun to another. Be
—and know at the same time Non-Being's condition. Or the Non-Being which
is the condition of Being. The nearest translation, perhaps, comes from the *Tao
Te Ching:*

The ten thousand things are born of being.
Being is born of non-being.

Eurydice has become the non-being from which being is born; he has planted
her, quietly, at the center of himself. In the peace that follows, and the tenderness, the ending of the poem is almost flippant: cancel the count.

Rilke lived for another five years past this moment. He wrote many more
poems, and the odd contradictions in his character persisted in his habits. He
maintained a fairly strict personal privacy and then devoted most of it to
voluminous social correspondence. One of the letters that he wrote during that
time is addressed to a young man who had asked for advice. "When I think
now of myself in my youth," Rilke writes, "I realize that it was for me
absolutely a case of having to go away at the risk of annoying and hurting. I
cannot describe to you our Austrian circumstances of that time . . . What I write
as an artist will probably be marked, to the end, by traces of that opposition
by means of which I set myself on my own course. And yet if you ask me, I
would not want *this* to be what emanated above all from my works. It is not
struggle and revolt, not the deserting of what surrounds and claims us that I
would wish young people to deduce from my writings, but rather that they
should bear in a new conciliatory spirit what is given, offered . . ." This is partly,
of course, the perpetual advice of middle age, but what a contrast to the
sometimes sanctimonious tone of *Letters to a Young Poet.* About his own work,
he is exactly right. It is everywhere marked by furious opposition. And if it is

the record of a man who wrestled with an angel, it is also the record of a very rare human victory.

All that really remained for him to do was to become his Eurydice. He set about the task scrupulously, specifying the churchyard at Raron near Muzot where he was to be buried, and even the gravestone, if it could be found, a very plain one, old and like his father's. He even wrote the small poem that became his epitaph:

> Rose, oh pure contradiction, joy
> of being No-one's sleep under so many
> lids.

Another shiver of pleasure. It is like the moment in "Song of Myself" when Walt Whitman says, ". . . look for me under your boot-soles." Rilke died on December 26, 1926, and was buried in the earth he had chosen.

—Robert Hass

FROM

THE BOOK
OF HOURS

(1905)

Ich bin, du Ängstlicher. Hörst du mich nicht
mit allen meinen Sinnen an dir branden?
Meine Gefühle, welche Flügel fanden,
umkreisen weiß dein Angesicht.
Siehst du nicht meine Seele, wie sie dicht
vor dir in einem Kleid aus Stille steht?
Reift nicht mein mailiches Gebet
an deinem Blicke wie an einem Baum?

Wenn du der Träumer bist, bin ich dein Traum.
Doch wenn du wachen willst, bin ich dein Wille
und werde mächtig aller Herrlichkeit
und ründe mich wie eine Sternenstille
über der wunderlichen Stadt der Zeit.

[I am, O Anxious One. Don't you hear my voice]

I am, O Anxious One. Don't you hear my voice
surging forth with all my earthly feelings?
They yearn so high that they have sprouted wings
and whitely fly in circles around your face.
My soul, dressed in silence, rises up
and stands alone before you: can't you see?
Don't you know that my prayer is growing ripe
upon your vision, as upon a tree?

If you are the dreamer, I am what you dream.
But when you want to wake, I am your wish,
and I grow strong with all magnificence
and turn myself into a star's vast silence
above the strange and distant city, Time.

Ich finde dich in allen diesen Dingen,
denen ich gut und wie ein Bruder bin;
als Samen sonnst du dich in den geringen
und in den großen giebst du groß dich hin.

Das ist das wundersame Spiel der Kräfte,
daß sie so dienend durch die Dinge gehn:
in Wurzeln wachsend, schwindend in die Schäfte
und in den Wipfeln wie ein Auferstehn.

[I find you, Lord, in all Things and in all]

I find you, Lord, in all Things and in all
my fellow creatures, pulsing with your life;
as a tiny seed you sleep in what is small
and in the vast you vastly yield yourself.

The wondrous game that power plays with Things
is to move in such submission through the world:
groping in roots and growing thick in trunks
and in treetops like a rising from the dead.

FROM

THE BOOK
OF PICTURES

(1902; 1906)

KLAGE

O wie ist alles fern
und lange vergangen.
Ich glaube, der Stern,
von welchem ich Glanz empfange,
ist seit Jahrtausenden tot.
Ich glaube, im Boot,
das vorüberfuhr,
hörte ich etwas Banges sagen.
Im Hause hat eine Uhr
geschlagen . . .
In welchem Haus? . . .
Ich möchte aus meinem Herzen hinaus
unter den großen Himmel treten.
Ich möchte beten.
Und einer von allen Sternen
müßte wirklich noch sein.
Ich glaube, ich wüßte,
welcher allein
gedauert hat,—
welcher wie eine weiße Stadt
am Ende des Strahls in den Himmeln steht . . .

LAMENT

Everything is far
and long gone by.
I think that the star
glittering above me
has been dead for a million years.
I think there were tears
in the car I heard pass
and something terrible was said.
A clock has stopped striking in the house
across the road . . .
When did it start? . . .
I would like to step out of my heart
and go walking beneath the enormous sky.
I would like to pray.
And surely of all the stars that perished
long ago,
one still exists.
I think that I know
which one it is—
which one, at the end of its beam in the sky,
stands like a white city . . .

HERBSTTAG

Herr: es ist Zeit. Der Sommer war sehr groß.
Leg deinen Schatten auf die Sonnenuhren,
und auf den Fluren laß die Winde los.

Befiehl den letzten Früchten voll zu sein;
gieb ihnen noch zwei südlichere Tage,
dränge sie zur Vollendung hin und jage
die letzte Süße in den schweren Wein.

Wer jetzt kein Haus hat, baut sich keines mehr.
Wer jetzt allein ist, wird es lange bleiben,
wird wachen, lesen, lange Briefe schreiben
und wird in den Alleen hin und her
unruhig wandern, wenn die Blätter treiben.

AUTUMN DAY

Lord: it is time. The huge summer has gone by.
Now overlap the sundials with your shadows,
and on the meadows let the wind go free.

Command the fruits to swell on tree and vine;
grant them a few more warm transparent days,
urge them on to fulfillment then, and press
the final sweetness into the heavy wine.

Whoever has no house now, will never have one.
Whoever is alone will stay alone,
will sit, read, write long letters through the evening,
and wander on the boulevards, up and down,
restlessly, while the dry leaves are blowing.

ABEND

Der Abend wechselt langsam die Gewänder,
die ihm ein Rand von alten Bäumen hält;
du schaust: und von dir scheiden sich die Länder,
ein himmelfahrendes und eins, das fällt;

und lassen dich, zu keinem ganz gehörend,
nicht ganz so dunkel wie das Haus, das schweigt,
nicht ganz so sicher Ewiges beschwörend
wie das, was Stern wird jede Nacht und steigt—

und lassen dir (unsäglich zu entwirrn)
dein Leben bang und riesenhaft und reifend,
so daß es, bald begrenzt und bald begreifend,
abwechselnd Stein in dir wird und Gestirn.

EVENING

The sky puts on the darkening blue coat
held for it by a row of ancient trees;
you watch: and the lands grow distant in your sight,
one journeying to heaven, one that falls;

and leave you, not at home in either one,
not quite so still and dark as the darkened houses,
not calling to eternity with the passion
of what becomes a star each night, and rises;

and leave you (inexpressibly to unravel)
your life, with its immensity and fear,
so that, now bounded, now immeasurable,
it is alternately stone in you and star.

DAS LIED DES BLINDEN

Ich bin blind, ihr draußen, das ist ein Fluch,
ein Widerwillen, ein Widerspruch,
etwas täglich Schweres.
Ich leg meine Hand auf den Arm der Frau,
meine graue Hand auf ihr graues Grau,
und sie führt mich durch lauter Leeres.

Ihr rührt euch und rückt und bildet euch ein
anders zu klingen als Stein auf Stein,
aber ihr irrt euch: ich allein
lebe und leide und lärme.
In mir ist ein endloses Schrein
und ich weiß nicht, schreit mir mein
Herz oder meine Gedärme.

Erkennt ihr die Lieder? Ihr sanget sie nicht
nicht ganz in dieser Betonung.
Euch kommt jeden Morgen das neue Licht
warm in die offene Wohnung.
Und ihr habt ein Gefühl von Gesicht zu Gesicht
und das verleitet zur Schonung.

THE BLINDMAN'S SONG

I am blind, you outsiders. It is a curse,
a contradiction, a tiresome farce,
and every day I despair.
I put my hand on the arm of my wife
(colorless hand on colorless sleeve)
and she walks me through empty air.

You push and shove and think that you've been
sounding different from stone against stone,
but you are mistaken: I alone
live and suffer and howl.
In me there is an endless outcry
and I can't tell what's crying, whether it's my
broken heart or my bowels.

Are the tunes familiar? You don't sing them like this:
how could you understand?
Each morning the sunlight comes into your house,
and you welcome it as a friend.
And you know what it's like to see face-to-face;
and that tempts you to be kind.

DAS LIED DES TRINKERS

Es war nicht in mir. Es ging aus und ein.
Da wollt ich es halten. Da hielt es der Wein.
(Ich weiß nicht mehr was es war.)
Dann hielt er mir jenes und hielt mir dies
bis ich mich ganz auf ihn verließ.
Ich Narr.

Jetzt bin ich in seinem Spiel und er streut
mich verächtlich herum und verliert mich noch heut
an dieses Vieh, an den Tod.
Wenn der mich, schmutzige Karte, gewinnt,
so kratzt er mit mir seinen grauen Grind
und wirft mich fort in den Kot.

THE DRUNKARD'S SONG

It wasn't in me. It went out and in.
I wanted to hold it. It held, with Wine.
(I no longer know what it was.)
Then Wine held this and held that for me
till I came to depend on him totally.
Like an ass.

Now I'm playing his game and he deals me out
with a sneer on his lips, and maybe tonight
he will lose me to Death, that boor.
When *he* wins me, filthiest card in the deck,
he'll take me and scratch the scabs on his neck,
then toss me into the mire.

DAS LIED DES IDIOTEN

Sie hindern mich nicht. Sie lassen mich gehn.
Sie sagen es könne nichts geschehn.
Wie gut.
Es kann nichts geschehn. Alles kommt und kreist
immerfort um den heiligen Geist,
um den gewissen Geist (du weißt)—,
wie gut.

Nein man muß wirklich nicht meinen es sei
irgend eine Gefahr dabei.
Da ist freilich das Blut.
Das Blut ist das Schwerste. Das Blut ist schwer.
Manchmal glaub ich, ich kann nicht mehr—.
(Wie gut.)

Ah was ist das für ein schöner Ball;
rot und rund wie ein Überall.
Gut, daß ihr ihn erschuft.
Ob der wohl kommt wenn man ruft?

Wie sich das alles seltsam benimmt,
ineinandertreibt, auseinanderschwimmt:
freundlich, ein wenig unbestimmt.
Wie gut.

THE IDIOT'S SONG

They're not in my way. They let me be.
They say that nothing can happen to me.
How good.
Nothing can happen. All things flow
from the Holy Ghost, and they come and go
around that particular Ghost (you know)—,
how good.

No we really mustn't imagine there is
any danger in any of this.
Of course, there's blood.
Blood is the hardest. Hard as stone.
Sometimes I think that I can't go on—.
(How good.)

Oh look at that beautiful ball over there:
red and round as an Everywhere.
Good that you made it be.
If I call, will it come to me?

How very strange the world can appear,
blending and breaking, far and near:
friendly, a little bit unclear.
How good.

DAS LIED DES ZWERGES

Meine Seele ist vielleicht grad und gut;
aber mein Herz, mein verbogenes Blut,
alles das, was mir wehe tut,
kann sie nicht aufrecht tragen.
Sie hat keinen Garten, sie hat kein Bett,
sie hängt an meinem scharfen Skelett
mit entsetztem Flügelschlagen.

Aus meinen Händen wird auch nichts mehr.
Wie verkümmert sie sind: sieh her:
zähe hüpfen sie, feucht und schwer,
wie kleine Kröten nach Regen.
Und das Andre an mir ist
abgetragen und alt und trist;
warum zögert Gott, auf den Mist
alles das hinzulegen.

Ob er mir zürnt für mein Gesicht
mit dem mürrischen Munde?
Es war ja so oft bereit, ganz licht
und klar zu werden im Grunde;
aber nichts kam ihm je so dicht
wie die großen Hunde.
Und die Hunde haben das nicht.

THE DWARF'S SONG

My soul itself may be straight and good;
ah, but my heart, my bent-over blood,
all the distortions that hurt me inside—
it buckles under these things.
It has no garden, it has no sun,
it hangs on my twisted skeleton
and, terrified, flaps its wings.

Nor are my hands of much use. Look here:
see how shrunken and shapeless they are:
clumsily hopping, clammy and fat,
like toads after the rain.
And everything else about me is torn,
sad and weather-beaten and worn;
why did God ever hesitate
to flush it all down the drain?

Is it because he's angry at me
for my face with its moping lips?
It was so often ready to be
light and clear in its depths;
but nothing came so close to it
as big dogs did.
And dogs don't have what I need.

FROM

NEW POEMS

(1907; 1908)

DER PANTHER

Im Jardin des Plantes, Paris

Sein Blick ist vom Vorübergehn der Stäbe
so müd geworden, daß er nichts mehr hält.
Ihm ist, als ob es tausend Stäbe gäbe
und hinter tausend Stäben keine Welt.

Der weiche Gang geschmeidig starker Schritte,
der sich im allerkleinsten Kreise dreht,
ist wie ein Tanz von Kraft um eine Mitte,
in der betäubt ein großer Wille steht.

Nur manchmal schiebt der Vorhang der Pupille
sich lautlos auf—. Dann geht ein Bild hinein,
geht durch der Glieder angespannte Stille—
und hört im Herzen auf zu sein.

THE PANTHER

In the Jardin des Plantes, Paris

His vision, from the constantly passing bars,
has grown so weary that it cannot hold
anything else. It seems to him there are
a thousand bars; and behind the bars, no world.

As he paces in cramped circles, over and over,
the movement of his powerful soft strides
is like a ritual dance around a center
in which a mighty will stands paralyzed.

Only at times, the curtain of the pupils
lifts, quietly—. An image enters in,
rushes down through the tensed, arrested muscles,
plunges into the heart and is gone.

DIE GAZELLE

Gazella Dorcas

Verzauberte: wie kann der Einklang zweier
erwählter Worte je den Reim erreichen,
der in dir kommt und geht, wie auf ein Zeichen.
Aus deiner Stirne steigen Laub und Leier,

und alles Deine geht schon im Vergleich
durch Liebeslieder, deren Worte, weich
wie Rosenblätter, dem, der nicht mehr liest,
sich auf die Augen legen, die er schließt:

um dich zu sehen: hingetragen, als
wäre mit Sprüngen jeder Lauf geladen
und schösse nur nicht ab, solang der Hals

das Haupt ins Horchen hält: wie wenn beim Baden
im Wald die Badende sich unterbricht:
den Waldsee im gewendeten Gesicht.

THE GAZELLE

Gazella Dorcas

Enchanted thing: how can two chosen words
ever attain the harmony of pure rhyme
that pulses through you as your body stirs?
Out of your forehead branch and lyre climb,

and all your features pass in simile, through
the songs of love whose words, as light as rose-
petals, rest on the face of someone who
has put his book away and shut his eyes:

to see you: tensed, as if each leg were a gun
loaded with leaps, but not fired while your neck
holds your head still, listening: as when,

while swimming in some isolated place,
a girl hears leaves rustle, and turns to look:
the forest pool reflected in her face.

DER SCHWAN

Diese Mühsal, durch noch Ungetanes
schwer und wie gebunden hinzugehn,
gleicht dem ungeschaffnen Gang des Schwanes.

Und das Sterben, dieses Nichtmehrfassen
jenes Grunds, auf dem wir täglich stehn,
seinem ängstlichen Sich-Niederlassen—:

in die Wasser, die ihn sanft empfangen
und die sich, wie glücklich und vergangen,
unter ihm zurückziehn, Flut um Flut;
während er unendlich still und sicher
immer mündiger und königlicher
und gelassener zu ziehn geruht.

THE SWAN

This laboring through what is still undone,
as though, legs bound, we hobbled along the way,
is like the awkward walking of the swan.

And dying—to let go, no longer feel
the solid ground we stand on every day—
is like his anxious letting himself fall

into the water, which receives him gently
and which, as though with reverence and joy,
draws back past him in streams on either side;
while, infinitely silent and aware,
in his full majesty and ever more
indifferent, he condescends to glide.

DIE ERWACHSENE

Das alles stand auf ihr und war die Welt
und stand auf ihr mit allem, Angst und Gnade,
wie Bäume stehen, wachsend und gerade,
ganz Bild und bildlos wie die Bundeslade
und feierlich, wie auf ein Volk gestellt.

Und sie ertrug es; trug bis obenhin
das Fliegende, Entfliehende, Entfernte,
das Ungeheuere, noch Unerlernte
gelassen wie die Wasserträgerin
den vollen Krug. Bis mitten unterm Spiel,
verwandelnd und auf andres vorbereitend,
der erste weiße Schleier, leise gleitend,
über das aufgetane Antlitz fiel

fast undurchsichtig und sich nie mehr hebend
und irgendwie auf alle Fragen ihr
nur eine Antwort vage wiedergebend:
In dir, du Kindgewesene, in dir.

THE GROWNUP

All this stood upon her and was the world
and stood upon her with all its fear and grace
as trees stand, growing straight up, imageless
yet wholly image, like the Ark of God,
and solemn, as if imposed upon a race.

And she endured it all: bore up under
the swift-as-flight, the fleeting, the far-gone,
the inconceivably vast, the still-to-learn,
serenely as a woman carrying water
moves with a full jug. Till in the midst of play,
transfiguring and preparing for the future,
the first white veil descended, gliding softly

over her opened face, almost opaque there,
never to be lifted off again, and somehow
giving to all her questions just one answer:
In you, who were a child once—in you.

DIE ERBLINDENDE

Sie saß so wie die anderen beim Tee.
Mir war zuerst, als ob sie ihre Tasse
ein wenig anders als die andern fasse.
Sie lächelte einmal. Es tat fast weh.

Und als man schließlich sich erhob und sprach
und langsam und wie es der Zufall brachte
durch viele Zimmer ging (man sprach und lachte),
da sah ich sie. Sie ging den andern nach,

verhalten, so wie eine, welche gleich
wird singen müssen und vor vielen Leuten;
auf ihren hellen Augen die sich freuten
war Licht von außen wie auf einem Teich.

Sie folgte langsam und sie brauchte lang
als wäre etwas noch nicht überstiegen;
und doch: als ob, nach einem Übergang,
sie nicht mehr gehen würde, sondern fliegen.

GOING BLIND

She sat just like the others at the table.
But on second glance, she seemed to hold her cup
a little differently as she picked it up.
She smiled once. It was almost painful.

And when they finished and it was time to stand
and slowly, as chance selected them, they left
and moved through many rooms (they talked and laughed),
I saw her. She was moving far behind

the others, absorbed, like someone who will soon
have to sing before a large assembly;
upon her eyes, which were radiant with joy,
light played as on the surface of a pool.

She followed slowly, taking a long time,
as though there were some obstacle in the way;
and yet: as though, once it was overcome,
she would be beyond all walking, and would fly.

VOR DEM SOMMERREGEN

Auf einmal ist aus allem Grün im Park
man weiß nicht was, ein Etwas, fortgenommen;
man fühlt ihn näher an die Fenster kommen
und schweigsam sein. Inständig nur und stark

ertönt aus dem Gehölz der Regenpfeifer,
man denkt an einen Hieronymus:
so sehr steigt irgend Einsamkeit und Eifer
aus dieser einen Stimme, die der Guß

erhören wird. Des Saales Wände sind
mit ihren Bildern von uns fortgetreten,
als dürften sie nicht hören was wir sagen.

Es spiegeln die verblichenen Tapeten
das ungewisse Licht von Nachmittagen,
in denen man sich fürchtete als Kind.

BEFORE SUMMER RAIN

Suddenly, from all the green around you,
something—you don't know what—has disappeared;
you feel it creeping closer to the window,
in total silence. From the nearby wood

you hear the urgent whistling of a plover,
reminding you of someone's *Saint Jerome:*
so much solitude and passion come
from that one voice, whose fierce request the downpour

will grant. The walls, with their ancient portraits, glide
away from us, cautiously, as though
they weren't supposed to hear what we are saying.

And reflected on the faded tapestries now:
the chill, uncertain sunlight of those long
childhood hours when you were so afraid.

LETZTER ABEND

(Aus dem Besitze Frau Nonnas)

Und Nacht und fernes Fahren; denn der Train
des ganzen Heeres zog am Park vorüber.
Er aber hob den Blick vom Clavecin
und spielte noch und sah zu ihr hinüber

beinah wie man in einen Spiegel schaut:
so sehr erfüllt von seinen jungen Zügen
und wissend, wie sie seine Trauer trügen,
schön und verführender bei jedem Laut.

Doch plötzlich wars, als ob sich das verwische:
sie stand wie mühsam in der Fensternische
und hielt des Herzens drängendes Geklopf.

Sein Spiel gab nach. Von draußen wehte Frische.
Und seltsam fremd stand auf dem Spiegeltische
der schwarze Tschako mit dem Totenkopf.

THE LAST EVENING

(By permission of Frau Nonna)

And night and distant rumbling; now the army's
carrier-train was moving out, to war.
He looked up from the harpsichord, and as
he went on playing, he looked across at her

almost as one might gaze into a mirror:
so deeply was her every feature filled
with his young features, which bore his pain and were
more beautiful and seductive with each sound.

Then, suddenly, the image broke apart.
She stood, as though distracted, near the window
and felt the violent drum-beats of her heart.

His playing stopped. From outside, a fresh wind blew.
And strangely alien on the mirror-table
stood the black shako with its ivory skull.

JUGEND-BILDNIS
MEINES VATERS

Im Auge Traum. Die Stirn wie in Berührung
mit etwas Fernem. Um den Mund enorm
viel Jugend, ungelächelte Verführung,
und vor der vollen schmückenden Verschnürung
der schlanken adeligen Uniform
der Säbelkorb und beide Hände—, die
abwarten, ruhig, zu nichts hingedrängt.
Und nun fast nicht mehr sichtbar: als ob sie
zuerst, die Fernes greifenden, verschwänden.
Und alles andre mit sich selbst verhängt
und ausgelöscht als ob wirs nicht verständen
und tief aus seiner eignen Tiefe trüb—.

Du schnell vergehendes Daguerreotyp
in meinen langsamer vergehenden Händen.

PORTRAIT OF MY FATHER
AS A YOUNG MAN

In the eyes: dream. The brow as if it could feel
something far off. Around the lips, a great
freshness—seductive, though there is no smile.
Under the rows of ornamental braid
on the slim Imperial officer's uniform:
the saber's basket-hilt. Both hands stay
folded upon it, going nowhere, calm
and now almost invisible, as if they
were the first to grasp the distance and dissolve.
And all the rest so curtained with itself,
so cloudy, that I cannot understand
this figure as it fades into the background—.

Oh quickly disappearing photograph
in my more slowly disappearing hand.

SELBSTBILDNIS AUS DEM
JAHRE 1906

Des alten lange adligen Geschlechtes
Feststehendes im Augenbogenbau.
Im Blicke noch der Kindheit Angst und Blau
und Demut da und dort, nicht eines Knechtes
doch eines Dienenden und einer Frau.
Der Mund als Mund gemacht, groß und genau,
nicht überredend, aber ein Gerechtes
Aussagendes. Die Stirne ohne Schlechtes
und gern im Schatten stiller Niederschau.

Das, als Zusammenhang, erst nur geahnt;
noch nie im Leiden oder im Gelingen
zusammgefaßt zu dauerndem Durchdringen,
doch so, als wäre mit zerstreuten Dingen
von fern ein Ernstes, Wirkliches geplant.

SELF-PORTRAIT,
1906

The stamina of an old, long-noble race
in the eyebrows' heavy arches. In the mild
blue eyes, the solemn anguish of a child
and, here and there, humility—not a fool's,
but feminine: the look of one who serves.
The mouth quite ordinary, large and straight,
composed, yet not unwilling to speak out
when necessary. The forehead still naive,
most comfortable in shadows, looking down.

This, as a whole, just hazily foreseen—
never, in any joy or suffering,
collected for a firm accomplishment;
and yet, as though, from far off, with scattered Things,
a serious, true work were being planned.

SPANISCHE TÄNZERIN

Wie in der Hand ein Schwefelzündholz, weiß,
eh es zur Flamme kommt, nach allen Seiten
zuckende Zungen streckt—: beginnt im Kreis
naher Beschauer hastig, hell und heiß
ihr runder Tanz sich zuckend auszubreiten.

Und plötzlich ist er Flamme, ganz und gar.

Mit einem Blick entzündet sie ihr Haar
und dreht auf einmal mit gewagter Kunst
ihr ganzes Kleid in diese Feuersbrunst,
aus welcher sich, wie Schlangen die erschrecken,
die nackten Arme wach und klappernd strecken.

Und dann: als würde ihr das Feuer knapp,
nimmt sie es ganz zusamm und wirft es ab
sehr herrisch, mit hochmütiger Gebärde
und schaut: da liegt es rasend auf der Erde
und flammt noch immer und ergiebt sich nicht—.
Doch sieghaft, sicher und mit einem süßen
grüßenden Lächeln hebt sie ihr Gesicht
und stampft es aus mit kleinen festen Füßen.

SPANISH DANCER

As on all its sides a kitchen-match darts white
flickering tongues before it bursts into flame:
with the audience around her, quickened, hot,
her dance begins to flicker in the dark room.

And all at once it is completely fire.

One upward glance and she ignites her hair
and, whirling faster and faster, fans her dress
into passionate flames, till it becomes a furnace
from which, like startled rattlesnakes, the long
naked arms uncoil, aroused and clicking.

And then: as if the fire were too tight
around her body, she takes and flings it out
haughtily, with an imperious gesture,
and watches: it lies raging on the floor,
still blazing up, and the flames refuse to die—.
Till, moving with total confidence and a sweet
exultant smile, she looks up finally
and stamps it out with powerful small feet.

HETÄREN-GRÄBER

In ihren langen Haaren liegen sie
mit braunen, tief in sich gegangenen Gesichtern.
Die Augen zu wie vor zu vieler Ferne.
Skelette, Munde, Blumen. In den Munden
die glatten Zähne wie ein Reise-Schachspiel
aus Elfenbein in Reihen aufgestellt.
Und Blumen, gelbe Perlen, schlanke Knochen,
Hände und Hemden, welkende Gewebe
über dem eingestürzten Herzen. Aber
dort unter jenen Ringen, Talismanen
und augenblauen Steinen (Lieblings-Angedenken)
steht noch die stille Krypta des Geschlechtes,
bis an die Wölbung voll mit Blumenblättern.
Und wieder gelbe Perlen, weitverrollte,—
Schalen gebrannten Tones, deren Bug
ihr eignes Bild geziert hat, grüne Scherben
von Salben-Vasen, die wie Blumen duften,
und Formen kleiner Götter: Hausaltäre,
Hetärenhimmel mit entzückten Göttern.
Gesprengte Gürtel, flache Skarabäen,
kleine Figuren riesigen Geschlechtes,
ein Mund der lacht und Tanzende und Läufer,
goldene Fibeln, kleinen Bogen ähnlich
zur Jagd auf Tier- und Vogelamulette,
und lange Nadeln, zieres Hausgeräte
und eine runde Scherbe roten Grundes,
darauf, wie eines Eingangs schwarze Aufschrift,
die straffen Beine eines Viergespannes.
Und wieder Blumen, Perlen, die verrollt sind,
die hellen Lenden einer kleinen Leier,
und zwischen Schleiern, die gleich Nebeln fallen,
wie ausgekrochen aus des Schuhes Puppe:
des Fußgelenkes leichter Schmetterling.

So liegen sie mit Dingen angefüllt,
kostbaren Dingen, Steinen, Spielzeug, Hausrat,

TOMBS OF THE HETAERAE

They lie in their long hair, and the brown faces
have long ago withdrawn into themselves.
Eyes shut, as though before too great a distance.
Skeletons, mouths, flowers. Inside the mouths,
the shiny teeth like rows of pocket chessmen.
And flowers, yellow pearls, slender bones,
hands and tunics, woven cloth decaying
over the shriveled heart. But there, beneath
those rings, beneath the talismans and gems
and precious stones like blue eyes (lovers' keepsakes),
there still remains the silent crypt of sex,
filled to its vaulted roof with flower-petals.
And yellow pearls again, unstrung and scattered,
vessels of fired clay on which their own
portraits once were painted, the green fragments
of perfume jars that smelled like flowers, and images
of little household gods upon their altars:
courtesan-heavens with enraptured gods.
Broken waistbands, scarabs carved in jade,
small statues with enormous genitals,
a laughing mouth, dancing-girls, runners,
golden clasps that look like tiny bows
for shooting bird- and beast-shaped amulets,
ornamented knives and spoons, long needles,
a roundish light-red potsherd upon which
the stiff legs of a team of horses stand
like the dark inscription above an entryway.
And flowers again, pearls that have rolled apart,
the shining flanks of a little gilded lyre;
and in between the veils that fall like mist,
as though it had crept out from the shoe's chrysalis:
the delicate pale butterfly of the ankle.

And so they lie, filled to the brim with Things,
expensive Things, jewels, toys, utensils,

zerschlagnem Tand (was alles in sie abfiel),
und dunkeln wie der Grund von einem Fluß.

Flußbetten waren sie,
darüber hin in kurzen schnellen Wellen
(die weiter wollten zu dem nächsten Leben)
die Leiber vieler Jünglinge sich stürzten
und in denen der Männer Ströme rauschten.
Und manchmal brachen Knaben aus den Bergen
der Kindheit, kamen zagen Falles nieder
und spielten mit den Dingen auf dem Grunde,
bis das Gefälle ihr Gefühl ergriff:

Dann füllten sie mit flachem klaren Wasser
die ganze Breite dieses breiten Weges
und trieben Wirbel an den tiefen Stellen;
und spiegelten zum ersten Mal die Ufer
und ferne Vogelrufe—, während hoch
die Sternennächte eines süßen Landes
in Himmel wuchsen, die sich nirgends schlossen.

broken trinkets (how much fell into them!)
and they darken as a river's bottom darkens.

For they *were* riverbeds once,
and over them in brief, impetuous waves
(each wanting to prolong itself, forever)
the bodies of countless adolescents surged;
and in them roared the currents of grown men.
And sometimes boys would burst forth from the mountains
of childhood, would descend in timid streams
and play with what they found on the river's bottom,
until the steep slope gripped their consciousness:

Then they filled, with clear, shallow water,
the whole breadth of this broad canal, and set
little whirlpools turning in the depths,
and for the first time mirrored the green banks
and distant calls of birds—, while in the sky
the starry nights of another, sweeter country
blossomed above them and would never close.

ORPHEUS. EURYDIKE. HERMES

Das war der Seelen wunderliches Bergwerk.
Wie stille Silbererze gingen sie
als Adern durch sein Dunkel. Zwischen Wurzeln
entsprang das Blut, das fortgeht zu den Menschen,
und schwer wie Porphyr sah es aus im Dunkel.
Sonst war nichts Rotes.

Felsen waren da
und wesenlose Wälder. Brücken über Leeres
und jener große graue blinde Teich,
der über seinem fernen Grunde hing
wie Regenhimmel über einer Landschaft.
Und zwischen Wiesen, sanft und voller Langmut,
erschien des einen Weges blasser Streifen,
wie eine lange Bleiche hingelegt.

Und dieses einen Weges kamen sie.

Voran der schlanke Mann im blauen Mantel,
der stumm und ungeduldig vor sich aussah.
Ohne zu kauen fraß sein Schritt den Weg
in großen Bissen; seine Hände hingen
schwer und verschlossen aus dem Fall der Falten
und wußten nicht mehr von der leichten Leier,
die in die Linke eingewachsen war
wie Rosenranken in den Ast des Ölbaums.
Und seine Sinne waren wie entzweit:
indes der Blick ihm wie ein Hund vorauslief,
umkehrte, kam und immer wieder weit
und wartend an der nächsten Wendung stand,—
blieb sein Gehör wie ein Geruch zurück.
Manchmal erschien es ihm als reichte es
bis an das Gehen jener beiden andern,
die folgen sollten diesen ganzen Aufstieg.
Dann wieder wars nur seines Steigens Nachklang
und seines Mantels Wind was hinter ihm war.

ORPHEUS. EURYDICE. HERMES

That was the deep uncanny mine of souls.
Like veins of silver ore, they silently
moved through its massive darkness. Blood welled up
among the roots, on its way to the world of men,
and in the dark it looked as hard as stone.
Nothing else was red.

There were cliffs there,
and forests made of mist. There were bridges
spanning the void, and that great gray blind lake
which hung above its distant bottom
like the sky on a rainy day above a landscape.
And through the gentle, unresisting meadows
one pale path unrolled like a strip of cotton.

Down this path they were coming.

In front, the slender man in the blue cloak—
mute, impatient, looking straight ahead.
In large, greedy, unchewed bites his walk
devoured the path; his hands hung at his sides,
tight and heavy, out of the falling folds,
no longer conscious of the delicate lyre
which had grown into his left arm, like a slip
of roses grafted onto an olive tree.
His senses felt as though they were split in two:
his sight would race ahead of him like a dog,
stop, come back, then rushing off again
would stand, impatient, at the path's next turn,—
but his hearing, like an odor, stayed behind.
Sometimes it seemed to him as though it reached
back to the footsteps of those other two
who were to follow him, up the long path home.
But then, once more, it was just his own steps' echo,
or the wind inside his cloak, that made the sound.

Er aber sagte sich, sie kämen doch;
sagte es laut und hörte sich verhallen.
Sie kämen doch, nur wärens zwei
die furchtbar leise gingen. Dürfte er
sich einmal wenden (wäre das Zurückschaun
nicht die Zersetzung dieses ganzen Werkes,
das erst vollbracht wird), müßte er sie sehen,
die beiden Leisen, die ihm schweigend nachgehn:

Den Gott des Ganges und der weiten Botschaft,
die Reisehaube über hellen Augen,
den schlanken Stab hertragend vor dem Leibe
und flügelschlagend an den Fußgelenken;
und seiner linken Hand gegeben: *sie*.

Die So-geliebte, daß aus einer Leier
mehr Klage kam als je aus Klagefrauen;
daß eine Welt aus Klage ward, in der
alles noch einmal da war: Wald und Tal
und Weg und Ortschaft, Feld und Fluß und Tier;
und daß um diese Klage-Welt, ganz so
wie um die andre Erde, eine Sonne
und ein gestirnter stiller Himmel ging,
ein Klage-Himmel mit entstellten Sternen—:
Diese So-geliebte.

Sie aber ging an jenes Gottes Hand,
den Schritt beschränkt von langen Leichenbändern,
unsicher, sanft und ohne Ungeduld.
Sie war in sich, wie Eine hoher Hoffnung,
und dachte nicht des Mannes, der voranging,
und nicht des Weges, der ins Leben aufstieg.
Sie war in sich. Und ihr Gestorbensein
erfüllte sie wie Fülle.
Wie eine Frucht von Süßigkeit und Dunkel,
so war sie voll von ihrem großen Tode,
der also neu war, daß sie nichts begriff.

He said to himself, they had to be behind him;
said it aloud and heard it fade away.
They had to be behind him, but their steps
were ominously soft. If only he could
turn around, just once (but looking back
would ruin this entire work, so near
completion), then he could not fail to see them,
those other two, who followed him so softly:

The god of speed and distant messages,
a traveler's hood above his shining eyes,
his slender staff held out in front of him,
and little wings fluttering at his ankles;
and on his left arm, barely touching it: *she.*

A woman so loved that from one lyre there came
more lament than from all lamenting women;
that a whole world of lament arose, in which
all nature reappeared: forest and valley,
road and village, field and stream and animal;
and that around this lament-world, even as
around the other earth, a sun revolved
and a silent star-filled heaven, a lament-
heaven, with its own, disfigured stars—:
So greatly was she loved.

But now she walked beside the graceful god,
her steps constricted by the trailing graveclothes,
uncertain, gentle, and without impatience.
She was deep within herself, like a woman heavy
with child, and did not see the man in front
or the path ascending steeply into life.
Deep within herself. Being dead
filled her beyond fulfillment. Like a fruit
suffused with its own mystery and sweetness,
she was filled with her vast death, which was so new,
she could not understand that it had happened.

Sie war in einem neuen Mädchentum
und unberührbar; ihr Geschlecht war zu
wie eine junge Blume gegen Abend,
und ihre Hände waren der Vermählung
so sehr entwöhnt, daß selbst des leichten Gottes
unendlich leise, leitende Berührung
sie kränkte wie zu sehr Vertraulichkeit.

Sie war schon nicht mehr diese blonde Frau,
die in des Dichters Liedern manchmal anklang,
nicht mehr des breiten Bettes Duft und Eiland
und jenes Mannes Eigentum nicht mehr.

Sie war schon aufgelöst wie langes Haar
und hingegeben wie gefallner Regen
und ausgeteilt wie hundertfacher Vorrat.

Sie war schon Wurzel.

Und als plötzlich jäh
der Gott sie anhielt und mit Schmerz im Ausruf
die Worte sprach: Er hat sich umgewendet—,
begriff sie nichts und sagte leise: *Wer?*

Fern aber, dunkel vor dem klaren Ausgang,
stand irgend jemand, dessen Angesicht
nicht zu erkennen war. Er stand und sah,
wie auf dem Streifen eines Wiesenpfades
mit trauervollem Blick der Gott der Botschaft
sich schweigend wandte, der Gestalt zu folgen,
die schon zurückging dieses selben Weges,
den Schritt beschränkt von langen Leichenbändern,
unsicher, sanft und ohne Ungeduld.

She had come into a new virginity
and was untouchable; her sex had closed
like a young flower at nightfall, and her hands
had grown so unused to marriage that the god's
infinitely gentle touch of guidance
hurt her, like an undesired kiss.

She was no longer that woman with blue eyes
who once had echoed through the poet's songs,
no longer the wide couch's scent and island,
and that man's property no longer.

She was already loosened like long hair,
poured out like fallen rain,
shared like a limitless supply.

She was already root.

And when, abruptly,
the god put out his hand to stop her, saying,
with sorrow in his voice: He has turned around—,
she could not understand, and softly answered
Who?

                              Far away,
dark before the shining exit-gates,
someone or other stood, whose features were
unrecognizable. He stood and saw
how, on the strip of road among the meadows,
with a mournful look, the god of messages
silently turned to follow the small figure
already walking back along the path,
her steps constricted by the trailing graveclothes,
uncertain, gentle, and without impatience.

ALKESTIS

Da plötzlich war der Bote unter ihnen,
hineingeworfen in das Überkochen
des Hochzeitsmahles wie ein neuer Zusatz.
Sie fühlten nicht, die Trinkenden, des Gottes
heimlichen Eintritt, welcher seine Gottheit
so an sich hielt wie einen nassen Mantel
und ihrer einer schien, der oder jener,
wie er so durchging. Aber plötzlich sah
mitten im Sprechen einer von den Gästen
den jungen Hausherrn oben an dem Tische
wie in die Höh gerissen, nicht mehr liegend,
und überall und mit dem ganzen Wesen
ein Fremdes spiegelnd, das ihn furchtbar ansprach.
Und gleich darauf, als klärte sich die Mischung,
war Stille; nur mit einem Satz am Boden
von trübem Lärm und einem Niederschlag
fallenden Lallens, schon verdorben riechend
nach dumpfem umgestandenen Gelächter.
Und da erkannten sie den schlanken Gott,
und wie er dastand, innerlich voll Sendung
und unerbittlich,—wußten sie es beinah.
Und doch, als es gesagt war, war es mehr
als alles Wissen, gar nicht zu begreifen.
Admet muß sterben. Wann? In dieser Stunde.

Der aber brach die Schale seines Schreckens
in Stücken ab und streckte seine Hände
heraus aus ihr, um mit dem Gott zu handeln.
Um Jahre, um ein einzig Jahr noch Jugend,
um Monate, um Wochen, um paar Tage,
ach, Tage nicht, um Nächte, nur um Eine,
um Eine Nacht, um diese nur: um die.
Der Gott verneinte, und da schrie er auf
und schrie's hinaus und hielt es nicht und schrie
wie seine Mutter aufschrie beim Gebären.

ALCESTIS

Then all at once the messenger was there,
amid the simmer of wedding guests: dropped in
like the last ingredient into a bubbling pot.
They kept on drinking and did not feel the stealthy
entrance of the god, who held his aura
as tight against his body as a wet cloak,
and seemed to be like any one of them
as he walked on. But abruptly, halfway through
a sentence, one guest saw how the young master
was startled from his couch at the table's head,
as though he had been snatched up into the air
and mirroring, all over, with all his being,
a strangeness that addressed him, horribly.
And then, as though the mixture cleared, there was
silence; on the bottom, just the dregs
of muddy noise and a precipitate
of falling babble, already giving off
the rancid smell of laughter that has turned.
For now they recognized the slender god,
and, as he stood before them, filled with his message
and unentreatable,—they almost knew.
And yet, when it was uttered, it was beyond
all understanding; none of them could grasp it.
Admetus must die. When? Within the hour.

But by this time he had broken through the shell
of his terror; and he thrust out both his hands
from the jagged holes, to bargain with the god.
For years, for only one more year of youth,
for months, for weeks, for just a few more days,
oh not for days: for nights, for just a night,
for one more night, for just this one: for this.
The god refused; and then *he* started screaming,
and screamed it out, held nothing back, screamed
as his own mother once had screamed in childbirth.

Und die trat zu ihm, eine alte Frau,
und auch der Vater kam, der alte Vater,
und beide standen, alt, veraltet, ratlos,
beim Schreienden, der plötzlich, wie noch nie
so nah, sie ansah, abbrach, schluckte, sagte:
Vater,
liegt dir denn viel daran an diesem Rest,
an diesem Satz, der dich beim Schlingen hindert?
Geh, gieß ihn weg. Und du, du alte Frau,
Matrone,
was tust du denn noch hier: du hast geboren.
Und beide hielt er sie wie Opfertiere
in Einem Griff. Auf einmal ließ er los
und stieß die Alten fort, voll Einfall, strahlend
und atemholend, rufend: Kreon, Kreon!
Und nichts als das; und nichts als diesen Namen.
Aber in seinem Antlitz stand das Andere,
das er nicht sagte, namenlos erwartend,
wie ers dem jungen Freunde, dem Geliebten,
erglühend hinhielt übern wirren Tisch.
Die Alten (stand da), siehst du, sind kein Loskauf,
sie sind verbraucht und schlecht und beinah wertlos,
du aber, du, in deiner ganzen Schönheit—

Da aber sah er seinen Freund nicht mehr.
Er blieb zurück, und das, was kam, war *sie,*
ein wenig kleiner fast als er sie kannte
und leicht und traurig in dem bleichen Brautkleid.
Die andern alle sind nur ihre Gasse,
durch die sie kommt und kommt—: (gleich wird sie da sein
in seinen Armen, die sich schmerzhaft auftun).

Doch wie er wartet, spricht sie; nicht zu ihm.
Sie spricht zum Gotte, und der Gott vernimmt sie,
und alle hörens gleichsam erst im Gotte:

Ersatz kann keiner für ihn sein. Ich *bins.*
Ich bin Ersatz. Denn keiner ist zu Ende

And she came up beside him, an old woman,
and his father came up also, his old father,
and both stood waiting—old, decrepit, helpless—
beside the screaming man, who, as never before
so closely, saw them, stopped, swallowed, said:
Father,
do you care about the wretched scrap of life
still left you, that will just stick in your throat?
Go spit it out. And you, old woman, old
Mother,
why should you stay here? you have given birth.
And grabbed them both, like sacrificial beasts,
in his harsh grip. Then suddenly let them go,
pushed the old couple off, inspired, beaming,
breathing hard and calling: Creon! Creon!
And nothing else; and nothing but that name.
Yet in his features stood the other name
he could not utter, namelessly expectant
as, glowing, he held it out to the young guest,
his dearest friend, across the bewildered table.
These two old people (it stood there) are no ransom,
they are used up, exhausted, nearly worthless,
but you, Creon, you, in all your beauty—

But now he could no longer see his friend,
who stayed behind; and what came forth was *she,*
almost a little smaller than as he knew her,
slight and sad in her pale wedding dress.
All the others are just her narrow path,
down which she comes and comes—: (soon she will be
there, in his arms, which painfully have opened).

But while he waits, she speaks; though not to him.
She is speaking to the god, and the god listens,
and all can hear, as though within the god:

No one can be his ransom: only I can.
I *am* his ransom. For no one else has finished

wie ich es bin. Was bleibt mir denn von dem
was ich hier war? Das *ists* ja, daß ich sterbe.
Hat sie dirs nicht gesagt, da sie dirs auftrug,
daß jenes Lager, das da drinnen wartet,
zur Unterwelt gehört? Ich nahm ja Abschied.
Abschied über Abschied.
Kein Sterbender nimmt mehr davon. Ich ging ja,
damit das Alles, unter Dem begraben
der jetzt mein Gatte ist, zergeht, sich auflöst—.
So führ mich hin: ich sterbe ja für ihn.

Und wie der Wind auf hoher See, der umspringt,
so trat der Gott fast wie zu einer Toten
und war auf einmal weit von ihrem Gatten,
dem er, versteckt in einem kleinen Zeichen,
die hundert Leben dieser Erde zuwarf.
Der stürzte taumelnd zu den beiden hin
und griff nach ihnen wie im Traum. Sie gingen
schon auf den Eingang zu, in dem die Frauen
verweint sich drängten. Aber einmal sah
er noch des Mädchens Antlitz, das sich wandte
mit einem Lächeln, hell wie eine Hoffnung,
die beinah ein Versprechen war: erwachsen
zurückzukommen aus dem tiefen Tode
zu ihm, dem Lebenden—

Da schlug er jäh
die Hände vors Gesicht, wie er so kniete,
um nichts zu sehen mehr nach diesem Lächeln.

with life as I have. What is left for me
of everything I once was? Just my dying.
Didn't she tell you when she sent you down here
that the bed waiting inside belongs to death?
For I have taken leave. No one dying
takes more than that. I left so that all this,
buried beneath the man who is now my husband,
might fade and vanish—. Come: lead me away:
already I have begun to die, for him.

And veering like a wind on the high seas,
the god approached as though she were already
dead, and instantly was there beside her,
far from her husband, to whom, with an abrupt
nod, he tossed the hundred lives of earth.
The young man hurried, staggering, toward the two
and grasped at them as in a dream. But now
they had nearly reached the entrance, which was crowded
with sobbing women. One more time he saw
the girl's face, for just a moment, turning toward him
with a smile that was as radiant as a hope
and almost was a promise: to return
from out of the abyss of death, grown fully,
to him, who was still alive—

At that, he flung
his hands before his own face, as he knelt there,
in order to see nothing but that smile.

ARCHAÏSCHER TORSO APOLLOS

Wir kannten nicht sein unerhörtes Haupt,
darin die Augenäpfel reiften. Aber
sein Torso glüht noch wie ein Kandelaber,
in dem sein Schauen, nur zurückgeschraubt,

sich hält und glänzt. Sonst könnte nicht der Bug
der Brust dich blenden, und im leisen Drehen
der Lenden könnte nicht ein Lächeln gehen
zu jener Mitte, die die Zeugung trug.

Sonst stünde dieser Stein entstellt und kurz
unter der Schultern durchsichtigem Sturz
und flimmerte nicht so wie Raubtierfelle;

und bräche nicht aus allen seinen Rändern
aus wie ein Stern: denn da ist keine Stelle,
die dich nicht sieht. Du mußt dein Leben ändern.

ARCHAIC TORSO OF APOLLO

We cannot know his legendary head
with eyes like ripening fruit. And yet his torso
is still suffused with brilliance from inside,
like a lamp, in which his gaze, now turned to low,

gleams in all its power. Otherwise
the curved breast could not dazzle you so, nor could
a smile run through the placid hips and thighs
to that dark center where procreation flared.

Otherwise this stone would seem defaced
beneath the translucent cascade of the shoulders
and would not glisten like a wild beast's fur:

would not, from all the borders of itself,
burst like a star: for here there is no place
that does not see you. You must change your life.

LEICHEN-WÄSCHE

Sie hatten sich an ihn gewöhnt. Doch als
die Küchenlampe kam und unruhig brannte
im dunkeln Luftzug, war der Unbekannte
ganz unbekannt. Sie wuschen seinen Hals,

und da sie nichts von seinem Schicksal wußten,
so logen sie ein anderes zusamm,
fortwährend waschend. Eine mußte husten
und ließ solang den schweren Essigschwamm

auf dem Gesicht. Da gab es eine Pause
auch für die zweite. Aus der harten Bürste
klopften die Tropfen; während seine grause
gekrampfte Hand dem ganzen Hause
beweisen wollte, daß ihn nicht mehr dürste.

Und er bewies. Sie nahmen wie betreten
eiliger jetzt mit einem kurzen Huster
die Arbeit auf, so daß an den Tapeten
ihr krummer Schatten in dem stummen Muster

sich wand und wälzte wie in einem Netze,
bis daß die Waschenden zu Ende kamen.
Die Nacht im vorhanglosen Fensterrahmen
war rücksichtslos. Und einer ohne Namen
lag bar und reinlich da und gab Gesetze.

WASHING THE CORPSE

They had, for a while, grown used to him. But after
they lit the kitchen lamp and in the dark
it began to burn, restlessly, the stranger
was altogether strange. They washed his neck,

and since they knew nothing about his life
they lied till they produced another one,
as they kept washing. One of them had to cough,
and while she coughed she left the vinegar sponge,

dripping, upon his face. The other stood
and rested for a minute. A few drops fell
from the stiff scrub-brush, as his horrible
contorted hand was trying to make the whole
room aware that he no longer thirsted.

And he did let them know. With a short cough,
as if embarrassed, they both began to work
more hurriedly now, so that across
the mute, patterned wallpaper their thick

shadows reeled and staggered as if bound
in a net; till they had finished washing him.
The night, in the uncurtained window-frame,
was pitiless. And one without a name
lay clean and naked there, and gave commands.

SCHWARZE KATZE

Ein Gespenst ist noch wie eine Stelle,
dran dein Blick mit einem Klange stößt;
aber da, an diesem schwarzen Felle
wird dein stärkstes Schauen aufgelöst:

wie ein Tobender, wenn er in vollster
Raserei ins Schwarze stampft,
jählings am benehmenden Gepolster
einer Zelle aufhört und verdampft.

Alle Blicke, die sie jemals trafen,
scheint sie also an sich zu verhehlen,
um darüber drohend und verdrossen
zuzuschauern und damit zu schlafen.
Doch auf einmal kehrt sie, wie geweckt,
ihr Gesicht und mitten in das deine:
und da triffst du deinen Blick im geelen
Amber ihrer runden Augensteine
unerwartet wieder: eingeschlossen
wie ein ausgestorbenes Insekt.

BLACK CAT

A ghost, though invisible, still is like a place
your sight can knock on, echoing; but here
within this thick black pelt, your strongest gaze
will be absorbed and utterly disappear:

just as a raving madman, when nothing else
can ease him, charges into his dark night
howling, pounds on the padded wall, and feels
the rage being taken in and pacified.

She seems to hide all looks that have ever fallen
into her, so that, like an audience,
she can look them over, menacing and sullen,
and curl to sleep with them. But all at once

as if awakened, she turns her face to yours;
and with a shock, you see yourself, tiny,
inside the golden amber of her eyeballs
suspended, like a prehistoric fly.

DIE FLAMINGOS

Jardin des Plantes, Paris

In Spiegelbildern wie von Fragonard
ist doch von ihrem Weiß und ihrer Röte
nicht mehr gegeben, als dir einer böte,
wenn er von seiner Freundin sagt: sie war

noch sanft von Schlaf. Denn steigen sie ins Grüne
und stehn, auf rosa Stielen leicht gedreht,
beisammen, blühend, wie in einem Beet,
verführen sie verführender als Phryne

sich selber; bis sie ihres Auges Bleiche
hinhalsend bergen in der eignen Weiche,
in welcher Schwarz und Fruchtrot sich versteckt.

Auf einmal kreischt ein Neid durch die Volière;
sie aber haben sich erstaunt gestreckt
und schreiten einzeln ins Imaginäre.

THE FLAMINGOS

Jardin des Plantes, Paris

With all the subtle paints of Fragonard
no more of their red and white could be expressed
than someone would convey about his mistress
by telling you, "She was lovely, lying there

still soft with sleep." They rise above the green
grass and lightly sway on their long pink stems,
side by side, like enormous feathery blossoms,
seducing (more seductively than Phryne)

themselves; till, necks curling, they sink their large
pale eyes into the softness of their down,
where apple-red and jet-black lie concealed.

A shriek of envy shakes the parrot cage;
but *they* stretch out, astonished, and one by one
stride into their imaginary world.

BUDDHA IN DER GLORIE

Mitte aller Mitten, Kern der Kerne,
Mandel, die sich einschließt und versüßt,—
dieses Alles bis an alle Sterne
ist dein Fruchtfleisch: Sei gegrüßt.

Sieh, du fühlst, wie nichts mehr an dir hängt;
im Unendlichen ist deine Schale,
und dort steht der starke Saft und drängt.
Und von außen hilft ihm ein Gestrahle,

denn ganz oben werden deine Sonnen
voll und glühend umgedreht.
Doch in dir ist schon begonnen,
was die Sonnen übersteht.

BUDDHA IN GLORY

Center of all centers, core of cores,
almond self-enclosed and growing sweet—
all this universe, to the furthest stars
and beyond them, is your flesh, your fruit.

Now you feel how nothing clings to you;
your vast shell reaches into endless space,
and there the rich, thick fluids rise and flow.
Illuminated in your infinite peace,

a billion stars go spinning through the night,
blazing high above your head.
But *in* you is the presence that
will be, when all the stars are dead.

FROM

REQUIEM

(1909)

REQUIEM FÜR EINE FREUNDIN

Ich habe Tote, und ich ließ sie hin
und war erstaunt, sie so getrost zu sehn,
so rasch zuhaus im Totsein, so gerecht,
so anders als ihr Ruf. Nur du, du kehrst
zurück; du streifst mich, du gehst um, du willst
an etwas stoßen, daß es klingt von dir
und dich verrät. O nimm mir nicht, was ich
langsam erlern. Ich habe recht; du irrst
wenn du gerührt zu irgend einem Ding
ein Heimweh hast. Wir wandeln dieses um;
es ist nicht hier, wir spiegeln es herein
aus unserm Sein, sobald wir es erkennen.

    Ich glaubte dich viel weiter. Mich verwirrts,
daß *du* gerade irrst und kommst, die mehr
verwandelt hat als irgend eine Frau.
Daß wir erschraken, da du starbst, nein, daß
dein starker Tod uns dunkel unterbrach,
das Bisdahin abreißend vom Seither:
das geht uns an; das einzuordnen wird
die Arbeit sein, die wir mit allem tun.
Doch daß du selbst erschrakst und auch noch jetzt
den Schrecken hast, wo Schrecken nicht mehr gilt;
daß du von deiner Ewigkeit ein Stück
verlierst und hier hereintrittst, Freundin, hier,
wo alles noch nicht *ist;* daß du zerstreut,
zum ersten Mal im All zerstreut und halb,
den Aufgang der unendlichen Naturen
nicht so ergriffst wie hier ein jedes Ding;
daß aus dem Kreislauf, der dich schon empfing,
die stumme Schwerkraft irgend einer Unruh
dich niederzieht zur abgezählten Zeit—:
dies weckt mich nachts oft wie ein Dieb, der einbricht.
Und dürft ich sagen, daß du nur geruhst,
daß du aus Großmut kommst, aus Überfülle,
weil du so sicher bist, so in dir selbst,

REQUIEM FOR A FRIEND

I have my dead, and I have let them go,
and was amazed to see them so contented,
so soon at home in being dead, so cheerful,
so unlike their reputation. Only you
return; brush past me, loiter, try to knock
against something, so that the sound reveals
your presence. Oh don't take from me what I
am slowly learning. I'm sure you have gone astray
if you are moved to homesickness for anything
in this dimension. We transform these Things;
they aren't real, they are only the reflections
upon the polished surface of our being.

    I thought you were much further on. It troubles me
that *you* should stray back, you, who have achieved
more transformation than any other woman.
That we were frightened when you died . . . no; rather:
that your stern death broke in upon us, darkly,
wrenching the till-then from the ever-since—
this concerns *us*: setting it all in order
is the task we have continually before us.
But that you too were frightened, and even now
pulse with your fear, where fear can have no meaning;
that you have lost even the smallest fragment
of your eternity, Paula, and have entered
here, where nothing yet exists; that out there,
bewildered for the first time, inattentive,
you didn't grasp the splendor of the infinite
forces, as on earth you grasped each Thing;
that, from the realm which already had received you,
the gravity of some old discontent
has dragged you back to measurable time—:
this often startles me out of dreamless sleep
at night, like a thief climbing in my window.
If I could say it is only out of kindness,
out of your great abundance, that you have come,
because you are so secure, so self-contained,

daß du herumgehst wie ein Kind, nicht bange
vor Örtern, wo man einem etwas tut—:
doch nein: du bittest. Dieses geht mir so
bis ins Gebein und querrt wie eine Säge.
Ein Vorwurf, den du trügest als Gespenst,
nachtrügest mir, wenn ich mich nachts zurückzieh
in meine Lunge, in die Eingeweide,
in meines Herzens letzte ärmste Kammer,—
ein solcher Vorwurf wäre nicht so grausam,
wie dieses Bitten ist. Was bittest du?

Sag, soll ich reisen? Hast du irgendwo
ein Ding zurückgelassen, das sich quält
und das dir nachwill? Soll ich in ein Land,
das du nicht sahst, obwohl es dir verwandt
war wie die andre Hälfte deiner Sinne?

Ich will auf seinen Flüssen fahren, will
an Land gehn und nach alten Sitten fragen,
will mit den Frauen in den Türen sprechen
und zusehn, wenn sie ihre Kinder rufen.
Ich will mir merken, wie sie dort die Landschaft
umnehmen draußen bei der alten Arbeit
der Wiesen und der Felder; will begehren,
vor ihren König hingeführt zu sein,
und will die Priester durch Bestechung reizen,
daß sie mich legen vor das stärkste Standbild
und fortgehn und die Tempeltore schließen.
Dann aber will ich, wenn ich vieles weiß,
einfach die Tiere anschaun, daß ein Etwas
von ihrer Wendung mir in die Gelenke
herübergleitet; will ein kurzes Dasein
in ihren Augen haben, die mich halten
und langsam lassen, ruhig, ohne Urteil.
Ich will mir von den Gärtnern viele Blumen
hersagen lassen, daß ich in den Scherben
der schönen Eigennamen einen Rest
herüberbringe von den hundert Düften.
Und Früchte will ich kaufen, Früchte, drin
das Land noch einmal ist, bis an den Himmel.
Denn Das verstandest du: die vollen Früchte.

that you can wander anywhere, like a child,
not frightened of any harm that might await you . . .
But no: you're pleading. This penetrates me, to
my very bones, and cuts at me like a saw.
The bitterest rebuke your ghost could bring me,
could scream to me, at night, when I withdraw
into my lungs, into my intestines,
into the last bare chamber of my heart,—
such bitterness would not chill me half so much
as this mute pleading. What is it that you want?

    Tell me, must I travel? Did you leave
some Thing behind, some place, that cannot bear
your absence? Must I set out for a country
you never saw, although it was as vividly
near to you as your own senses were?

    I will sail its rivers, search its valleys, inquire
about its oldest customs; I will stand
for hours, talking with women in their doorways
and watching, while they call their children home.
I will see the way they wrap the land around them
in their ancient work in field and meadow; will ask
to be led before their king; will bribe the priests
to take me to their temple, before the most
powerful of the statues in their keeping,
and to leave me there, shutting the gates behind them.

And only then, when I have learned enough,
I will go to watch the animals, and let
something of their composure slowly glide
into my limbs; will see my own existence
deep in their eyes, which hold me for a while
and let me go, serenely, without judgment.
I will have the gardeners come to me and recite
many flowers, and in the small clay pots
of their melodious names I will bring back
some remnant of the hundred fragrances.
And fruits: I will buy fruits, and in their sweetness
that country's earth and sky will live again.

    For that is what you understood: ripe fruits.

Die legtest du auf Schalen vor dich hin
und wogst mit Farben ihre Schwere auf.
Und so wie Früchte sahst du auch die Fraun
und sahst die Kinder so, von innen her
getrieben in die Formen ihres Daseins.
Und sahst dich selbst zuletzt wie eine Frucht,
nahmst dich heraus aus deinen Kleidern, trugst
dich vor den Spiegel, ließest dich hinein
bis auf dein Schauen; das blieb groß davor
und sagte nicht: das bin ich; nein: dies ist.
So ohne Neugier war zuletzt dein Schaun
und so besitzlos, von so wahrer Armut,
daß es dich selbst nicht mehr begehrte: heilig.

So will ich dich behalten, wie du dich
hinstelltest in den Spiegel, tief hinein
und fort von allem. Warum kommst du anders?
Was widerrufst du dich? Was willst du mir
einreden, daß in jenen Bernsteinkugeln
um deinen Hals noch etwas Schwere war
von jener Schwere, wie sie nie im Jenseits
beruhigter Bilder ist; was zeigst du mir
in deiner Haltung eine böse Ahnung;
was heißt dich die Konturen deines Leibes
auslegen wie die Linien einer Hand,
daß ich sie nicht mehr sehn kann ohne Schicksal?

Komm her ins Kerzenlicht. Ich bin nicht bang,
die Toten anzuschauen. Wenn sie kommen,
so haben sie ein Recht, in unserm Blick
sich aufzuhalten, wie die andern Dinge.

Komm her; wir wollen eine Weile still sein.
Sieh diese Rose an auf meinem Schreibtisch;
ist nicht das Licht um sie genau so zaghaft
wie über dir: sie dürfte auch nicht hier sein.
Im Garten draußen, unvermischt mit mir,
hätte sie bleiben müssen oder hingehn,—
nun währt sie so: was ist ihr mein Bewußtsein?

You set them before the canvas, in white bowls,
and weighed out each one's heaviness with your colors.
Women too, you saw, were fruits; and children, molded
from inside, into the shapes of their existence.
And at last, you saw yourself as a fruit, you stepped
out of your clothes and brought your naked body
before the mirror, you let yourself inside
down to your gaze; which stayed in front, immense,
and didn't say: I am that; no: this is.
So free of curiosity your gaze
had become, so unpossessive, of such true
poverty, it had no desire even
for you yourself; it wanted nothing: holy.

    And that is how I have cherished you—deep inside
the mirror, where you put yourself, far away
from all the world. Why have you come like this
and so denied yourself? Why do you want
to make me think that in the amber beads
you wore in your self-portrait, there was still
a kind of heaviness that can't exist
in the serene heaven of paintings? Why do you show me
an evil omen in the way you stand?
What makes you read the contours of your body
like the lines engraved inside a palm, so that
I cannot see them now except as fate?

    Come into the candlelight. I'm not afraid
to look the dead in the face. When they return,
they have a right, as much as other Things do,
to pause and refresh themselves within our vision.

    Come; and we will be silent for a while.
Look at this rose on the corner of my desk:
isn't the light around it just as timid
as the light on you? It too should not be here,
it should have bloomed or faded in the garden,
outside, never involved with me. But now
it lives on in its small porcelain vase:
what meaning does it find in my awareness?

Erschrick nicht, wenn ich jetzt begreife, ach,
da steigt es in mir auf: ich kann nicht anders,
ich muß begreifen, und wenn ich dran stürbe.
Begreifen, daß du hier bist. Ich begreife.
Ganz wie ein Blinder rings ein Ding begreift,
fühl ich dein Los und weiß ihm keinen Namen.
Laß uns zusammen klagen, daß dich einer
aus deinem Spiegel nahm. Kannst du noch weinen?
Du kannst nicht. Deiner Tränen Kraft und Andrang
hast du verwandelt in dein reifes Anschaun
und warst dabei, jeglichen Saft in dir
so umzusetzen in ein starkes Dasein,
das steigt und kreist, im Gleichgewicht und blindlings.
Da riß ein Zufall dich, dein letzter Zufall
riß dich zurück aus deinem fernsten Fortschritt
in eine Welt zurück, wo Säfte *wollen*.
Riß dich nicht ganz; riß nur ein Stück zuerst,
doch als um dieses Stück von Tag zu Tag
die Wirklichkeit so zunahm, daß es schwer ward,
da brauchtest du dich ganz: da gingst du hin
und brachst in Brocken dich aus dem Gesetz
mühsam heraus, weil du dich brauchtest. Da
trugst du dich ab und grubst aus deines Herzens
nachtwarmem Erdreich die noch grünen Samen,
daraus dein Tod aufkeimen sollte: deiner,
dein eigner Tod zu deinem eignen Leben.
Und aßest sie, die Körner deines Todes,
wie alle andern, aßest seine Körner,
und hattest Nachgeschmack in dir von Süße,
die du nicht meintest, hattest süße Lippen,
du: die schon innen in den Sinnen süß war.

O laß uns klagen. Weißt du, wie dein Blut
aus einem Kreisen ohnegleichen zögernd
und ungern wiederkam, da du es abriefst?
Wie es verwirrt des Leibes kleinen Kreislauf
noch einmal aufnahm; wie es voller Mißtraun
und Staunen eintrat in den Mutterkuchen
und von dem weiten Rückweg plötzlich müd war.

Don't be frightened if I understand it now;
it's rising in me, ah, I'm trying to grasp it,
must grasp it, even if I die of it. Must grasp
that you are here. As a blind man grasps an object,
I feel your fate, although I cannot name it.
Let us lament together that someone pulled you
out of your mirror's depths. Can you still cry?
No: I see you can't. You turned your tears'
strength and pressure into your ripe gaze,
and were transforming every fluid inside you
into a strong reality, which would rise
and circulate, in equilibrium, blindly.
Then, for the last time, chance came in and tore you
back, from the last step forward on your path,
into a world where bodies have their will.
Not all at once: tore just a shred at first;
but when, around this shred, day after day,
the objective world expanded, swelled, grew heavy—
you needed your whole self; and so you went
and broke yourself, out of its grip, in pieces,
painfully, because your need was great.
Then from the night-warm soilbed of your heart
you dug the seeds, still green, from which your death
would sprout: your own, your perfect death, the one
that was your whole life's perfect consummation.
And swallowed down the kernels of your death,
like all the other ones, swallowed them, and were
startled to find an aftertaste of sweetness
you hadn't planned on, a sweetness on your lips, you
who inside your senses were so sweet already.

Ah let us lament. Do you know how hesitantly,
how reluctantly your blood, when you called it back,
returned from its incomparable circuit?
How confused it was to take up once again
the body's narrow circulation; how,
full of mistrust and astonishment, it came
flowing into the placenta and suddenly
was exhausted by the long journey home.

Du triebst es an, du stießest es nach vorn,
du zerrtest es zur Feuerstelle, wie
man eine Herde Tiere zerrt zum Opfer;
und wolltest noch, es sollte dabei froh sein.
Und du erzwangst es schließlich: es war froh
und lief herbei und gab sich hin. Dir schien,
weil du gewohnt warst an die andern Maße,
es wäre nur für eine Weile; aber
nun warst du in der Zeit, und Zeit ist lang.
Und Zeit geht hin, und Zeit nimmt zu, und Zeit
ist wie ein Rückfall einer langen Krankheit.

Wie war dein Leben kurz, wenn du's vergleichst
mit jenen Stunden, da du saßest und
die vielen Kräfte deiner vielen Zukunft
schweigend herabbogst zu dem neuen Kindkeim,
der wieder Schicksal war. O wehe Arbeit.
O Arbeit über alle Kraft. Du tatest
sie Tag für Tag, du schlepptest dich zu ihr
und zogst den schönen Einschlag aus dem Webstuhl
und brauchtest alle deine Fäden anders.
Und endlich hattest du noch Mut zum Fest.

Denn da's getan war, wolltest du belohnt sein,
wie Kinder, wenn sie bittersüßen Tee
getrunken haben, der vielleicht gesund macht.
So lohntest du dich: denn von jedem andern
warst du zu weit, auch jetzt noch; keiner hätte
ausdenken können, welcher Lohn dir wohltut.
Du wußtest es. Du saßest auf im Kindbett,
und vor dir stand ein Spiegel, der dir alles
ganz wiedergab. Nun war das alles *Du*
und ganz *davor*, und drinnen war nur Täuschung,
die schöne Täuschung jeder Frau, die gern
Schmuck umnimmt und das Haar kämmt und verändert.

So starbst du, wie die Frauen früher starben,
altmodisch starbst du in dem warmen Hause
den Tod der Wöchnerinnen, welche wieder
sich schließen wollen und es nicht mehr können,
weil jenes Dunkel, das sie mitgebaren,
noch einmal wiederkommt und drängt und eintritt.

You drove it on, you pushed it forward, you dragged it
up to the hearth, as one would drag a terrified
animal to the sacrificial altar;
and wanted it, after all that, to be happy.
Finally, you forced it: it was happy,
it ran up and surrendered. And you thought,
because you had grown used to other measures,
that this would be for just a little while.
But now you were in time, and time is long.
And time goes on, and time grows large, and time
is like a relapse after a long illness.

How short your life seems, if you now compare it
with those empty hours you passed in silence, bending
the abundant strengths of your abundant future
out of their course, into the new child-seed
that once again was fate. A painful task:
a task beyond all strength. But you performed it
day after day, you dragged yourself in front of it;
you pulled the lovely weft out of the loom
and wove your threads into a different pattern.
And still had courage enough for celebration.

When it was done, you wished to be rewarded,
like children when they have swallowed down the draught
of bittersweet tea that perhaps will make them well.
So you chose your own reward, being still so far
removed from people, even then, that no one
could have imagined what reward would please you.
But you yourself knew. You sat up in your childbed
and in front of you was a mirror, which gave back
everything. And this everything was you,
and right in front; inside was mere deception,
the sweet deception of every woman who smiles
as she puts her jewelry on and combs her hair.

And so you died as women used to die,
at home, in your own warm bedroom, the old-fashioned
death of women in labor, who try to close
themselves again but can't, because that ancient
darkness which they have also given birth to
returns for them, thrusts its way in, and enters.

Ob man nicht dennoch hätte Klagefrauen
auftreiben müssen? Weiber, welche weinen
für Geld, und die man so bezahlen kann,
daß sie die Nacht durch heulen, wenn es still wird.
Gebräuche her! wir haben nicht genug
Gebräuche. Alles geht und wird verredet.
So mußt du kommen, tot, und hier mit mir
Klagen nachholen. Hörst du, daß ich klage?
Ich möchte meine Stimme wie ein Tuch
hinwerfen über deines Todes Scherben
und zerrn an ihr, bis sie in Fetzen geht,
und alles, was ich sage, müßte so
zerlumpt in dieser Stimme gehn und frieren;
blieb es beim Klagen. Doch jetzt klag ich an:
den Einen nicht, der dich aus dir zurückzog,
(ich find ihn nicht heraus, er ist wie alle)
doch alle klag ich in ihm an: den Mann.

Wenn irgendwo ein Kindgewesensein
tief in mir aufsteigt, das ich noch nicht kenne,
vielleicht das reinste Kindsein meiner Kindheit:
ich wills nicht wissen. Einen Engel will
ich daraus bilden ohne hinzusehn
und will ihn werfen in die erste Reihe
schreiender Engel, welche Gott erinnern.

Denn dieses Leiden dauert schon zu lang,
und keiner kanns; es ist zu schwer für uns,
das wirre Leiden von der falschen Liebe,
die, bauend auf Verjährung wie Gewohnheit,
ein Recht sich nennt und wuchert aus dem Unrecht.
Wo ist ein Mann, der Recht hat auf Besitz?
Wer kann besitzen, was sich selbst nicht hält,
was sich von Zeit zu Zeit nur selig auffängt
und wieder hinwirft wie ein Kind den Ball.
Sowenig wie der Feldherr eine Nike
festhalten kann am Vorderbug des Schiffes,
wenn das geheime Leichtsein ihrer Gottheit
sie plötzlich weghebt in den hellen Meerwind:
so wenig kann einer von uns die Frau

Once, ritual lament would have been chanted;
women would have been paid to beat their breasts
and howl for you all night, when all is silent.
Where can we find such customs now? So many
have long since disappeared or been disowned.
That's what you had to come for: to retrieve
the lament that we omitted. Can you hear me?
I would like to fling my voice out like a cloth
over the fragments of your death, and keep
pulling at it until it is torn to pieces,
and all my words would have to walk around
shivering, in the tatters of that voice;
if lament were enough. But now I must accuse:
not the man who withdrew you from yourself
(I cannot find him; he looks like everyone),
but in this one man, I accuse: all men.

    When somewhere, from deep within me, there arises
the vivid sense of having been a child,
the purity and essence of that childhood
where I once lived: then I don't want to know it.
I want to form an angel from that sense
and hurl him upward, into the front row
of angels who scream out, reminding God.

    For this suffering has lasted far too long;
none of us can bear it; it is too heavy—
this tangled suffering of spurious love
which, building on convention like a habit,
calls itself just, and fattens on injustice.
Show me a man with the right to his possession.
Who can possess what cannot hold its own self,
but only, now and then, will blissfully
catch itself, then quickly throw itself
away, like a child playing with a ball.
As little as a captain can hold the carved
Nikē facing outward from his ship's prow
when the lightness of her godhead suddenly
lifts her up, into the bright sea-wind:
so little can one of us call back the woman

anrufen, die uns nicht mehr sieht und die
auf einem schmalen Streifen ihres Daseins
wie durch ein Wunder fortgeht, ohne Unfall:
er hätte denn Beruf und Lust zur Schuld.

    Denn *das* ist Schuld, wenn irgendeines Schuld ist:
die Freiheit eines Lieben nicht vermehren
um alle Freiheit, die man in sich aufbringt.
Wir haben, wo wir lieben, ja nur dies:
einander lassen; denn daß wir uns halten,
das fällt uns leicht und ist nicht erst zu lernen.

    Bist du noch da? In welcher Ecke bist du?—
Du hast so viel gewußt von alledem
und hast so viel gekonnt, da du so hingingst
für alles offen, wie ein Tag, der anbricht.
Die Frauen leiden: lieben heißt allein sein,
und Künstler ahnen manchmal in der Arbeit,
daß sie verwandeln müssen, wo sie lieben.
Beides begannst du; beides ist in Dem,
was jetzt ein Ruhm entstellt, der es dir fortnimmt.
Ach du warst weit von jedem Ruhm. Du warst
unscheinbar; hattest leise deine Schönheit
hineingenommen, wie man eine Fahne
einzieht am grauen Morgen eines Werktags,
und wolltest nichts, als eine lange Arbeit,—
die nicht getan ist: dennoch nicht getan.
    Wenn du noch da bist, wenn in diesem Dunkel
noch eine Stelle ist, an der dein Geist
empfindlich mitschwingt auf den flachen Schallwelln,
die eine Stimme, einsam in der Nacht,
aufregt in eines hohen Zimmers Strömung:
So hör mich: Hilf mir. Sieh, wir gleiten so,
nicht wissend wann, zurück aus unserm Fortschritt
in irgendwas, was wir nicht meinen; drin
wir uns verfangen wie in einem Traum
und drin wir sterben, ohne zu erwachen.
Keiner ist weiter. Jedem, der sein Blut
hinaufhob in ein Werk, das lange wird,

who, now no longer seeing us, walks on
along the narrow strip of her existence
as though by miracle, in perfect safety—
unless, that is, he wishes to do wrong.

For *this* is wrong, if anything is wrong:
not to enlarge the freedom of a love
with all the inner freedom one can summon.
We need, in love, to practice only this:
letting each other go. For holding on
comes easily; we do not need to learn it.

Are you still here? Are you standing in some corner?—
You knew so much of all this, you were able
to do so much; you passed through life so open
to all things, like an early morning. I know:
women suffer; for love means being alone;
and artists in their work sometimes intuit
that they must keep transforming, where they love.
You began both; both exist in that
which any fame takes from you and disfigures.
Oh you were far beyond all fame; were almost
invisible; had withdrawn your beauty, softly,
as one would lower a brightly-colored flag
on the gray morning after a holiday.
You had just one desire: a years-long work—
which was not finished; was somehow never finished.
If you are still here with me, if in this darkness
there is still some place where your spirit resonates
on the shallow soundwaves stirred up by my voice:
hear me; help me. We can so easily
slip back from what we have struggled to attain,
abruptly, into a life we never wanted;
can find that we are trapped, as in a dream,
and die there, without ever waking up.
This can occur. Anyone who has lifted
his blood into a years-long work may find

kann es geschehen, daß ers nicht mehr hochhält
und daß es geht nach seiner Schwere, wertlos.
Denn irgendwo ist eine alte Feindschaft
zwischen dem Leben und der großen Arbeit.
Daß ich sie einseh und sie sage: hilf mir.

    Komm nicht zurück. Wenn du's erträgst, so sei
tot bei den Toten. Tote sind beschäftigt.
Doch hilf mir so, daß es dich nicht zerstreut,
wie mir das Fernste manchmal hilft: in mir.

that he can't sustain it, the force of gravity
is irresistible, and it falls back, worthless.
For somewhere there is an ancient enmity
between our daily life and the great work.
Help me, in saying it, to understand it.

Do not return. If you can bear to, stay
dead with the dead. The dead have their own tasks.
But help me, if you can without distraction,
as what is farthest sometimes helps: in me.

FROM

THE NOTEBOOKS OF MALTE LAURIDS BRIGGE

(1910)

. . . Ach, aber mit Versen ist so wenig getan, wenn man sie früh schreibt. Man sollte warten damit und Sinn und Süßigkeit sammeln ein ganzes Leben lang und ein langes womöglich, und dann, ganz zum Schluß, vielleicht könnte man dann zehn Zeilen schreiben, die gut sind. Denn Verse sind nicht, wie die Leute meinen, Gefühle (die hat man früh genug),—es sind Erfahrungen. Um eines Verses willen muß man viele Städte sehen, Menschen und Dinge, man muß die Tiere kennen, man muß fühlen, wie die Vögel fliegen, und die Gebärde wissen, mit welcher die kleinen Blumen sich auftun am Morgen. Man muß zurückdenken können an Wege in unbekannten Gegenden, an unerwartete Begegnungen und an Abschiede, die man lange kommen sah,—an Kindheitstage, die noch unaufgeklärt sind, an die Eltern, die man kränken mußte, wenn sie einem eine Freude brachten und man begriff sie nicht (es war eine Freude für einen anderen—), an Kinderkrankheiten, die so seltsam anheben mit so vielen tiefen und schweren Verwandlungen, an Tage in stillen, verhaltenen Stuben und an Morgen am Meer, an das Meer überhaupt, an Meere, an Reisenächte, die hoch dahinrauschten und mit allen Sternen flogen,—und es ist noch nicht genug, wenn man an alles das denken darf. Man muß Erinnerungen haben an viele Liebesnächte, von denen keine der andern glich, an Schreie von Kreißenden und an leichte, weiße, schlafende Wöchnerinnen, die sich schließen. Aber auch bei Sterbenden muß man gewesen sein, muß bei Toten gesessen haben in der Stube mit dem offenen Fenster und den stoßweisen Geräuschen. Und es genügt auch noch nicht, daß man Erinnerungen hat. Man muß sie vergessen können, wenn es viele sind, und man muß die große Geduld haben, zu warten, daß sie wiederkommen. Denn die Erinnerungen selbst *sind* es noch nicht. Erst wenn sie Blut werden in uns, Blick und Gebärde, namenlos und nicht mehr zu unterscheiden von uns selbst, erst dann kann es geschehen, daß in einer sehr seltenen Stunde das erste Wort eines Verses aufsteht in ihrer Mitte und aus ihnen ausgeht.

[FOR THE SAKE OF A SINGLE POEM]

... Ah, poems amount to so little when you write them too early in your life. You ought to wait and gather sense and sweetness for a whole lifetime, and a long one if possible, and then, at the very end, you might perhaps be able to write ten good lines. For poems are not, as people think, simply emotions (one has emotions early enough)—they are experiences. For the sake of a single poem, you must see many cities, many people and Things, you must understand animals, must feel how birds fly, and know the gesture which small flowers make when they open in the morning. You must be able to think back to streets in unknown neighborhoods, to unexpected encounters, and to partings you had long seen coming; to days of childhood whose mystery is still unexplained, to parents whom you had to hurt when they brought in a joy and you didn't pick it up (it was a joy meant for somebody else—); to childhood illnesses that began so strangely with so many profound and difficult transformations, to days in quiet, restrained rooms and to mornings by the sea, to the sea itself, to seas, to nights of travel that rushed along high overhead and went flying with all the stars,—and it is still not enough to be able to think of all that. You must have memories of many nights of love, each one different from all the others, memories of women screaming in labor, and of light, pale, sleeping girls who have just given birth and are closing again. But you must also have been beside the dying, must have sat beside the dead in the room with the open window and the scattered noises. And it is not yet enough to have memories. You must be able to forget them when they are many, and you must have the immense patience to wait until they return. For the memories themselves are not important. Only when they have changed into our very blood, into glance and gesture, and are nameless, no longer to be distinguished from ourselves—only then can it happen that in some very rare hour the first word of a poem arises in their midst and goes forth from them.

Habe ich es schon gesagt? Ich lerne sehen. Ja, ich fange an. Es geht noch schlecht. Aber ich will meine Zeit ausnutzen.

Daß es mir zum Beispiel niemals zum Bewußtsein gekommen ist, wieviel Gesichter es giebt. Es giebt eine Menge Menschen, aber noch viel mehr Gesichter, denn jeder hat mehrere. Da sind Leute, die tragen ein Gesicht jahrelang, natürlich nutzt es sich ab, es wird schmutzig, es bricht in den Falten, es weitet sich aus wie Handschuhe, die man auf der Reise getragen hat. Das sind sparsame, einfache Leute; sie wechseln es nicht, sie lassen es nicht einmal reinigen. Es sei gut genug, behaupten sie, und wer kann ihnen das Gegenteil nachweisen? Nun fragt es sich freilich, da sie mehrere Gesichter haben, was tun sie mit den andern? Sie heben sie auf. Ihre Kinder sollen sie tragen. Aber es kommt auch vor, daß ihre Hunde damit ausgehen. Weshalb auch nicht? Gesicht ist Gesicht.

Andere Leute setzen unheimlich schnell ihre Gesichter auf, eins nach dem andern, und tragen sie ab. Es scheint ihnen zuerst, sie hätten für immer, aber sie sind kaum vierzig; da ist schon das letzte. Das hat natürlich seine Tragik. Sie sind nicht gewohnt, Gesichter zu schonen, ihr letztes ist in acht Tagen durch, hat Löcher, ist an vielen Stellen dünn wie Papier, und da kommt dann nach und nach die Unterlage heraus, das Nichtgesicht, und sie gehen damit herum.

Aber die Frau, die Frau: sie war ganz in sich hineingefallen, vornüber in ihre Hände. Es war an der Ecke rue Notre-Dame-des-Champs. Ich fing an, leise zu gehen, sowie ich sie gesehen hatte. Wenn arme Leute nachdenken, soll man sie nicht stören. Vielleicht fällt es ihnen doch ein.

Die Straße war zu leer, ihre Leere langweilte sich und zog mir den Schritt unter den Füßen weg und klappte mit ihm herum, drüben und da, wie mit einem Holzschuh. Die Frau erschrak und hob sich aus sich ab, zu schnell, zu heftig, so daß das Gesicht in den zwei Händen blieb. Ich konnte es darin liegen sehen, seine hohle Form. Es kostete mich unbeschreibliche Anstrengung, bei diesen Händen zu bleiben und nicht zu schauen, was sich aus ihnen abgerissen hatte. Mir graute, ein Gesicht von innen zu sehen, aber ich fürchtete mich doch noch viel mehr vor dem bloßen wunden Kopf ohne Gesicht.

[FACES]

Have I said it before? I am learning to see. Yes, I am beginning. It's still going badly. But I intend to make the most of my time.

For example, it never occurred to me before how many faces there are. There are multitudes of people, but there are many more faces, because each person has several of them. There are people who wear the same face for years; naturally it wears out, gets dirty, splits at the seams, stretches like gloves worn during a long journey. They are thrifty, uncomplicated people; they never change it, never even have it cleaned. It's good enough, they say, and who can convince them of the contrary? Of course, since they have several faces, you might wonder what they do with the other ones. They keep them in storage. Their children will wear them. But sometimes it also happens that their dogs go out wearing them. And why not? A face is a face.

Other people change faces incredibly fast, put on one after another, and wear them out. At first, they think they have an unlimited supply; but when they are barely forty years old they come to their last one. There is, to be sure, something tragic about this. They are not accustomed to taking care of faces; their last one is worn through in a week, has holes in it, is in many places as thin as paper, and then, little by little, the lining shows through, the non-face, and they walk around with that on.

But the woman, the woman: she had completely fallen into herself, forward into her hands. It was on the corner of rue Notre-Dame-des-Champs. I began to walk quietly as soon as I saw her. When poor people are thinking, they shouldn't be disturbed. Perhaps their idea will still occur to them.

The street was too empty; its emptiness had gotten bored and pulled my steps out from under my feet and clattered around in them, all over the street, as if they were wooden clogs. The woman sat up, frightened, she pulled out of herself, too quickly, too violently, so that her face was left in her two hands. I could see it lying there: its hollow form. It cost me an indescribable effort to stay with those two hands, not to look at what had been torn out of them. I shuddered to see a face from the inside, but I was much more afraid of that bare flayed head waiting there, faceless.

Ich liege in meinem Bett, fünf Treppen hoch, und mein Tag, den nichts unterbricht, ist wie ein Zifferblatt ohne Zeiger. Wie ein Ding, das lange verloren war, eines Morgens auf seiner Stelle liegt, geschont und gut, neuer fast als zur Zeit des Verlustes, ganz als ob es bei irgend jemandem in Pflege gewesen wäre—: so liegt da und da auf meiner Bettdecke Verlorenes aus der Kindheit und ist wie neu. Alle verlorenen Ängste sind wieder da.

Die Angst, daß ein kleiner Wollfaden, der aus dem Saum der Decke heraussteht, hart sei, hart und scharf wie eine stählerne Nadel; die Angst, daß dieser kleine Knopf meines Nachthemdes größer sei als mein Kopf, groß und schwer; die Angst, daß dieses Krümchen Brot, das jetzt von meinem Bette fällt, gläsern und zerschlagen unten ankommen würde, und die drückende Sorge, daß damit eigentlich alles zerbrochen sei, alles für immer; die Angst, daß der Streifen Rand eines aufgerissenen Briefes etwas Verbotenes sei, das niemand sehen dürfe, etwas unbeschreiblich Kostbares, für das keine Stelle in der Stube sicher genug sei; die Angst, daß ich, wenn ich einschliefe, das Stück Kohle verschlucken würde, das vor dem Ofen liegt; die Angst, daß irgendeine Zahl in meinem Gehirn zu wachsen beginnt, bis sie nicht mehr Raum hat in mir; die Angst, daß das Granit sei, worauf ich liege, grauer Granit; die Angst, daß ich schreien könnte und daß man vor meiner Türe zusammenliefe und sie schließlich aufbräche, die Angst, daß ich mich verraten könnte und alles das sagen, wovor ich mich fürchte, und die Angst, daß ich nichts sagen könnte, weil alles unsagbar ist, —und die anderen Ängste . . . die Ängste.

Ich habe um meine Kindheit gebeten, und sie ist wiedergekommen, und ich fühle, daß sie immer noch so schwer ist wie damals und daß es nichts genützt hat, älter zu werden.

[FEARS]

I am lying in my bed five flights up, and my day, which nothing interrupts, is like a clock-face without hands. As something that has been lost for a long time reappears one morning in its old place, safe and sound, almost newer than when it vanished, just as if someone had been taking care of it—: so, here and there on my blanket, lost feelings out of my childhood lie and are like new. All the lost fears are here again.

The fear that a small woolen thread sticking out of the hem of my blanket may be hard, hard and sharp as a steel needle; the fear that this little button on my night-shirt may be bigger than my head, bigger and heavier; the fear that the breadcrumb which just dropped off my bed may turn into glass, and shatter when it hits the floor, and the sickening worry that when it does, everything will be broken, for ever; the fear that the ragged edge of a letter which was torn open may be something forbidden, which no one ought to see, something indescribably precious, for which no place in the room is safe enough; the fear that if I fell asleep I might swallow the piece of coal lying in front of the stove; the fear that some number may begin to grow in my brain until there is no more room for it inside me; the fear that I may be lying on granite, on gray granite; the fear that I may start screaming, and people will come running to my door and finally force it open, the fear that I might betray myself and tell everything I dread, and the fear that I might not be able to say anything, because everything is unsayable,—and the other fears . . . the fears.

I prayed to rediscover my childhood, and it has come back, and I feel that it is just as difficult as it used to be, and that growing older has served no purpose at all.

Ich unterschätze es nicht. Ich weiß, es gehört Mut dazu. Aber nehmen wir
für einen Augenblick an, es hätte ihn einer, diesen Courage de luxe, ihnen
nachzugehen, um dann für immer (denn wer könnte das wieder vergessen oder
verwechseln?) zu wissen, wo sie hernach hineinkriechen und was sie den vielen
übrigen Tag beginnen und ob sie schlafen bei Nacht. Dies ganz besonders wäre
festzustellen: ob sie schlafen. Aber mit dem Mut ist es noch nicht getan. Denn
sie kommen und gehen nicht wie die übrigen Leute, denen zu folgen eine
Kleinigkeit wäre. Sie sind da und wieder fort, hingestellt und weggenommen
wie Bleisoldaten. Es sind ein wenig abgelegene Stellen, wo man sie findet, aber
durchaus nicht versteckte. Die Büsche treten zurück, der Weg wendet sich ein
wenig um den Rasenplatz herum: da stehen sie und haben eine Menge durchsich-
tigen Raumes um sich, als ob sie unter einem Glassturz stünden. Du könntest
sie für nachdenkliche Spaziergänger halten, diese unscheinbaren Männer von
kleiner, in jeder Beziehung bescheidener Gestalt. Aber du irrst. Siehst du die
linke Hand, wie sie nach etwas greift in der schiefen Tasche des alten Überzie-
hers; wie sie es findet und herausholt und den kleinen Gegenstand linkisch und
auffällig in die Luft hält? Es dauert keine Minute, so sind zwei, drei Vögel da,
Spatzen, die neugierig heranhüpfen. Und wenn es dem Manne gelingt, ihrer sehr
genauen Auffassung von Unbeweglichkeit zu entsprechen, so ist kein Grund,
warum sie nicht noch näher kommen sollen. Und schließlich steigt der erste und
schwirrt eine Weile nervös in der Höhe jener Hand, die (weiß Gott) ein kleines
Stück abgenutzten süßen Brotes mit anspruchslosen, ausdrücklich verzichtenden
Fingern hinbietet. Und je mehr Menschen sich um ihn sammeln, in entsprechen-
dem Abstand natürlich, desto weniger hat er mit ihnen gemein. Wie ein
Leuchter steht er da, der ausbrennt, und leuchtet mit dem Rest von Docht und
ist ganz warm davon und hat sich nie gerührt. Und wie er lockt, wie er anlockt,
das können die vielen, kleinen, dummen Vögel gar nicht beurteilen. Wenn die
Zuschauer nicht wären und man ließe ihn lange genug dastehn, ich bin sicher,
daß auf einmal ein Engel käme und überwände sich und äße den alten, süß-
lichen Bissen aus der verkümmerten Hand. Dem sind nun, wie immer, die Leute
im Wege. Sie sorgen dafür, daß nur Vögel kommen; sie finden das reichlich,
und sie behaupten, er erwarte sich nichts anderes. Was sollte sie auch erwarten,
diese alte, verregnete Puppe, die ein wenig schräg in der Erde steckt wie die
Schiffsfiguren in den kleinen Gärten zuhause; kommt auch bei ihr diese Haltung
davon her, daß sie einmal irgendwo vorne gestanden hat auf ihrem Leben, wo
die Bewegung am größten ist? Ist sie nun so verwaschen, weil sie einmal bunt
war? Willst du sie fragen?

[THE BIRD-FEEDERS]

I don't underestimate it. I know it takes courage. But let us suppose for a moment that someone had it, this *courage de luxe* to follow them, in order to know for ever (for who could forget it again or confuse it with anything else?) where they creep off to afterward and what they do with the rest of the long day and whether they sleep at night. That especially should be ascertained: whether they sleep. But it will take more than courage. For they don't come and go like other people, whom it would be child's play to follow. They are here and then gone, put down and snatched away like toy soldiers. The places where they can be found are somewhat out-of-the-way, but by no means hidden. The bushes recede, the path curves slightly around the lawn: there they are, with a large transparent space around them, as if they were standing under a glass dome. You might think they were pausing, absorbed in their thoughts, these inconspicuous men, with such small, in every way unassuming bodies. But you are wrong. Do you see the left hand, how it is grasping for something in the slanted pocket of the old coat? how it finds it and takes it out and holds the small object in the air, awkwardly, attracting attention? In less than a minute, two or three birds appear, sparrows, which come hopping up inquisitively. And if the man succeeds in conforming to their very exact idea of immobility, there is no reason why they shouldn't come even closer. Finally one of them flies up, and flutters nervously for a while at the level of that hand, which is holding out God knows what crumbs of used-up bread in its unpretentious, explicitly renunciatory fingers. And the more people gather around him—at a suitable distance, of course—the less he has in common with them. He stands there like a candle that is almost consumed and burns with the small remnant of its wick and is all warm with it and has never moved. And all those small, foolish birds can't understand how he attracts, how he tempts them. If there were no onlookers and he were allowed to stand there long enough, I'm certain that an angel would suddenly appear and, overcoming his disgust, would eat the stale, sweetish breadcrumbs from that stunted hand. But now, as always, people keep that from happening. They make sure that only birds come; they find this quite sufficient and assert that he expects nothing else. What else could it expect, this old, weather-beaten doll, stuck into the ground at a slight angle, like a painted figurehead in an old sea-captain's garden? Does it stand like that because it too had once been placed somewhere on the forward tip of its life, at the point where motion is greatest? Is it now so washed out because it was once so bright? Will you go ask it?

Nur die Frauen frag nichts, wenn du eine füttern siehst. Denen könnte man sogar folgen; sie tun es so im Vorbeigehen; es wäre ein Leichtes. Aber laß sie. Sie wissen nicht, wie es kam. Sie haben auf einmal eine Menge Brot in ihrem Handsack, und sie halten große Stücke hinaus aus ihrer dünnen Mantille, Stücke, die ein bißchen gekaut sind und feucht. Das tut ihnen wohl, daß ihr Speichel ein wenig in die Welt kommt, daß die kleinen Vögel mit diesem Beigeschmack herumfliegen, wenn sie ihn natürlich auch gleich wieder vergessen.

Only don't ask the women anything when you see them feeding the birds. You could even follow them; they do it just in passing; it would be easy. But leave them alone. They don't know how it happens. All at once they have a whole purseful of bread, and they hold out large pieces from under their flimsy shawls, pieces that are a bit chewed and soggy. It does them good to think that their saliva is getting out into the world a little, that the small birds will fly off with the taste of it in their mouths, even though a moment later they naturally forget it again.

Da saß ich an deinen Büchern, Eigensinniger, und versuchte sie zu meinen wie die andern, die dich nicht beisammen lassen und sich ihren Anteil genommen haben, befriedigt. Denn da begriff ich noch nicht den Ruhm, diesen öffentlichen Abbruch eines Werdenden, in dessen Bauplatz die Menge einbricht, ihm die Steine verschiebend.

Junger Mensch irgendwo, in dem etwas aufsteigt, was ihn erschauern macht, nütz es, daß dich keiner kennt. Und wenn sie dir widersprechen, die dich für nichts nehmen, und wenn sie dich ganz aufgeben, die, mit denen du umgehst, und wenn sie dich ausrotten wollen, um deiner lieben Gedanken willen, was ist diese deutliche Gefahr, die dich zusammenhält in dir, gegen die listige Feindschaft später des Ruhms, die dich unschädlich macht, indem sie dich ausstreut.

Bitte keinen, daß er von dir spräche, nicht einmal verächtlich. Und wenn die Zeit geht und du merkst, wie dein Name herumkommt unter den Leuten, nimm ihn nicht ernster als alles, was du in ihrem Munde findest. Denk: er ist schlecht geworden, und tu ihn ab. Nimm einen andern an, irgendeinen, damit Gott dich rufen kann in der Nacht. Und verbirg ihn vor allen.

Du Einsamster, Abseitiger, wie haben sie dich eingeholt auf deinem Ruhm. Wie lang ist es her, da waren sie wider dich von Grund aus, und jetzt gehen sie mit dir um, wie mit ihresgleichen. Und deine Worte führen sie mit sich in den Käfigen ihres Dünkels und zeigen sie auf den Plätzen und reizen sie ein wenig von ihrer Sicherheit aus. Alle deine schrecklichen Raubtiere.

Da las ich dich erst, da sie mir ausbrachen und mich anfielen in meiner Wüste, die Verzweifelten. Verzweifelt, wie du selber warst am Schluß, du, dessen Bahn falsch eingezeichnet steht in allen Karten. Wie ein Sprung geht sie durch die Himmel, diese hoffnungslose Hyperbel deines Weges, die sich nur einmal heranbiegt an uns und sich entfernt voll Entsetzen. Was lag dir daran, ob eine Frau bleibt oder fortgeht und ob einen der Schwindel ergreift und einen der Wahnsinn und ob Tote lebendig sind und Lebendige scheintot: was lag dir daran? Dies alles war so natürlich für dich; da gingst du durch, wie man durch einen Vorraum geht, und hieltst dich nicht auf. Aber dort weiltest du und warst gebückt, wo unser Geschehen kocht und sich niederschlägt und die Farbe verändert, innen. Innerer als dort, wo je einer war; eine Tür war dir aufgesprungen, und nun warst du bei den Kolben im Feuerschein. Dort, wohin du nie einen mitnahmst, Mißtrauischer, dort saßest du und unterschiedest Übergänge. Und

[IBSEN]

There I sat before your books, obstinate man, trying to understand them as the others do, who don't leave you in one piece but chip off their little portion and go away satisfied. For I still didn't understand fame, that public demolition of someone who is in the process of becoming, whose building-site the mob breaks into, knocking down his stones.

Young man anywhere, in whom something is welling up that makes you shiver, be grateful that no one knows you. And if those who think you are worthless contradict you, and if those whom you call your friends abandon you, and if they want to destroy you because of your precious ideas: what is this obvious danger, which concentrates you inside yourself, compared with the cunning enmity of fame, later, which makes you innocuous by scattering you all around?

Don't ask anyone to speak about you, not even contemptuously. And when time passes and you notice that your name is circulating among men, don't take this more seriously than anything else you might find in their mouths. Think rather that it has become cheapened, and throw it away. Take another name, *any* other, so that God can call you in the night. And hide it from everyone.

Loneliest of men, holding aloof from them all, how quickly they have caught up with you because of your fame. A little while ago they were against you body and soul; and now they treat you as their equal. And they pull your words around with them in the cages of their presumption, and exhibit them in the streets, and tease them a little, from a safe distance. All your terrifying wild beasts.

When I first read you, these words broke loose and fell upon me in my wilderness, in all their desperation. As desperate as you yourself became in the end, you whose course is drawn incorrectly on every chart. Like a crack it crosses the heavens, this hopeless hyperbola of your path, which curves toward us only once, then recedes again in terror. What did you care if a woman stayed or left, if this man was seized by vertigo and that one by madness, if the dead were alive and the living seemed dead: what did you care? It was all so natural for you; you passed through it the way someone might walk through a vestibule, and didn't stop. But you lingered, bent over, where our life boils and precipitates and changes color: inside. Farther in than anyone has ever been; a door had sprung open before you, and now you were among the alembics in the firelight. In there, where, mistrustful, you wouldn't take anyone with you, in there you

dort, weil das Aufzeigen dir im Blute war und nicht das Bilden oder das Sagen, dort faßtest du den ungeheuren Entschluß, dieses Winzige, das du selber zuerst nur durch Gläser gewahrtest, ganz allein gleich so zu vergrößern, daß es vor Tausenden sei, riesig, vor allen. Dein Theater entstand. Du konntest nicht warten, daß dieses fast raumlose von den Jahrhunderten zu Tropfen zusammengepreßte Leben von den anderen Künsten gefunden und allmählich versichtbart werde für einzelne, die sich nach und nach zusammenfinden zur Einsicht und die endlich verlangen, gemeinsam die erlauchten Gerüchte bestätigt zu sehen im Gleichnis der vor ihnen aufgeschlagenen Szene. Dies konntest du nicht abwarten, du warst da, du mußtest das kaum Meßbare: ein Gefühl, das um einen halben Grad stieg, den Ausschlagswinkel eines von fast nichts beschwerten Willens, den du ablasest von ganz nah, die leichte Trübung in einem Tropfen Sehnsucht und dieses Nichts von Farbenwechsel in einem Atom von Zutrauen: dieses mußtest du feststellen und aufbehalten; denn in solchen Vorgängen war jetzt das Leben, unser Leben, das in uns hineingeglitten war, das sich nach innen zurückgezogen hatte, so tief, daß es kaum noch Vermutungen darüber gab.

So wie du warst, auf das Zeigen angelegt, ein zeitlos tragischer Dichter, mußtest du dieses Kapillare mit einem Schlag umsetzen in die überzeugendsten Gebärden, in die vorhandensten Dinge. Da gingst du an die beispiellose Gewalttat deines Werkes, das immer ungeduldiger, immer verzweifelter unter dem Sichtbaren nach den Äquivalenten suchte für das innen Gesehene. Da war ein Kaninchen, ein Bodenraum, ein Saal, in dem einer auf und nieder geht: da war ein Glasklirren im Nebenzimmer, ein Brand vor den Fenstern, da war die Sonne. Da war eine Kirche und ein Felsental, das einer Kirche glich. Aber das reichte nicht aus; schließlich mußten die Türme herein und die ganzen Gebirge; und die Lawinen, die die Landschaften begraben, verschütteten die mit Greifbarem überladene Bühne um des Unfaßlichen willen. Da konntst du nicht mehr. Die beiden Enden, die du zusammengebogen hattest, schnellten auseinander; deine wahnsinnige Kraft entsprang aus dem elastischen Stab, und dein Werk war wie nicht.

Wer begriffe es sonst, daß du zum Schluß nicht vom Fenster fortwolltest, eigensinnig wie du immer warst. Die Vorübergehenden wolltest du sehen; denn es war dir der Gedanke gekommen, ob man nicht eines Tages etwas machen könnte aus ihnen, wenn man sich entschlösse anzufangen.

sat and discerned transitions. And there, since your blood drove you not to form or to speak, but to reveal, there you made the enormous decision to so magnify these tiny events, which you yourself first perceived only in test tubes, that they would be seen by thousands of people, immense before them all. Your theater came into being. You couldn't wait until this life almost without spatial reality, this life which had been condensed by the weight of the centuries into a few small drops, could be discovered by the other arts: until it could gradually be made visible to a few connoisseurs who, little by little, acquire insight and finally demand to see these august rumors confirmed in the parable of the scene opened in front of them. You couldn't wait for that; you were there, and everything that is barely measurable—an emotion that rises by half a degree, the angle of deflection, read off from up close, of a will burdened by an almost infinitesimal weight, the slight cloudiness in a drop of longing, and that barely perceptible color-change in an atom of confidence—all this you had to determine and record. For it is in such reactions that life existed, *our* life, which had slipped into us, had drawn back inside us so deeply that it was hardly possible even to make conjectures about it any more.

Because you were a revealer, a timelessly tragic poet, you had to transform this capillary action all at once into the most convincing gestures, into the most available forms. So you began that unprecedented act of violence in your work, which, more and more impatiently, desperately, sought equivalents in the visible world for what you had seen inside. There was a rabbit there, an attic, a room where someone was pacing back and forth; there was a clatter of glass in a nearby bedroom, a fire outside the windows; there was the sun. There was a church, and a rock-strewn valley that was like a church. But this wasn't enough: finally towers had to come in and whole mountain-ranges; and the avalanches that bury landscapes spilled onto a stage overwhelmed with what is tangible, for the sake of what cannot be grasped. Then you could do no more. The two ends, which you had bent together until they touched, sprang apart; your demented strength escaped from the flexible wand, and your work was as if it had never existed.

If this hadn't happened, who could understand why in the end you refused to go away from the window, obstinate as you always were? You wanted to see the people passing by; for the thought had occurred to you that someday you might make something out of them, if you decided to begin.

Wie begreif ich jetzt die wunderlichen Bilder, darinnen Dinge von beschränkten und regelmäßigen Gebrauchen sich ausspannen und sich lüstern und neugierig aneinander versuchen, zuckend in der ungefähren Unzucht der Zerstreuung. Diese Kessel, die kochend herumgehen, diese Kolben, die auf Gedanken kommen, und die müßigen Trichter, die sich in ein Loch drängen zu ihrem Vergnügen. Und da sind auch schon, vom eifersüchtigen Nichts heraufgeworfen, Gliedmaßen und Glieder unter ihnen und Gesichter, die warm in sie hineinvomieren, und blasende Gesäße, die ihnen den Gefallen tun.

Und der Heilige krümmt sich und zieht sich zusammen; aber in seinen Augen war noch ein Blick, der dies für möglich hielt: er hat hingesehen. Und schon schlagen sich seine Sinne nieder aus der hellen Lösung seiner Seele. Schon entblättert sein Gebet und steht ihm aus dem Mund wie ein eingegangener Strauch. Sein Herz ist umgefallen und ausgeflossen ins Trübe hinein. Seine Geißel trifft ihn schwach wie ein Schwanz, der Fliegen verjagt. Sein Geschlecht ist wieder nur an einer Stelle, und wenn eine Frau aufrecht durch das Gehudel kommt, den offenen Busen voll Brüste, so zeigt es auf sie wie ein Finger.

Es gab Zeiten, da ich diese Bilder für veraltet hielt. Nicht, als ob ich an ihnen zweifelte. Ich konnte mir denken, daß dies den Heiligen geschah, damals, den eifernden Voreiligen, die gleich mit Gott anfangen wollten um jeden Preis. Wir muten uns dies nicht mehr zu. Wir ahnen, daß er zu schwer ist für uns, daß wir ihn hinausschieben müssen, um langsam die lange Arbeit zu tun, die uns von ihm trennt. Nun aber weiß ich, daß diese Arbeit genau so bestritten ist wie das Heiligsein; daß dies da um jeden entsteht, der um ihretwillen einsam ist, wie es sich bildete um die Einsamen Gottes in ihren Höhlen und leeren Herbergen, einst.

[THE TEMPTATION OF THE SAINT]

How well I understand those strange pictures in which Things meant for limited and ordinary uses stretch out and stroke one another, lewd and curious, quivering in the random lechery of distraction. Those kettles that walk around steaming, those pistons that start to think, and the indolent funnel that squeezes into a hole for its pleasure. And already, tossed up by the jealous void, and among them, there are arms and legs, and faces that warmly vomit onto them, and windy buttocks that offer them satisfaction.

And the saint writhes and pulls back into himself; yet in his eyes there was still a look which thought this was possible: he had glimpsed it. And already his senses are precipitating out of the clear solution of his soul. His prayer is already losing its leaves and stands up out of his mouth like a withered shrub. His heart has fallen over and poured out into the muck. His whip strikes him as weakly as a tail flicking away flies. His sex is once again in one place only, and when a woman comes toward him, upright through the huddle, with her naked bosom full of breasts, it points at her like a finger.

There was a time when I considered these pictures obsolete. Not that I doubted their reality. I could imagine that long ago such things had happened to saints, those overhasty zealots, who wanted to begin with God, right away, whatever the cost. We no longer make such demands on ourselves. We suspect that he is too difficult for us, that we must postpone him, so that we can slowly do the long work that separates us from him. Now, however, I know that this work leads to combats just as dangerous as the combats of the saint; that such difficulties appear around everyone who is solitary for the sake of that work, as they took form around God's solitaries in their caves and empty shelters, long ago.

Man wird mich schwer davon überzeugen, daß die Geschichte des verlorenen Sohnes nicht die Legende dessen ist, der nicht geliebt werden wollte. Da er ein Kind war, liebten ihn alle im Hause. Er wuchs heran, er wußte es nicht anders und gewöhnte sich in ihre Herzweiche, da er ein Kind war.

Aber als Knabe wollte er seine Gewohnheiten ablegen. Er hätte es nicht sagen können, aber wenn er draußen herumstrich den ganzen Tag und nicht einmal mehr die Hunde mithaben wollte, so wars, weil auch sie ihn liebten; weil in ihren Blicken Beobachtung war und Teilnahme, Erwartung und Besorgtheit; weil man auch vor ihnen nichts tun konnte, ohne zu freuen oder zu kränken. Was er aber damals meinte, das war die innige Indifferenz seines Herzens, die ihn manchmal früh in den Feldern mit solcher Reinheit ergriff, daß er zu laufen begann, um nicht Zeit und Atem zu haben, mehr zu sein als ein leichter Moment, in dem der Morgen zum Bewußtsein kommt.

Das Geheimnis seines noch nie gewesenen Lebens breitete sich vor ihm aus. Unwillkürlich verließ er den Fußpfad und lief weiter feldein, die Arme ausgestreckt, als könnte er in dieser Breite mehrere Richtungen auf einmal bewältigen. Und dann warf er sich irgendwo hinter eine Hecke, und niemand legte Wert auf ihn. Er schälte sich eine Flöte, er schleuderte einen Stein nach einem kleinen Raubtier, er neigte sich vor und zwang einen Käfer umzukehren: dies alles wurde kein Schicksal, und die Himmel gingen wie über Natur. Schließlich kam der Nachmittag mit lauter Einfällen; man war ein Bucanier auf der Insel Tortuga, und es lag keine Verpflichtung darin, es zu sein; man belagerte Campêche, man eroberte Vera-Cruz; es war möglich, das ganze Heer zu sein oder ein Anführer zu Pferd oder ein Schiff auf dem Meer: je nachdem man sich fühlte. Fiel es einem aber ein, hinzuknien, so war man rasch Deodat von Gozon und hatte den Drachen erlegt und vernahm, ganz heiß, daß dieses Heldentum hoffährtig war, ohne Gehorsam. Denn man ersparte sich nichts, was zur Sache gehörte. Soviel Einbildungen sich aber auch einstellten, zwischendurch war immer noch Zeit, nichts als ein Vogel zu sein, ungewiß welcher. Nur daß der Heimweg dann kam.

Mein Gott, was war da alles abzulegen und zu vergessen; denn richtig vergessen, das war nötig; sonst verriet man sich, wenn sie drängten. Wie sehr man auch zögerte und sich umsah, schließlich kam doch der Giebel herauf. Das erste Fenster oben faßte einen ins Auge, es mochte wohl jemand dort stehen.

[THE PRODIGAL SON]

It would be difficult to persuade me that the story of the Prodigal Son is not the legend of a man who didn't want to be loved. When he was a child, everyone in the house loved him. He grew up not knowing it could be any other way and got used to their tenderness, when he was a child.

But as a boy he tried to lay aside these habits. He wouldn't have been able to say it, but when he spent the whole day roaming around outside and didn't even want to have the dogs with him, it was because they too loved him; because in their eyes he could see observation and sympathy, expectation, concern; because in their presence too he couldn't do anything without giving pleasure or pain. But what he wanted in those days was that profound indifference of heart which sometimes, early in the morning, in the fields, seized him with such purity that he had to start running, in order to have no time or breath to be more than a weightless moment in which the morning becomes conscious of itself.

The secret of that life of his which had never yet come into being, spread out before him. Involuntarily he left the footpath and went running across the fields, with outstretched arms, as if in this wide reach he would be able to master several directions at once. And then he flung himself down behind some bush and didn't matter to anyone. He peeled himself a willow flute, threw a pebble at some small animal, he leaned over and forced a beetle to turn around: none of this became fate, and the sky passed over him as over nature. Finally afternoon came with all its inspirations; you could become a buccaneer on the isle of Tortuga, and there was no obligation to be that; you could besiege Campeche, take Vera Cruz by storm; you could be a whole army or an officer on horseback or a ship on the ocean: according to the way you felt. If you thought of kneeling, right away you were Deodatus of Gozon and had slain the dragon and understood that this heroism was pure arrogance, without an obedient heart. For you didn't spare yourself anything that belonged to the game. But no matter how many scenes arose in your imagination, in between them there was always enough time to be nothing but a bird, you didn't even know what kind. Though afterward, you had to go home.

My God, how much there was then to leave behind and forget. For you really had to forget; otherwise you would betray yourself when they insisted. No matter how much you lingered and looked around, the gable always came into sight at last. The first window up there kept its eye on you; someone might

Die Hunde, in denen die Erwartung den ganzen Tag angewachsen war, preschten durch die Büsche und trieben einen zusammen zu dem, den sie meinten. Und den Rest tat das Haus. Man mußte nur eintreten in seinen vollen Geruch, schon war das Meiste entschieden. Kleinigkeiten konnten sich noch ändern; im ganzen war man schon der, für den sie einen hier hielten; der, dem sie aus seiner kleinen Vergangenheit und ihren eigenen Wünschen längst ein Leben gemacht hatten; das gemeinsame Wesen, das Tag und Nacht unter der Suggestion ihrer Liebe stand, zwischen ihrer Hoffnung und ihrem Argwohn, vor ihrem Tadel oder Beifall.

So einem nützt es nichts, mit unsäglicher Vorsicht die Treppen zu steigen. Alle werden im Wohnzimmer sein, und die Türe muß nur gehn, so sehen sie hin. Er bleibt im Dunkel, er will ihre Fragen abwarten. Aber dann kommt das Ärgste. Sie nehmen ihn bei den Händen, sie ziehen ihn an den Tisch, und alle, soviel ihrer da sind, strecken sich neugierig vor die Lampe. Sie haben es gut, sie halten sich dunkel, und auf ihn allein fällt, mit dem Licht, alle Schande, ein Gesicht zu haben.

Wird er bleiben und das ungefähre Leben nachlügen, das sie ihm zuschreiben, und ihnen allen mit dem ganzen Gesicht ähnlich werden? Wird er sich teilen zwischen der zarten Wahrhaftigkeit seines Willens und dem plumpen Betrug, der sie ihm selber verdirbt? Wird er es aufgeben, *das* zu werden, was denen aus seiner Familie, die nur noch ein schwaches Herz haben, schaden könnte?

Nein, er wird fortgehen. Zum Beispiel während sie alle beschäftigt sind, ihm den Geburtstagstisch zu bestellen mit den schlecht erratenen Gegenständen, die wieder einmal alles ausgleichen sollen. Fortgehen für immer. Viel später erst wird ihm klar werden, wie sehr er sich damals vornahm, niemals zu lieben, um keinen in die entsetzliche Lage zu bringen, geliebt zu sein. Jahre hernach fällt es ihm ein und, wie andere Vorsätze, so ist auch dieser unmöglich gewesen. Denn er hat geliebt und wieder geliebt in seiner Einsamkeit; jedesmal mit Verschwendung seiner ganzen Natur und unter unsäglicher Angst um die Freiheit des andern. Langsam hat er gelernt, den geliebten Gegenstand mit den Strahlen seines Gefühls zu durchscheinen, statt ihn darin zu verzehren. Und er war verwöhnt von dem Entzücken, durch die immer transparentere Gestalt der Geliebten die Weiten zu erkennen, die sie seinem unendlichen Besitzenwollen auftat.

Wie konnte er dann nächtelang weinen vor Sehnsucht, selbst so durchleuchtet zu sein. Aber eine Geliebte, die nachgibt, ist noch lang keine Liebende. O, trostlose Nächte, da er seine flutenden Gaben in Stücken wiederempfing, schwer von Vergänglichkeit. Wie gedachte er dann der Troubadours, die nichts mehr fürchteten als erhört zu sein. Alles erworbene und

be standing there. The dogs, in whom expectation had been growing all day long, ran through the hedges and drove you together into the one they recognized. And the house did the rest. Once you walked in to its full smell, most matters were already decided. A few details might still be changed; but on the whole you were already the person they thought you were; the person for whom they had long ago fashioned a life, out of his small past and their own desires; the creature belonging to them all, who stood day and night under the influence of their love, between their hope and their mistrust, before their approval or their blame.

It is useless for such a person to walk up the front steps with infinite caution. They will all be in the living room, and as soon as the door opens they will all look his way. He remains in the dark, wants to wait for their questions. But then comes the worst. They take him by the hands, lead him over to the table, and all of them, as many as are there, gather inquisitively in front of the lamp. They have the best of it; they stay in the shadows, and on him alone falls, along with the light, all the shame of having a face.

Can he stay and conform to this lying life of approximations which they have assigned to him, and come to resemble them all in every feature of his face? Can he divide himself between the delicate truthfulness of his will and the coarse deceit which corrupts it in his own eyes? Can he give up becoming what might hurt those of his family who have nothing left but a weak heart?

No, he will go away. For example, while they are all busy setting out on his birthday table those badly guessed presents which, once again, are supposed to make up for everything. He will go away for ever. Not until long afterward would he realize how thoroughly he had decided never to love, in order not to put anyone in the terrible position of being loved. He remembered this years later and, like other good intentions, it too had proved impossible. For he had loved again and again in his solitude, each time squandering his whole nature and in unspeakable fear for the freedom of the other person. Slowly he learned to let the rays of his emotion shine through into the beloved object, instead of consuming the emotion in her. And he was pampered by the joy of recognizing, through the more and more transparent form of the beloved, the expanses that she opened to his infinite desire for possession.

Sometimes he would spend whole nights in tears, longing to be filled with such rays himself. But a woman loved, who yields, is still far from being a woman who loves. Oh nights of no consolation, which returned his flooding gifts in pieces heavy with transience. How often he thought then of the Troubadours, who feared nothing more than having their prayers answered. All the

vermehrte Geld gab er dafür hin, dies nicht noch zu erfahren. Er kränkte sie mit seiner groben Bezahlung, von Tag zu Tag bang, sie könnten versuchen, auf seine Liebe einzugehen. Denn er hatte die Hoffnung nicht mehr, die Liebende zu erleben, die ihn durchbrach.

Selbst in der Zeit, da die Armut ihn täglich mit neuen Härten erschreckte, da sein Kopf das Lieblingsding des Elends war und ganz abgegriffen, da sich überall an seinem Leibe Geschwüre aufschlugen wie Notaugen gegen die Schwärze der Heimsuchung, da ihm graute vor dem Unrat, auf dem man ihn verlassen hatte, weil er seinesgleichen war: selbst da noch, wenn er sich besann, war es sein größestes Entsetzen, erwidert worden zu sein. Was waren alle Finsternisse seither gegen die dichte Traurigkeit jener Umarmungen, in denen sich alles verlor. Wachte man nicht auf mit dem Gefühl, ohne Zukunft zu sein? Ging man nicht sinnlos umher ohne Anrecht auf alle Gefahr? Hatte man nicht hundertmal versprechen müssen, nicht zu sterben? Vielleicht war es der Eigensinn dieser argen Erinnerung, die sich von Wiederkunft zu Wiederkunft eine Stelle erhalten wollte, was sein Leben unter den Abfällen währen ließ. Schließlich fand man ihn wieder. Und erst dann, erst in den Hirtenjahren, beruhigte sich seine viele Vergangenheit.

Wer beschreibt, was ihm damals geschah? Welcher Dichter hat die Überredung, seiner damaligen Tage Länge zu vertragen mit der Kürze des Lebens? Welche Kunst ist weit genug, zugleich seine schmale, vermantelte Gestalt hervorzurufen und den ganzen Überraum seiner riesigen Nächte.

Das war die Zeit, die damit begann, daß er sich allgemein und anonym fühlte wie ein zögernd Genesender. Er liebte nicht, es sei denn, daß er es liebte, zu sein. Die niedrige Liebe seiner Schafe lag ihm nicht an; wie Licht, das durch Wolken fällt, zerstreute sie sich um ihn her und schimmerte sanft über den Wiesen. Auf der schuldlosen Spur ihres Hungers schritt er schweigend über die Weiden der Welt. Fremde sahen ihn auf der Akropolis, und vielleicht war er lange einer der Hirten in den Baux und sah die versteinerte Zeit das hohe Geschlecht überstehen, das mit allem Erringen von Sieben und Drei die sechzehn Strahlen seines Sterns nicht zu bezwingen vermochte. Oder soll ich ihn denken zu Orange, an das ländliche Triumphtor geruht? Soll ich ihn sehen im seelengewohnten Schatten der Allyscamps, wie sein Blick zwischen den Gräbern, die offen sind wie die Gräber Auferstandener, eine Libelle verfolgt?

Gleichviel. Ich seh mehr als ihn, ich sehe sein Dasein, das damals die lange Liebe zu Gott begann, die stille, ziellose Arbeit. Denn über ihn, der sich für

money he had acquired and increased, he gave away so as not to experience that himself. He hurt them by so grossly offering payment, more and more afraid that they might try to respond to his love. For he had lost hope of ever meeting the woman whose love could pierce him.

Even during the time when poverty terrified him every day with new hardships, when his head was the favorite toy of misery, and utterly worn ragged by it, when ulcers broke out all over his body like emergency eyes against the blackness of tribulation, when he shuddered at the filth to which he had been abandoned because he was just as foul himself: even then, when he thought about it, his greatest terror was that someone would respond to him. What were all the darknesses of that time, compared with the thick sorrow of those embraces in which everything was lost? Didn't you wake up feeling that you had no future? Didn't you walk around drained of all meaning, without the right to even the slightest danger? Didn't you have to promise, a hundred times, not to die? Perhaps it was the stubbornness of this most painful memory, which wanted to reserve a place in him to return to again and again, that allowed him, amid the dunghills, to continue living. Finally, he found his freedom again. And not until then, not until his years as a shepherd, was there any peace in his crowded past.

Who can describe what happened to him then? What poet has the eloquence to reconcile the length of those days with the brevity of life? What art is broad enough to simultaneously evoke his thin, cloaked form and the vast spaciousness of his gigantic nights?

This was the time which began with his feeling as general and anonymous as a slowly recovering convalescent. He didn't love anything, unless it could be said that he loved existing. The humble love that his sheep felt for him was no burden; like sunlight falling through clouds, it dispersed around him and softly shimmered upon the meadows. On the innocent trail of their hunger, he walked silently over the pastures of the world. Strangers saw him on the Acropolis, and perhaps for many years he was one of the shepherds in Les Baux, and saw petrified time outlast that noble family which, in spite of all their conquests under the holy numbers seven and three, could not overcome the fatal sixteen-rayed star on their own coat-of-arms. Or should I imagine him at Orange, resting against the rustic triumphal arch? Should I see him in the soul-inhabited shade of Alyscamps, where, among the tombs that lie open as the tombs of the resurrected, his glance chases a dragonfly?

It doesn't matter. I see more than him: I see his whole existence, which was then beginning its long love toward God, that silent work undertaken

immer hatte verhalten wollen, kam noch einmal das anwachsende Nichtanders-können seines Herzens. Und diesmal hoffte er auf Erhörung. Sein ganzes, im langen Alleinsein ahnend und unbeirrbar gewordenes Wesen versprach ihm, daß jener, den er jetzt meinte, zu lieben verstünde mit durchdringender, strahlender Liebe. Aber während er sich sehnte, endlich so meisterhaft geliebt zu sein, begriff sein an Fernen gewohntes Gefühl Gottes äußersten Abstand. Nächte kamen, da er meinte, sich auf ihn zuzuwerfen in den Raum; Stunden voller Entdeckung, in denen er sich stark genug fühlte, nach der Erde zu tauchen, um sie hinaufzureißen auf der Sturmflut seines Herzens. Er war wie einer, der eine herrliche Sprache hört und fiebernd sich vornimmt, in ihr zu dichten. Noch stand ihm die Bestürzung bevor, zu erfahren, wie schwer diese Sprache sei; er wollte es nicht glauben zuerst, daß ein langes Leben darüber hingehen könne, die ersten, kurzen Scheinsätze zu bilden, die ohne Sinn sind. Er stürzte sich ins Erlernen wie ein Läufer in die Wette; aber die Dichte dessen, was zu überwinden war, verlangsamte ihn. Es war nichts auszudenken, was demütigender sein konnte als diese Anfängerschaft. Er hatte den Stein der Weisen gefunden, und nun zwang man ihn, das rasch gemachte Gold seines Glücks unaufhörlich zu verwandeln in das klumpige Blei der Geduld. Er, der sich dem Raum ange-paßt hatte, zog wie ein Wurm krumme Gänge ohne Ausgang und Richtung. Nun, da er so mühsam und kummervoll lieben lernte, wurde ihm gezeigt, wie nachlässig und gering bisher alle Liebe gewesen war, die er zu leisten vermeinte. Wie aus keiner etwas hatte werden können, weil er nicht begonnen hatte, an ihr Arbeit zu tun und sie zu verwirklichen.

In diesen Jahren gingen in ihm die großen Veränderungen vor. Er vergaß Gott beinah über der harten Arbeit, sich ihm zu nähern, und alles, was er mit der Zeit vielleicht bei ihm zu erreichen hoffte, war » sa patience de supporter une âme «. Die Zufälle des Schicksals, auf die die Menschen halten, waren schon längst von ihm abgefallen, aber nun verlor, selbst was an Lust und Schmerz notwendig war, den gewürzhaften Beigeschmack und wurde rein und nahrhaft für ihn. Aus den Wurzeln seines Seins entwickelte sich die feste, überwinternde Pflanze einer fruchtbaren Freudigkeit. Er ging ganz darin auf, zu bewältigen, was sein Binnenleben ausmachte, er wollte nichts überspringen, denn er zwei-felte nicht, daß in alledem seine Liebe war und zunahm. Ja, seine innere Fassung ging so weit, daß er beschloß, das Wichtigste von dem, was er früher nicht hatte leisten können, was einfach nur durchwartet worden war, nachzuholen. Er dachte vor allem an die Kindheit, sie kam ihm, je ruhiger er sich besann, desto

without thought of ever reaching its goal. For though he had wanted to hold himself back for ever, he was now once again overcome by the growing urgency of his heart. And this time he hoped to be answered. His whole being, which during his long solitude had become prescient and imperturbable, promised him that the one he was now turning to would be capable of loving with a penetrating, radiant love. But even while he longed to be loved in so masterful a way, his emotion, which had grown accustomed to great distances, realized how extremely remote God was. There were nights when he thought he would be able to fling himself into space, toward God; hours full of disclosure, when he felt strong enough to dive back to earth and pull it up with him on the tidal wave of his heart. He was like someone who hears a glorious language and feverishly decides to write poetry in it. Before long he would, to his dismay, find out how very difficult this language was; at first he was unwilling to believe that a person might spend a whole life putting together the words of the first short meaningless exercises. He threw himself into this learning like a runner into a race; but the density of what had to be mastered slowed him down. It would be hard to imagine anything more humiliating than this apprenticeship. He had found the philosopher's stone, and now he was being forced to ceaselessly transform the quickly produced gold of his happiness into the gross lead of patience. He, who had adapted himself to infinite space, had now become like a worm crawling through crooked passageways, without exit or direction. Now that he was learning to love, learning so laboriously and with so much pain, he could see how careless and trivial all the love had been which he thought he had achieved; how nothing could have come of it, because he had not begun to devote to it the work necessary to make it real.

During those years the great transformations were taking place inside him. He almost forgot God in the difficult work of approaching him, and all that he hoped to perhaps attain with him in time was "sa patience de supporter une âme." The accidents of fate, which most men cling to, had long ago fallen away from him; but now even the necessary pleasures and pains lost their spicy aftertaste and became pure and nourishing for him. From the roots of his being grew the sturdy evergreen plant of a fruitful joyousness. He became totally absorbed in mastering what constituted his inner life; he didn't want to omit anything, for he had no doubt that in all this his love existed and was growing. Indeed, his inward composure went so far that he decided to retrieve the most important of the experiences which he had been unable to accomplish before, those that had merely been waited through. Above all, he thought of his childhood, and the more calmly he recalled it, the more unfinished it seemed; all its

ungetaner vor; alle ihre Erinnerungen hatten das Vage von Ahnungen an sich, und daß sie als vergangen galten, machte sie nahezu zukünftig. Dies alles noch einmal und nun wirklich auf sich zu nehmen, war der Grund, weshalb der Entfremdete heimkehrte. Wir wissen nicht, ob er blieb; wir wissen nur, daß er wiederkam.

Die die Geschichte erzählt haben, versuchen es an dieser Stelle, uns an das Haus zu erinnern, wie es war; denn dort ist nur wenig Zeit vergangen, ein wenig gezählter Zeit, alle im Haus können sagen, wieviel. Die Hunde sind alt geworden, aber sie leben noch. Es wird berichtet, daß einer aufheulte. Eine Unterbrechung geht durch das ganze Tagwerk. Gesichter erscheinen an den Fenstern, gealterte und erwachsene Gesichter von rührender Ähnlichkeit. Und in einem ganz alten schlägt plötzlich blaß das Erkennen durch. Das Erkennen? Wirklich nur das Erkennen? —Das Verzeihen. Das Verzeihen wovon? —Die Liebe. Mein Gott: die Liebe.

Er, der Erkannte, er hatte daran nicht mehr gedacht, beschäftigt wie er war: daß sie noch sein könne. Es ist begreiflich, daß von allem, was nun geschah, nur noch dies überliefert ward: seine Gebärde, die unerhörte Gebärde, die man nie vorher gesehen hatte; die Gebärde des Flehens, mit der er sich an ihre Füße warf, sie beschwörend, daß sie nicht liebten. Erschrocken und schwankend hoben sie ihn zu sich herauf. Sie legten sein Ungestüm nach ihrer Weise aus, indem sie verziehen. Es muß für ihn unbeschreiblich befreiend gewesen sein, daß ihn alle mißverstanden, trotz der verzweifelten Eindeutigkeit seiner Haltung. Wahrscheinlich konnte er bleiben. Denn er erkannte von Tag zu Tag mehr, daß die Liebe ihn nicht betraf, auf die sie so eitel waren und zu der sie einander heimlich ermunterten. Fast mußte er lächeln, wenn sie sich anstrengten, und es wurde klar, wie wenig sie ihn meinen konnten.

Was wußten sie, wer er war. Er war jetzt furchtbar schwer zu lieben, und er fühlte, daß nur Einer dazu imstande sei. Der aber wollte noch nicht.

memories had the vagueness of premonitions, and the fact that they were past made them almost arise as future. To take all this past upon himself once more, and this time really, was the reason why, from the midst of his estrangement, he returned home. We don't know whether he stayed there; we only know that he came back.

Those who have told the story try at this point to remind us of the house as it was then; there, only a short time has passed, a short period of counted time, everyone in the house knows exactly how much. The dogs have grown old, but they are still alive. It is reported that one of them let out a howl. All the daily tasks stop. Faces appear in the window, faces that have aged or grown up and touchingly resemble how they used to look. And in one old face, grown suddenly pale, recognition breaks through. Recognition? Is it really just recognition? —Forgiveness. Forgiveness of what? —Love. My God: it is love.

He, the one who was recognized, had no longer thought, preoccupied as he was, that love could still exist. It is easy to understand how, of everything that happened then, only this has been handed down to us: his gesture, the incredible gesture which had never been seen before, the gesture of supplication with which he threw himself at their feet, imploring them not to love. Dizzy with fright, they made him stand up, embraced him. They interpreted his outburst in their own way, forgiving him. It must have been an indescribable relief for him that, in spite of the desperate clarity of his posture, they all misunderstood him. He was probably able to stay. For every day he recognized more clearly that their love, of which they were so vain and to which they secretly encouraged one another, had nothing to do with him. He almost had to smile at their exertions, and it was obvious how little they could have him in mind.

How could they know who he was? He was now terribly difficult to love, and he felt that only One would be capable of it. But He was not yet willing.

UNCOLLECTED
POEMS

1913–1918

DIE SPANISCHE TRILOGIE

[I]

Aus dieser Wolke, siehe: die den Stern
so wild verdeckt, der eben war—(und mir),
aus diesem Bergland drüben, das jetzt Nacht,
Nachtwinde hat für eine Zeit—(und mir),
aus diesem Fluß im Talgrund, der den Schein
zerrissner Himmels-Lichtung fängt—(und mir);
aus mir und alledem ein einzig Ding
zu machen, Herr: aus mir und dem Gefühl,
mit dem die Herde, eingekehrt im Pferch,
das große dunkle Nichtmehrsein der Welt
ausatmend hinnimmt—, mir und jedem Licht
im Finstersein der vielen Häuser, Herr:
ein Ding zu machen; aus den Fremden, denn
nicht Einen kenn ich, Herr, und mir und mir
ein Ding zu machen; aus den Schlafenden,
den fremden alten Männern im Hospiz,
die wichtig in den Betten husten, aus
schlaftrunknen Kindern an so fremder Brust,
aus vielen Ungenaun und immer mir,
aus nichts als mir und dem, was ich nicht kenn,
das Ding zu machen, Herr Herr Herr, das Ding,
das welthaft-irdisch wie ein Meteor
in seiner Schwere nur die Summe Flugs
zusammennimmt: nichts wiegend als die Ankunft.

[II]

Warum muß einer gehn und fremde Dinge
so auf sich nehmen, wie vielleicht der Träger
den fremdlings mehr und mehr gefüllten Marktkorb
von Stand zu Stand hebt und beladen nachgeht
und kann nicht sagen: Herr, wozu das Gastmahl?

THE SPANISH TRILOGY

I

From this cloud, look!, which has so wildly covered
the star that just now shone there—(and from me),
from these dark clustered hills which hold the night,
the night-winds, for a while—(and from me),
from this stream in the valley which has caught
the jagged glow of the night sky—(and from me);
from me, Lord, and from all of this, to make
one single Thing; from me and the slow breathing
with which the flock, penned in the fold at dusk,
endures the great dark absence of the world—,
from me and every candle flickering
in the dimness of the many houses, Lord:
to make one Thing; from strangers, for I know
no one here, Lord, and from me, from me,
to make *one* Thing; from sleepers in these houses,
from old men left alone at the asylum
who cough in bed, importantly, from children
drunk with sleep upon the breasts of strangers,
from so much that is uncertain and from me,
from me alone and from what I do not know,
to make the Thing, Lord Lord Lord, the Thing
which, earthly and cosmic, like a meteor
gathers within its heaviness no more than
the sum of flight: and weighs nothing but arrival.

II

Why must a man be always taking on
Things not his own, as if he were a servant
whose marketing-bag grows heavier and heavier
from stall to stall and, loaded down, he follows
and doesn't dare ask: Master, why this banquet?

Warum muß einer dastehn wie ein Hirt,
so ausgesetzt dem Übermaß von Einfluß,
beteiligt so an diesem Raum voll Vorgang,
daß er gelehnt an einen Baum der Landschaft
sein Schicksal hätte, ohne mehr zu handeln.
Und hat doch nicht im viel zu großen Blick
die stille Milderung der Herde. Hat
nichts als Welt, hat Welt in jedem Aufschaun,
in jeder Neigung Welt. Ihm dringt, was andern
gerne gehört, unwirtlich wie Musik
und blind ins Blut und wandelt sich vorüber.

Da steht er nächtens auf und hat den Ruf
des Vogels draußen schon in seinem Dasein
und fühlt sich kühn, weil er die ganzen Sterne
in sein Gesicht nimmt, schwer—, o nicht wie einer,
der der Geliebten diese Nacht bereitet
und sie verwöhnt mit den gefühlten Himmeln.

[III]

Daß mir doch, wenn ich wieder der Städte Gedräng
und verwickelten Lärmknäul und die
Wirrsal des Fahrzeugs um mich habe, einzeln,
daß mir doch über das dichte Getrieb
Himmel erinnerte und der erdige Bergrand,
den von drüben heimwärts die Herde betrat.
Steinig sei mir zu Mut
und das Tagwerk des Hirten scheine mir möglich,
wie er einhergeht und bräunt und mit messendem Steinwurf
seine Herde besäumt, wo sie sich ausfranst.
Langsamen Schrittes, nicht leicht, nachdenklichen Körpers,
aber im Stehn ist er herrlich. Noch immer dürfte ein Gott
heimlich in diese Gestalt und würde nicht minder.
Abwechselnd weilt er und zieht, wie selber der Tag,
und Schatten der Wolken
durchgehn ihn, als dächte der Raum
langsam Gedanken für ihn.

Why must a man keep standing like a shepherd,
exposed, in such an overflow of power,
so much a part of this event-filled landscape,
that if he were to lean back against a tree trunk
he would complete his destiny, forever.
Yet does not have, in his too open gaze,
the silent comfort of the flock: has nothing
but world; has world each time he lifts his head;
each time he looks down—world. What gladly yields
to others, pierces him like music, blindly
enters his blood, changes, disappears.

At night he stands up, the distant call of birds
already deep inside him; and feels bold
because he has taken all the galaxies
into his face, not lightly—, oh not like someone
who prepares a night like this for his beloved
and treats her to the skies that he has known.

III

Let me, though, when again I have all around me
the chaos of cities, the tangled
skein of commotion, the blare of the traffic, alone,
let me, above the most dense confusion,
remember this sky and the darkening rim of the valley
where the flock appeared, echoing, on its way home.
Let my courage be like a rock,
let the daily task of the shepherd seem possible to me,
as he moves about and, throwing a stone to measure it,
fixes the hem of his flock where it has grown ragged.
His solemn, unhurried steps, his contemplative body,
his majesty when he stands: even today a god
could secretly enter this form and not be diminished.
He alternately lingers and moves, like the day itself,
and shadows of clouds
pass through him, like thoughts which space
is thinking, slowly, for him.

Sei er wer immer für euch. Wie das wehende Nachtlicht
in den Mantel der Lampe stell ich mich innen in ihn.
Ein Schein wird ruhig. Der Tod
fände sich reiner zurecht.

Let him be whomever you wish. Like a fluttering candle
into a stormlamp, I place myself there inside him.
A glow becomes peaceful. May death
more easily find its way.

DER GEIST ARIEL

(Nach der Lesung von Shakespeares Sturm)

Man hat ihn einmal irgendwo befreit
mit jenem Ruck, mit dem man sich als Jüngling
ans Große hinriß, weg von jeder Rücksicht.
Da ward er willens, sieh: und seither dient er,
nach jeder Tat gefaßt auf seine Freiheit.
Und halb sehr herrisch, halb beinah verschämt,
bringt mans ihm vor, daß man für dies und dies
ihn weiter brauche, ach, und muß es sagen,
was man ihm half. Und dennoch fühlt man selbst,
wie alles das, was man mit ihm zurückhält,
fehlt in der Luft. Verführend fast und süß:
ihn hinzulassen—, um dann, nicht mehr zaubernd,
ins Schicksal eingelassen wie die andern,
zu wissen, daß sich seine leichte Freundschaft,
jetzt ohne Spannung, nirgends mehr verpflichtet,
ein Überschuß zu dieses Atmens Raum,
gedankenlos im Element beschäftigt.
Abhängig fürder, länger nicht begabt,
den dumpfen Mund zu jenem Ruf zu formen,
auf den er stürzte. Machtlos, alternd, arm
und doch *ihn* atmend wie unfaßlich weit
verteilten Duft, der erst das Unsichtbare
vollzählig macht. Auflächelnd, daß man dem
so winken durfte, in so großen Umgang
so leicht gewöhnt. Aufweinend vielleicht auch,
wenn man bedenkt, wie's einen liebte und
fortwollte, beides, immer ganz in Einem.

(Ließ ich es schon? Nun schreckt mich dieser Mann,
der wieder Herzog wird. Wie er sich sanft
den Draht ins Haupt zieht und sich zu den andern
Figuren hängt und künftighin das Spiel
um Milde bittet. . . . Welcher Epilog
vollbrachter Herrschaft. Abtun, bloßes Dastehn
mit nichts als eigner Kraft: »und das ist wenig.«)

ARIEL

(After reading Shakespeare's Tempest*)*

Once, somewhere, somehow, you had set him free
with that sharp jolt which as a young man tore you
out of your life and vaulted you to greatness.
Then he grew willing; and, since then, he serves,
after each task impatient for his freedom.
And half imperious, half almost ashamed,
you make excuses, say that you still need him
for this and that, and, ah, you must describe
how you helped him. Yet you feel, yourself,
that everything held back by his detention
is missing from the air. How sweet, how tempting:
to let him go—to give up all your magic,
submit yourself to destiny like the others,
and know that his light friendship, without strain now,
with no more obligations, anywhere,
an intensifying of this space you breathe,
is working in the element, thoughtlessly.
Henceforth dependent, never again empowered
to shape the torpid mouth into that call
at which he dived. Defenseless, aging, poor,
and yet still breathing *him* in, like a fragrance
spread endlessly, which makes the invisible
complete for the first time. Smiling that you ever
could summon him and feel so much at home
in that vast intimacy. Weeping too, perhaps,
when you remember how he loved and yet
wished to leave you: always both, at once.

(Have I let go already? I look on,
terrified by this man who has become
a duke again. How easily he draws
the wire through his head and hangs himself
up with the other puppets; then steps forward
to ask the audience for their applause
and their indulgence. . . . What consummate power:
to lay aside, to stand there nakedly
with no strength but one's own, "which is most faint.")

So angestrengt wider die starke Nacht
werfen sie ihre Stimmen ins Gelächter,
das schlecht verbrennt. O aufgelehnte Welt
voll Weigerung. Und atmet doch den Raum,
in dem die Sterne gehen. Siehe, dies
bedürfte nicht und könnte, der Entfernung
fremd hingegeben, in dem Übermaß
von Fernen sich ergehen, fort von uns.
Und nun geruhts und reicht uns ans Gesicht
wie der Geliebten Aufblick; schlägt sich auf
uns gegenüber und zerstreut vielleicht
an uns sein Dasein. Und wir sinds nicht wert.
Vielleicht entziehts den Engeln etwas Kraft,
daß nach uns her der Sternenhimmel nachgiebt
und uns hereinhängt ins getrübte Schicksal.
Umsonst. Denn wer gewahrts? Und wo es einer
gewärtig wird: wer darf noch an den Nacht-Raum
die Stirne lehnen wie ans eigne Fenster?
Wer hat dies nicht verleugnet? Wer hat nicht
in dieses eingeborne Element
gefälschte, schlechte, nachgemachte Nächte
hereingeschleppt und sich daran begnügt?
Wir lassen Götter stehn um gohren Abfall,
denn Götter locken nicht. Sie haben Dasein
und nichts als Dasein, Überfluß von Dasein,
doch nicht Geruch, nicht Wink. Nichts ist so stumm
wie eines Gottes Mund. Schön wie ein Schwan
auf seiner Ewigkeit grundlosen Fläche:
so zieht der Gott und taucht und schont sein Weiß.

Alles verführt. Der kleine Vogel selbst
tut Zwang an uns aus seinem reinen Laubwerk,
die Blume hat nicht Raum und drängt herüber;
was will der Wind nicht alles? Nur der Gott,
wie eine Säule, läßt vorbei, verteilend
hoch oben, wo er trägt, nach beiden Seiten
die leichte Wölbung seines Gleichmuts.

[Straining so hard against the strength of night]

Straining so hard against the strength of night,
they fling their tiny voices on the laughter
that will not burn. Oh disobedient world,
full of refusal. And yet it breathes the space
in which the stars revolve. It doesn't need us,
and, at any time, abandoned to the distance,
could spin off in remoteness, far from us.
And now it deigns to touch our faces, softly,
like a loved woman's glance; it opens up
in front of us, and may be spilling out
its essence on us. And we are not worth it.
Perhaps the angels' power is slightly lessened
when the sky with all its stars bends down to us
and hangs us here, into our cloudy fate.
In vain. For who has noticed it? And even
if someone has: who dares to lean his forehead
against the night as on a bedroom window?
Who has not disavowed it? Who has not
dragged into this pure inborn element
nights shammed and counterfeited, tinsel-nights,
and been content (how easily) with those?
We ignore the gods and fill our minds with trash.
For gods do not entice. They have their being,
and nothing else: an overflow of being.
Not scent or gesture. Nothing is so mute
as a god's mouth. As lovely as a swan
on its eternity of unfathomed surface,
the god glides by, plunges, and spares his whiteness.

Everything tempts. Even the little bird,
unseen among the pure leaves, can compel us;
the flower needs space and forces its way over;
what doesn't the wind lay claim to? Only the god,
like a pillar, lets us pass, distributing
high up, where he supports, to either side
the light arch of his equanimity.

DIE GROSSE NACHT

Oft anstaunt ich dich, stand an gestern begonnenem Fenster,
stand und staunte dich an. Noch war mir die neue
Stadt wie verwehrt, und die unüberredete Landschaft
finsterte hin, als wäre ich nicht. Nicht gaben die nächsten
Dinge sich Müh, mir verständlich zu sein. An der Laterne
drängte die Gasse herauf: ich sah, daß sie fremd war.
Drüben—ein Zimmer, mitfühlbar, geklärt in der Lampe—,
schon nahm ich teil; sie empfandens, schlossen die Läden.
Stand. Und dann weinte ein Kind. Ich wußte die Mütter
rings in den Häusern, was sie vermögen—, und wußte
alles Weinens zugleich die untröstlichen Gründe.
Oder es sang eine Stimme und reichte ein Stück weit
aus der Erwartung heraus, oder es hustete unten
voller Vorwurf ein Alter, als ob sein Körper im Recht sei
wider die mildere Welt. Dann schlug eine Stunde—,
aber ich zählte zu spät, sie fiel mir vorüber.—
Wie ein Knabe, ein fremder, wenn man endlich ihn zuläßt,
doch den Ball nicht fängt und keines der Spiele
kann, die die andern so leicht an einander betreiben,
dasteht und wegschaut,—wohin—?: stand ich und plötzlich,
daß *du* umgehst mit mir, spielest, begriff ich, erwachsene
Nacht, und staunte dich an. Wo die Türme
zürnten, wo abgewendeten Schicksals
eine Stadt mich umstand und nicht zu erratende Berge
wider mich lagen, und im genäherten Umkreis
hungernde Fremdheit umzog das zufällige Flackern
meiner Gefühle—: da war es, du Hohe,
keine Schande für dich, daß du mich kanntest. Dein Atem
ging über mich. Dein auf weite Ernste verteiltes
Lächeln trat in mich ein.

THE VAST NIGHT

Often I gazed at you in wonder: stood at the window begun
the day before, stood and gazed at you in wonder. As yet
the new city seemed forbidden to me, and the strange
unpersuadable landscape darkened as though
I didn't exist. Even the nearest Things
didn't care whether I understood them. The street
thrust itself up to the lamppost: I saw it was foreign.
Over there—a room, feelable, clear in the lamplight—,
I already took part; they noticed, and closed the shutters.
Stood. Then a child began crying. I knew what the mothers
all around, in the houses, were capable of—, and knew
the inconsolable origins of all tears.
Or a woman's voice sang and reached a little beyond
expectation, or downstairs an old man let out
a cough that was full of reproach, as though his body were right
and the gentler world mistaken. And then the hour
struck—, but I counted too late, it tumbled on past me.—
Like a new boy at school, who is finally allowed to join in,
but he can't catch the ball, is helpless at all the games
the others pursue with such ease, and he stands there staring
into the distance,—where—?: I stood there and suddenly
grasped that it was you: *you* were playing with me, grown-up
Night, and I gazed at you in wonder. Where the towers
were raging, where with averted fate
a city surrounded me, and indecipherable mountains
camped against me, and strangeness, in narrowing circles,
prowled around my randomly flickering emotions—:
it was then that in all your magnificence
you were not ashamed to know me. Your breath moved tenderly
over my face. And, spread across solemn distances,
your smile entered my heart.

Du im Voraus
verlorne Geliebte, Nimmergekommene,
nicht weiß ich, welche Töne dir lieb sind.
Nicht mehr versuch ich, dich, wenn das Kommende wogt,
zu erkennen. Alle die großen
Bilder in mir, im Fernen erfahrene Landschaft,
Städte und Türme und Brücken und un-
vermutete Wendung der Wege
und das Gewaltige jener von Göttern
einst durchwachsenen Länder:
steigt zur Bedeutung in mir
deiner, Entgehende, an.

Ach, die Gärten bist du,
ach, ich sah sie mit solcher
Hoffnung. Ein offenes Fenster
im Landhaus—, und du tratest beinahe
mir nachdenklich heran. Gassen fand ich,—
du warst sie gerade gegangen,
und die Spiegel manchmal der Läden der Händler
waren noch schwindlich von dir und gaben erschrocken
mein zu plötzliches Bild.—Wer weiß, ob derselbe
Vogel nicht hinklang durch uns
gestern, einzeln, im Abend?

[You who never arrived]

You who never arrived
in my arms, Beloved, who were lost
from the start,
I don't even know what songs
would please you. I have given up trying
to recognize you in the surging wave of the next
moment. All the immense
images in me—the far-off, deeply-felt landscape,
cities, towers, and bridges, and un-
suspected turns in the path,
and those powerful lands that were once
pulsing with the life of the gods—
all rise within me to mean
you, who forever elude me.

You, Beloved, who are all
the gardens I have ever gazed at,
longing. An open window
in a country house—, and you almost
stepped out, pensive, to meet me. Streets that I chanced upon,—
you had just walked down them and vanished.
And sometimes, in a shop, the mirrors
were still dizzy with your presence and, startled, gave back
my too-sudden image. Who knows? perhaps the same
bird echoed through both of us
yesterday, separate, in the evening . . .

WENDUNG

Der Weg von der Innigkeit zur Größe
geht durch das Opfer.   Kassner

Lange errang ers im Anschaun.
Sterne brachen ins Knie
unter dem ringenden Aufblick.
Oder er anschaute knieend,
und seines Instands Duft
machte ein Göttliches müd,
daß es ihm lächelte schlafend.

Türme schaute er so,
daß sie erschraken:
wieder sie bauend, hinan, plötzlich, in Einem!
Aber wie oft, die vom Tag
überladene Landschaft
ruhete hin in sein stilles Gewahren, abends.

Tiere traten getrost
in den offenen Blick, weidende,
und die gefangenen Löwen
starrten hinein wie in unbegreifliche Freiheit;
Vögel durchflogen ihn grad,
den gemütigen; Blumen
wiederschauten in ihn
groß wie in Kinder.

Und das Gerücht, daß ein Schauender sei,
rührte die minder,
fraglicher Sichtbaren,
rührte die Frauen.

Schauend wie lang?
Seit wie lange schon innig entbehrend,
flehend im Grunde des Blicks?

TURNING-POINT

The road from intensity to greatness
passes through sacrifice.   —Kassner

For a long time he attained it in looking.
Stars would fall to their knees
beneath his compelling vision.
Or as he looked on, kneeling,
his urgency's fragrance
tired out a god until
it smiled at him in its sleep.

Towers he would gaze at so
that they were terrified:
building them up again, suddenly, in an instant!
But how often the landscape,
overburdened by day,
came to rest in his silent awareness, at nightfall.

Animals trusted him, stepped
into his open look, grazing,
and the imprisoned lions
stared in as if into an incomprehensible freedom;
birds, as it felt them, flew headlong
through it; and flowers, as enormous
as they are to children, gazed back
into it, on and on.

And the rumor that there was someone
who knew how to look,
stirred those less
visible creatures:
stirred the women.

Looking how long?
For how long now, deeply deprived,
beseeching in the depths of his glance?

Wenn er, ein Wartender, saß in der Fremde; des Gasthofs
zerstreutes, abgewendetes Zimmer
mürrisch um sich, und im vermiedenen Spiegel
wieder das Zimmer
und später vom quälenden Bett aus
wieder:
da beriets in der Luft,
unfaßbar beriet es
über sein fühlbares Herz,
über sein durch den schmerzhaft verschütteten Körper
dennoch fühlbares Herz
beriet es und richtete:
daß es der Liebe nicht habe.

(Und verwehrte ihm weitere Weihen.)

Denn des Anschauns, siehe, ist eine Grenze.
Und die geschautere Welt
will in der Liebe gedeihn.

Werk des Gesichts ist getan,
tue nun Herz-Werk
an den Bildern in dir, jenen gefangenen; denn du
überwältigtest sie: aber nun kennst du sie nicht.
Siehe, innerer Mann, dein inneres Mädchen,
dieses errungene aus
tausend Naturen, dieses
erst nur errungene, nie
noch geliebte Geschöpf.

When he, whose vocation was Waiting, sat far from home—
the hotel's distracted unnoticing bedroom
moody around him, and in the avoided mirror
once more the room, and later
from the tormenting bed
once more:
then in the air the voices
discussed, beyond comprehension,
his heart, which could still be felt;
debated what through the painfully buried body
could somehow be felt—his heart;
debated and passed their judgment:
that it did not have love.

(And denied him further communions.)

For there is a boundary to looking.
And the world that is looked at so deeply
wants to flourish in love.

Work of the eyes is done, now
go and do heart-work
on all the images imprisoned within you; for you
overpowered them: but even now you don't know them.
Learn, inner man, to look on your inner woman,
the one attained from a thousand
natures, the merely attained but
not yet beloved form.

KLAGE

Wem willst du klagen, Herz? Immer gemiedener
ringt sich dein Weg durch die unbegreiflichen
Menschen. Mehr noch vergebens vielleicht,
da er die Richtung behält,
Richtung zur Zukunft behält,
zu der verlorenen.

Früher. Klagtest? Was wars? Eine gefallene
Beere des Jubels, unreife.
Jetzt aber bricht mir mein Jubel-Baum,
bricht mir im Sturme mein langsamer
Jubel-Baum.
Schönster in meiner unsichtbaren
Landschaft, der du mich kenntlicher
machtest Engeln, unsichtbaren.

LAMENT

Whom will you cry to, heart? More and more lonely,
your path struggles on through incomprehensible
mankind. All the more futile perhaps
for keeping to its direction,
keeping on toward the future,
toward what has been lost.

Once. You lamented? What was it? A fallen berry
of jubilation, unripe.
But now the whole tree of my jubilation
is breaking, in the storm it is breaking, my slow
tree of joy.
Loveliest in my invisible
landscape, you that made me more known
to the invisible angels.

›MAN MUSS STERBEN WEIL MAN SIE KENNT‹

(›Papyrus Prisse‹. Aus den Sprüchen des Ptah-hotep,
Handschrift um 2000 v. Ch.)

›Man muß sterben weil man sie kennt.‹ Sterben
an der unsäglichen Blüte des Lächelns. Sterben
an ihren leichten Händen. Sterben
an Frauen.

Singe der Jüngling die tödlichen,
wenn sie ihm hoch durch den Herzraum
wandeln. Aus seiner blühenden Brust
sing er sie an:
unerreichbare! Ach, wie sie fremd sind.
Über den Gipfeln
seines Gefühls gehn sie hervor und ergießen
süß verwandelte Nacht ins verlassene
Tal seiner Arme. Es rauscht
Wind ihres Aufgangs im Laub seines Leibes. Es glänzen
seine Bäche dahin.

Aber der Mann
schweige erschütterter. Er, der
pfadlos die Nacht im Gebirg
seiner Gefühle geirrt hat:
schweige.

Wie der Seemann schweigt, der ältere,
und die bestandenen
Schrecken spielen in ihm wie in zitternden Käfigen.

'WE MUST DIE BECAUSE WE HAVE KNOWN THEM'

(Papyrus Prisse. From the sayings of Ptah-hotep, manuscript from ca. 2000 B.C.)

'We must die because we have known them.' Die
of their smile's unsayable flower. Die
of their delicate hands. Die
of women.

Let the young man sing of them, praise
these death-bringers, when they move through his heart-space,
high overhead. From his blossoming breast
let him sing to them:
unattainable! Ah, how distant they are.
Over the peaks
of his feeling, they float and pour down
sweetly transfigured night into the abandoned
valley of his arms. The wind
of their rising rustles in the leaves of his body. His brooks run
sparkling into the distance.

But the grown man
shudders and is silent. The man who
has wandered pathless at night
in the mountain-range of his feelings:
is silent.

As the old sailor is silent,
and the terrors that he has endured
play inside him as though in quivering cages.

AN HÖLDERLIN

Verweilung, auch am Vertrautesten nicht,
ist uns gegeben; aus den erfüllten
Bildern stürzt der Geist zu plötzlich zu füllenden; Seeen
sind erst im Ewigen. Hier ist Fallen
das Tüchtigste. Aus dem gekonnten Gefühl
überfallen hinab ins geahndete, weiter.

Dir, du Herrlicher, war, dir war, du Beschwörer, ein ganzes
Leben das dringende Bild, wenn du es aussprachst,
die Zeile schloß sich wie Schicksal, ein Tod war
selbst in der lindesten, und du betratest ihn; aber
der vorgehende Gott führte dich drüben hervor.

O du wandelnder Geist, du wandelndster! Wie sie doch alle
wohnen im warmen Gedicht, häuslich, und lang
bleiben im schmalen Vergleich. Teilnehmende. Du nur
ziehst wie der Mond. Und unten hellt und verdunkelt
deine nächtliche sich, die heilig erschrockene Landschaft,
die du in Abschieden fühlst. Keiner
gab sie erhabener hin, gab sie ans Ganze
heiler zurück, unbedürftiger. So auch
spieltest du heilig durch nicht mehr gerechnete Jahre
mit dem unendlichen Glück, als wär es nicht innen, läge
keinem gehörend im sanften
Rasen der Erde umher, von göttlichen Kindern verlassen.
Ach, was die Höchsten begehren, du legtest es wunschlos
Baustein auf Baustein: es stand. Doch selber sein Umsturz
irrte dich nicht.

Was, da ein solcher, Ewiger, war, mißtraun wir
immer dem Irdischen noch? Statt am Vorläufigen ernst
die Gefühle zu lernen für welche
Neigung, künftig im Raum?

TO HÖLDERLIN

We are not permitted to linger, even with what is most
intimate. From images that are full, the spirit
plunges on to others that suddenly must be filled;
there are no lakes till eternity. Here,
falling is best. To fall from the mastered emotion
into the guessed-at, and onward.

To you, O majestic poet, to you the compelling image,
O caster of spells, was a life, entire; when you uttered it
a line snapped shut like fate, there was a death
even in the mildest, and you walked straight into it; but
the god who preceded you led you out and beyond it.

O wandering spirit, most wandering of all! How snugly
the others live in their heated poems and stay,
content, in their narrow similes. Taking part. Only you
move like the moon. And underneath brightens and darkens
the nocturnal landscape, the holy, the terrified landscape,
which you feel in departures. No one
gave it away more sublimely, gave it back
more fully to the universe, without any need to hold on.
Thus for years that you no longer counted, holy, you played
with infinite joy, as though it were not inside you,
but lay, belonging to no one, all around
on the gentle lawns of the earth, where the godlike children had left it.
Ah, what the greatest have longed for: you built it, free of desire,
stone upon stone, till it stood. And when it collapsed,
even then you weren't bewildered.

Why, after such an eternal life, do we still
mistrust the earthly? Instead of patiently learning from transience
the emotions for what future
slopes of the heart, in pure space?

Ausgesetzt auf den Bergen des Herzens. Siehe, wie klein dort,
siehe: die letzte Ortschaft der Worte, und höher,
aber wie klein auch, noch ein letztes
Gehöft von Gefühl. Erkennst du's?
Ausgesetzt auf den Bergen des Herzens. Steingrund
unter den Händen. Hier blüht wohl
einiges auf; aus stummem Absturz
blüht ein unwissendes Kraut singend hervor.
Aber der Wissende? Ach, der zu wissen begann
und schweigt nun, ausgesetzt auf den Bergen des Herzens.
Da geht wohl, heilen Bewußtseins,
manches umher, manches gesicherte Bergtier,
wechselt und weilt. Und der große geborgene Vogel
kreist um der Gipfel reine Verweigerung.—Aber
ungeborgen, hier auf den Bergen des Herzens. . . .

[Exposed on the cliffs of the heart]

Exposed on the cliffs of the heart. Look, how tiny down there,
look: the last village of words and, higher,
(but how tiny) still one last
farmhouse of feeling. Can you see it?
Exposed on the cliffs of the heart. Stoneground
under your hands. Even here, though,
something can bloom; on a silent cliff-edge
an unknowing plant blooms, singing, into the air.
But the one who knows? Ah, he began to know
and is quiet now, exposed on the cliffs of the heart.
While, with their full awareness,
many sure-footed mountain animals pass
or linger. And the great sheltered bird flies, slowly
circling, around the peak's pure denial.—But
without a shelter, here on the cliffs of the heart. . . .

DER TOD

Da steht der Tod, ein bläulicher Absud
in einer Tasse ohne Untersatz.
Ein wunderlicher Platz für eine Tasse:
steht auf dem Rücken einer Hand. Ganz gut
erkennt man noch an dem glasierten Schwung
den Bruch des Henkels. Staubig. Und: ›*Hoff-nung*‹
an ihrem Bug in aufgebrauchter Schrift.

Das hat der Trinker, den der Trank betrifft,
bei einem fernen Frühstück ab-gelesen.

Was sind denn das für Wesen,
die man zuletzt wegschrecken muß mit Gift?

Blieben sie sonst? Sind sie denn hier vernarrt
in dieses Essen voller Hindernis?
Man muß ihnen die harte Gegenwart
ausnehmen, wie ein künstliches Gebiß.
Dann lallen sie. Gelall, Gelall . . . .
. . . .

O Sternenfall,
von einer Brücke einmal eingesehn—:
Dich nicht vergessen. Stehn!

DEATH

There stands death, a bluish distillate
in a cup without a saucer. Such a strange
place to find a cup: standing on
the back of a hand. One recognizes clearly
the line along the glazed curve, where the handle
snapped. Covered with dust. And *HOPE* is written
across the side, in faded Gothic letters.

The man who was to drink out of that cup
read it aloud at breakfast, long ago.

What kind of beings are they then,
who finally must be scared away by poison?

Otherwise would they stay here? Would they keep
chewing so foolishly on their own frustration?
The hard present moment must be pulled
out of them, like a set of false teeth. Then
they mumble. They go on mumbling, mumbling . . . .
. . . .

O shooting star
that fell into my eyes and through my body—:
Not to forget you. To endure.

AN DIE MUSIK

Musik: Atem der Statuen. Vielleicht:
Stille der Bilder. Du Sprache wo Sprachen
enden. Du Zeit,
die senkrecht steht auf der Richtung vergehender Herzen.

Gefühle zu wem? O du der Gefühle
Wandlung in was?—: in hörbare Landschaft.
Du Fremde: Musik. Du uns entwachsener
Herzraum. Innigstes unser,
das, uns übersteigend, hinausdrängt,—
heiliger Abschied:
da uns das Innre umsteht
als geübteste Ferne, als andre
Seite der Luft:
rein,
riesig,
nicht mehr bewohnbar.

TO MUSIC

Music: breathing of statues. Perhaps:
silence of paintings. You language where all language
ends. You time
standing vertically on the motion of mortal hearts.

Feelings for whom? O you the transformation
of feelings into what?—: into audible landscape.
You stranger: music. You heart-space
grown out of us. The deepest space *in* us,
which, rising above us, forces its way out,—
holy departure:
when the innermost point in us stands
outside, as the most practiced distance, as the other
side of the air:
pure,
boundless,
no longer habitable.

DUINO ELEGIES

(1923)

The property of Princess
Marie von Thurn und Taxis-Hohenlohe

(1912/1922)

DIE ERSTE ELEGIE

Wer, wenn ich schriee, hörte mich denn aus der Engel
Ordnungen? und gesetzt selbst, es nähme
einer mich plötzlich ans Herz: ich verginge von seinem
stärkeren Dasein. Denn das Schöne ist nichts
als des Schrecklichen Anfang, den wir noch grade ertragen,
und wir bewundern es so, weil es gelassen verschmäht,
uns zu zerstören. Ein jeder Engel ist schrecklich.
    Und so verhalt ich mich denn und verschlucke den Lockruf
dunkelen Schluchzens. Ach, wen vermögen
wir denn zu brauchen? Engel nicht, Menschen nicht,
und die findigen Tiere merken es schon,
daß wir nicht sehr verläßlich zu Haus sind
in der gedeuteten Welt. Es bleibt uns vielleicht
irgend ein Baum an dem Abhang, daß wir ihn täglich
wiedersähen; es bleibt uns die Straße von gestern
und das verzogene Treusein einer Gewohnheit,
der es bei uns gefiel, und so blieb sie und ging nicht.
    O und die Nacht, die Nacht, wenn der Wind voller Weltraum
uns am Angesicht zehrt—, wem bliebe sie nicht, die ersehnte,
sanft enttäuschende, welche dem einzelnen Herzen
mühsam bevorsteht. Ist sie den Liebenden leichter?
Ach, sie verdecken sich nur mit einander ihr Los.
    Weißt du's *noch* nicht? Wirf aus den Armen die Leere
zu den Räumen hinzu, die wir atmen; vielleicht daß die Vögel
die erweiterte Luft fühlen mit innigerm Flug.

Ja, die Frühlinge brauchten dich wohl. Es muteten manche
Sterne dir zu, daß du sie spürtest. Es hob
sich eine Woge heran im Vergangenen, oder
da du vorüberkamst am geöffneten Fenster,
gab eine Geige sich hin. Das alles war Auftrag.
Aber bewältigtest du's? Warst du nicht immer
noch von Erwartung zerstreut, als kündigte alles
eine Geliebte dir an? (Wo willst du sie bergen,
da doch die großen fremden Gedanken bei dir
aus und ein gehn und öfters bleiben bei Nacht.)

THE FIRST ELEGY

Who, if I cried out, would hear me among the angels'
hierarchies? and even if one of them pressed me
suddenly against his heart: I would be consumed
in that overwhelming existence. For beauty is nothing
but the beginning of terror, which we still are just able to endure,
and we are so awed because it serenely disdains
to annihilate us. Every angel is terrifying.
    And so I hold myself back and swallow the call-note
of my dark sobbing. Ah, whom can we ever turn to
in our need? Not angels, not humans,
and already the knowing animals are aware
that we are not really at home in
our interpreted world. Perhaps there remains for us
some tree on a hillside, which every day we can take
into our vision; there remains for us yesterday's street
and the loyalty of a habit so much at ease
when it stayed with us that it moved in and never left.
    Oh and night: there is night, when a wind full of infinite space
gnaws at our faces. Whom would it not remain for—that longed-after,
mildly disillusioning presence, which the solitary heart
so painfully meets. Is it any less difficult for lovers?
But they keep on using each other to hide their own fate.
    Don't you know *yet*? Fling the emptiness out of your arms
into the spaces we breathe; perhaps the birds
will feel the expanded air with more passionate flying.

Yes—the springtimes needed you. Often a star
was waiting for you to notice it. A wave rolled toward you
out of the distant past, or as you walked
under an open window, a violin
yielded itself to your hearing. All this was mission.
But could you accomplish it? Weren't you always
distracted by expectation, as if every event
announced a beloved? (Where can you find a place
to keep her, with all the huge strange thoughts inside you
going and coming and often staying all night.)

Sehnt es dich aber, so singe die Liebenden; lange
noch nicht unsterblich genug ist ihr berühmtes Gefühl.
Jene, du neidest sie fast, Verlassenen, die du
so viel liebender fandst als die Gestillten. Beginn
immer von neuem die nie zu erreichende Preisung;
denk: es erhält sich der Held, selbst der Untergang war ihm
nur ein Vorwand, zu sein: seine letzte Geburt.
Aber die Liebenden nimmt die erschöpfte Natur
in sich zurück, als wären nicht zweimal die Kräfte,
dieses zu leisten. Hast du der Gaspara Stampa
denn genügend gedacht, daß irgend ein Mädchen,
dem der Geliebte entging, am gesteigerten Beispiel
dieser Liebenden fühlt: daß ich würde wie sie?
Sollen nicht endlich uns diese ältesten Schmerzen
fruchtbarer werden? Ist es nicht Zeit, daß wir liebend
uns vom Geliebten befrein und es bebend bestehn:
wie der Pfeil die Sehne besteht, um gesammelt im Absprung
mehr zu sein als er selbst. Denn Bleiben ist nirgends.

Stimmen, Stimmen. Höre, mein Herz, wie sonst nur
Heilige hörten: daß sie der riesige Ruf
aufhob vom Boden; sie aber knieten,
Unmögliche, weiter und achtetens nicht:
So waren sie hörend. Nicht, daß du *Gottes* ertrügest
die Stimme, bei weitem. Aber das Wehende höre,
die ununterbrochene Nachricht, die aus Stille sich bildet.
Es rauscht jetzt von jenen jungen Toten zu dir.
Wo immer du eintratst, redete nicht in Kirchen
zu Rom and Neapel ruhig ihr Schicksal dich an?
Oder es trug eine Inschrift sich erhaben dir auf,
wie neulich die Tafel in Santa Maria Formosa.
Was sie mir wollen? leise soll ich des Unrechts
Anschein abtun, der ihrer Geister
reine Bewegung manchmal ein wenig behindert.

But when you feel longing, sing of women in love;
for their famous passion is still not immortal. Sing
of women abandoned and desolate (you envy them, almost)
who could love so much more purely than those who were gratified.
Begin again and again the never-attainable praising;
remember: the hero lives on; even his downfall was
merely a pretext for achieving his final birth.
But Nature, spent and exhausted, takes lovers back
into herself, as if there were not enough strength
to create them a second time. Have you imagined
Gaspara Stampa intensely enough so that any girl
deserted by her beloved might be inspired
by that fierce example of soaring, objectless love
and might say to herself, "Perhaps I can be like her"?
Shouldn't this most ancient of sufferings finally grow
more fruitful for us? Isn't it time that we lovingly
freed ourselves from the beloved and, quivering, endured:
as the arrow endures the bowstring's tension, so that
gathered in the snap of release it can be more than
itself. For there is no place where we can remain.

Voices. Voices. Listen, my heart, as only
saints have listened: until the gigantic call lifted them
off the ground; yet they kept on, impossibly,
kneeling and didn't notice at all:
so complete was their listening. Not that you could endure
God's voice—far from it. But listen to the voice of the wind
and the ceaseless message that forms itself out of silence.
It is murmuring toward you now from those who died young.
Didn't their fate, whenever you stepped into a church
in Naples or Rome, quietly come to address you?
Or high up, some eulogy entrusted you with a mission,
as, last year, on the plaque in Santa Maria Formosa.
What they want of me is that I gently remove the appearance
of injustice about their death—which at times
slightly hinders their souls from proceeding onward.

Freilich ist es seltsam, die Erde nicht mehr zu bewohnen,
kaum erlernte Gebräuche nicht mehr zu üben,
Rosen, und andern eigens versprechenden Dingen
nicht die Bedeutung menschlicher Zukunft zu geben;
das, was man war in unendlich ängstlichen Händen,
nicht mehr zu sein, und selbst den eigenen Namen
wegzulassen wie ein zerbrochenes Spielzeug.
Seltsam, die Wünsche nicht weiterzuwünschen. Seltsam,
alles, was sich bezog, so lose im Raume
flattern zu sehen. Und das Totsein ist mühsam
und voller Nachholn, daß man allmählich ein wenig
Ewigkeit spürt.—Aber Lebendige machen
alle den Fehler, daß sie zu stark unterscheiden.
Engel (sagt man) wüßten oft nicht, ob sie unter
Lebenden gehn oder Toten. Die ewige Strömung
reißt durch beide Bereiche alle Alter
immer mit sich und übertönt sie in beiden.

Schließlich brauchen sie uns nicht mehr, die Früheentrückten,
man entwöhnt sich des Irdischen sanft, wie man den Brüsten
milde der Mutter entwächst. Aber wir, die so große
Geheimnisse brauchen, denen aus Trauer so oft
seliger Fortschritt entspringt—: *könnten* wir sein ohne sie?
Ist die Sage umsonst, daß einst in der Klage um Linos
wagende erste Musik dürre Erstarrung durchdrang;
daß erst im erschrockenen Raum, dem ein beinah göttlicher Jüngling
plötzlich für immer enttrat, das Leere in jene
Schwingung geriet, die uns jetzt hinreißt und tröstet und hilft.

Of course, it is strange to inhabit the earth no longer,
to give up customs one barely had time to learn,
not to see roses and other promising Things
in terms of a human future; no longer to be
what one was in infinitely anxious hands; to leave
even one's own first name behind, forgetting it
as easily as a child abandons a broken toy.
Strange to no longer desire one's desires. Strange
to see meanings that clung together once, floating away
in every direction. And being dead is hard work
and full of retrieval before one can gradually feel
a trace of eternity.— Though the living are wrong to believe
in the too-sharp distinctions which they themselves have created.
Angels (they say) don't know whether it is the living
they are moving among, or the dead. The eternal torrent
whirls all ages along in it, through both realms
forever, and their voices are drowned out in its thunderous roar.

In the end, those who were carried off early no longer need us:
they are weaned from earth's sorrows and joys, as gently as children
outgrow the soft breasts of their mothers. But we, who do need
such great mysteries, we for whom grief is so often
the source of our spirit's growth—: could we exist without *them*?
Is the legend meaningless that tells how, in the lament for Linus,
the daring first notes of song pierced through the barren numbness;
and then in the startled space which a youth as lovely as a god
had suddenly left forever, the Void felt for the first time
that harmony which now enraptures and comforts and helps us.

DIE ZWEITE ELEGIE

Jeder Engel ist schrecklich. Und dennoch, weh mir,
ansing ich euch, fast tödliche Vögel der Seele,
wissend um euch. Wohin sind die Tage Tobiae,
da der Strahlendsten einer stand an der einfachen Haustür,
zur Reise ein wenig verkleidet und schon nicht mehr furchtbar;
(Jüngling dem Jüngling, wie er neugierig hinaussah).
Träte der Erzengel jetzt, der gefährliche, hinter den Sternen
eines Schrittes nur nieder und herwärts: hochauf-
schlagend erschlüg uns das eigene Herz. Wer seid ihr?

Frühe Geglückte, ihr Verwöhnten der Schöpfung,
Höhenzüge, morgenrötliche Grate
aller Erschaffung,—Pollen der blühenden Gottheit,
Gelenke des Lichtes, Gänge, Treppen, Throne,
Räume aus Wesen, Schilde aus Wonne, Tumulte
stürmisch entzückten Gefühls und plötzlich, einzeln,
Spiegel: die die entströmte eigene Schönheit
wiederschöpfen zurück in das eigene Antlitz.

Denn wir, wo wir fühlen, verflüchtigen; ach wir
atmen uns aus und dahin; von Holzglut zu Holzglut
geben wir schwächern Geruch. Da sagt uns wohl einer:
ja, du gehst mir ins Blut, dieses Zimmer, der Frühling
füllt sich mit dir . . . Was hilfts, er kann uns nicht halten,
wir schwinden in ihm und um ihn. Und jene, die schön sind,
o wer hält sie zurück? Unaufhörlich steht Anschein
auf in ihrem Gesicht und geht fort. Wie Tau von dem Frühgras
hebt sich das Unsre von uns, wie die Hitze von einem
heißen Gericht. O Lächeln, wohin? O Aufschaun:
neue, warme, entgehende Welle des Herzens—;
weh mir: wir *sinds* doch. Schmeckt denn der Weltraum,
in den wir uns lösen, nach uns? Fangen die Engel
wirklich nur Ihriges auf, ihnen Entströmtes,
oder ist manchmal, wie aus Versehen, ein wenig
unseres Wesens dabei? Sind wir in ihre
Züge soviel nur gemischt wie das Vage in die Gesichter

THE SECOND ELEGY

Every angel is terrifying. And yet, alas,
I invoke you, almost deadly birds of the soul,
knowing about you. Where are the days of Tobias,
when one of you, veiling his radiance, stood at the front door,
slightly disguised for the journey, no longer appalling;
(a young man like the one who curiously peeked through the window).
But if the archangel now, perilous, from behind the stars
took even one step down toward us: our own heart, beating
higher and higher, would beat us to death. Who *are* you?

Early successes, Creation's pampered favorites,
mountain-ranges, peaks growing red in the dawn
of all Beginning,—pollen of the flowering godhead,
joints of pure light, corridors, stairways, thrones,
space formed from essence, shields made of ecstasy, storms
of emotion whirled into rapture, and suddenly, alone:
mirrors, which scoop up the beauty that has streamed from their face
and gather it back, into themselves, entire.

But we, when moved by deep feeling, evaporate; we
breathe ourselves out and away; from moment to moment
our emotion grows fainter, like a perfume. Though someone may tell us:
"Yes, you've entered my bloodstream, the room, the whole springtime
is filled with you . . ."—what does it matter? he can't contain us,
we vanish inside him and around him. And those who are beautiful,
oh who can retain them? Appearance ceaselessly rises
in their face, and is gone. Like dew from the morning grass,
what is ours floats into the air, like steam from a dish
of hot food. O smile, where are you going? O upturned glance:
new warm receding wave on the sea of the heart . . .
alas, but that is what we *are*. Does the infinite space
we dissolve into, taste of us then? Do the angels really
reabsorb only the radiance that streamed out from themselves, or
sometimes, as if by an oversight, is there a trace
of our essence in it as well? Are we mixed in with their
features even as slightly as that vague look

schwangerer Frauen? Sie merken es nicht in dem Wirbel
ihrer Rückkehr zu sich. (Wie sollten sie's merken.)

Liebende könnten, verstünden sie's, in der Nachtluft
wunderlich reden. Denn es scheint, daß uns alles
verheimlicht. Siehe, die Bäume *sind;* die Häuser,
die wir bewohnen, bestehn noch. Wir nur
ziehen allem vorbei wie ein luftiger Austausch.
Und alles ist einig, uns zu verschweigen, halb als
Schande vielleicht und halb als unsägliche Hoffnung.

Liebende, euch, ihr in einander Genügten,
frag ich nach uns. Ihr greift euch. Habt ihr Beweise?
Seht, mir geschiehts, daß meine Hände einander
inne werden oder daß mein gebrauchtes
Gesicht in ihnen sich schont. Das giebt mir ein wenig
Empfindung. Doch wer wagte darum schon zu *sein*?
Ihr aber, die ihr im Entzücken des anderen
zunehmt, bis er euch überwältigt
anfleht: nicht *mehr*—; die ihr unter den Händen
euch reichlicher werdet wie Traubenjahre;
die ihr manchmal vergeht, nur weil der andre
ganz überhand nimmt: euch frag ich nach uns. Ich weiß,
ihr berührt euch so selig, weil die Liebkosung verhält,
weil die Stelle nicht schwindet, die ihr, Zärtliche,
zudeckt; weil ihr darunter das reine
Dauern verspürt. So versprecht ihr euch Ewigkeit fast
von der Umarmung. Und doch, wenn ihr der ersten
Blicke Schrecken besteht und die Sehnsucht am Fenster,
und den ersten gemeinsamen Gang, *ein* Mal durch den Garten:
Liebende, *seid* ihrs dann noch? Wenn ihr einer dem andern
euch an den Mund hebt und ansetzt—: Getränk an Getränk:
o wie entgeht dann der Trinkende seltsam der Handlung.

Erstaunte euch nicht auf attischen Stelen die Vorsicht
menschlicher Geste? war nicht Liebe und Abschied
so leicht auf die Schultern gelegt, als wär es aus anderm
Stoffe gemacht als bei uns? Gedenkt euch der Hände,

in the faces of pregnant women? They do not notice it
(how could they notice) in their swirling return to themselves.

Lovers, if they knew how, might utter strange, marvelous
words in the night air. For it seems that everything
hides us. Look: trees do exist; the houses
that we live in still stand. We alone
fly past all things, as fugitive as the wind.
And all things conspire to keep silent about us, half
out of shame perhaps, half as unutterable hope.

Lovers, gratified in each other, I am asking *you*
about us. You hold each other. Where is your proof?
Look, sometimes I find that my hands have become aware
of each other, or that my time-worn face
shelters itself inside them. That gives me a slight
sensation. But who would dare to exist, just for that?
You, though, who in the other's passion
grow until, overwhelmed, he begs you:
"No *more* . . ."; you who beneath his hands
swell with abundance, like autumn grapes;
you who may disappear because the other has wholly
emerged: I am asking *you* about us. I know,
you touch so blissfully because the caress preserves,
because the place you so tenderly cover
does not vanish; because underneath it
you feel pure duration. So you promise eternity, almost,
from the embrace. And yet, when you have survived
the terror of the first glances, the longing at the window,
and the first walk together, once only, through the garden:
lovers, *are* you the same? When you lift yourselves up
to each other's mouth and your lips join, drink against drink:
oh how strangely each drinker seeps away from his action.

Weren't you astonished by the caution of human gestures
on Attic gravestones? Wasn't love and departure
placed so gently on shoulders that it seemed to be made
of a different substance than in our world? Remember the hands,

wie sie drucklos beruhen, obwohl in den Torsen die Kraft steht.
Diese Beherrschten wußten damit: so weit sind wirs,
dieses ist unser, uns *so* zu berühren; stärker
stemmen die Götter uns an. Doch dies ist Sache der Götter.

Fänden auch wir ein reines, verhaltenes, schmales
Menschliches, einen unseren Streifen Fruchtlands
zwischen Strom und Gestein. Denn das eigene Herz übersteigt uns
noch immer wie jene. Und wir können ihm nicht mehr
nachschaun in Bilder, die es besänftigen, noch in
göttliche Körper, in denen es größer sich mäßigt.

how weightlessly they rest, though there is power in the torsos.
These self-mastered figures know: "We can go this far,
this is ours, to touch one another this lightly; the gods
can press down harder upon us. But that is the gods' affair."

If only we too could discover a pure, contained,
human place, our own strip of fruit-bearing soil
between river and rock. For our own heart always exceeds us,
as theirs did. And we can no longer follow it, gazing
into images that soothe it or into the godlike bodies
where, measured more greatly, it achieves a greater repose.

DIE DRITTE ELEGIE

Eines ist, die Geliebte zu singen. Ein anderes, wehe,
jenen verborgenen schuldigen Fluß-Gott des Bluts.
Den sie von weitem erkennt, ihren Jüngling, was weiß er
selbst von dem Herren der Lust, der aus dem Einsamen oft,
ehe das Mädchen noch linderte, oft auch als wäre sie nicht,
ach, von welchem Unkenntlichen triefend, das Gotthaupt
aufhob, aufrufend die Nacht zu unendlichem Aufruhr.
O des Blutes Neptun, o sein furchtbarer Dreizack.
O der dunkele Wind seiner Brust aus gewundener Muschel.
Horch, wie die Nacht sich muldet und höhlt. Ihr Sterne,
stammt nicht von euch des Liebenden Lust zu dem Antlitz
seiner Geliebten? Hat er die innige Einsicht
in ihr reines Gesicht nicht aus dem reinen Gestirn?

Du nicht hast ihm, wehe, nicht seine Mutter
hat ihm die Bogen der Braun so zur Erwartung gespannt.
Nicht an dir, ihn fühlendes Mädchen, an dir nicht
bog seine Lippe sich zum fruchtbarern Ausdruck.
Meinst du wirklich, ihn hätte dein leichter Auftritt
also erschüttert, du, die wandelt wie Frühwind?
Zwar du erschrakst ihm das Herz; doch ältere Schrecken
stürzten in ihn bei dem berührenden Anstoß.
Ruf ihn . . . du rufst ihn nicht ganz aus dunkelem Umgang.
Freilich, er *will,* er entspringt; erleichtert gewöhnt er
sich in dein heimliches Herz und nimmt und beginnt sich.
Aber begann er sich je?
Mutter, *du* machtest ihn klein, du warsts, die ihn anfing;
dir war er neu, du beugtest über die neuen
Augen die freundliche Welt und wehrtest der fremden.
Wo, ach, hin sind die Jahre, da du ihm einfach
mit der schlanken Gestalt wallendes Chaos vertratst?
Vieles verbargst du ihm so; das nächtlich-verdächtige Zimmer
machtest du harmlos, aus deinem Herzen voll Zuflucht
mischtest du menschlichern Raum seinem Nacht-Raum hinzu.
Nicht in die Finsternis, nein, in dein näheres Dasein
hast du das Nachtlicht gestellt, und es schien wie aus Freundschaft.

THE THIRD ELEGY

It is one thing to sing the beloved. Another, alas,
to invoke that hidden, guilty river-god of the blood.
Her young lover, whom she knows from far away—what does he know of
the lord of desire who often, up from the depths of his solitude,
even before she could soothe him, and as though she didn't exist,
held up his head, ah, dripping with the unknown,
erect, and summoned the night to an endless uproar.
Oh the Neptune inside our blood, with his appalling trident.
Oh the dark wind from his breast out of that spiraled conch.
Listen to the night as it makes itself hollow. O stars,
isn't it from you that the lover's desire for the face
of his beloved arises? Doesn't his secret insight
into her pure features come from the pure constellations?

Not you, his mother: alas, you were not the one
who bent the arch of his eyebrows into such expectation.
Not for you, girl so aware of him, not for your mouth
did his lips curve themselves into a more fruitful expression.
Do you really think that your gentle steps could have shaken him
with such violence, you who move like the morning breeze?
Yes, you did frighten his heart; but more ancient terrors
plunged into him at the shock of that feeling. Call him . . .
but you can't quite call him away from those dark companions.
Of course, he *wants* to escape, and he does; relieved, he nestles
into your sheltering heart, takes hold, and begins himself.
But did he ever begin himself, really?
Mother, *you* made him small, it was you who started him;
in *your* sight he was new, over his new eyes you arched
the friendly world and warded off the world that was alien.
Ah, where are the years when you shielded him just by placing
your slender form between him and the surging abyss?
How much you hid from him then. The room that filled with suspicion
at night: you made it harmless; and out of the refuge of your heart
you mixed a more human space in with his night-space.
And you set down the lamp, not in that darkness, but in
your own nearer presence, and it glowed at him like a friend.

Nirgends ein Knistern, das du nicht lächelnd erklärtest,
so als wüßtest du längst, *wann* sich die Diele benimmt . . .
Und er horchte und linderte sich. So vieles vermochte
zärtlich dein Aufstehn; hinter den Schrank trat
hoch im Mantel sein Schicksal, und in die Falten des Vorhangs
paßte, die leicht sich verschob, seine unruhige Zukunft.

Und er selbst, wie er lag, der Erleichterte, unter
schläfernden Lidern deiner leichten Gestaltung
Süße lösend in den gekosteten Vorschlaf—:
schien ein Gehüteter . . . Aber *innen:* wer wehrte,
hinderte innen in ihm die Fluten der Herkunft?
Ach, da *war* keine Vorsicht im Schlafenden; schlafend,
aber träumend, aber in Fiebern: wie er sich ein-ließ.
Er, der Neue, Scheuende, wie er verstrickt war,
mit des innern Geschehns weiterschlagenden Ranken
schon zu Mustern verschlungen, zu würgendem Wachstum, zu tierhaft
jagenden Formen. Wie er sich hingab—. Liebte.
Liebte sein Inneres, seines Inneren Wildnis,
diesen Urwald in ihm, auf dessen stummem Gestürztsein
lichtgrün sein Herz stand. Liebte. Verließ es, ging die
eigenen Wurzeln hinaus in gewaltigen Ursprung,
wo seine kleine Geburt schon überlebt war. Liebend
stieg er hinab in das ältere Blut, in die Schluchten,
wo das Furchtbare lag, noch satt von den Vätern. Und jedes
Schreckliche kannte ihn, blinzelte, war wie verständigt.
Ja, das Entsetzliche lächelte . . . Selten
hast du so zärtlich gelächelt, Mutter. Wie sollte
er es nicht lieben, da es ihm lächelte. *Vor* dir
hat ers geliebt, denn, da du ihn trugst schon,
war es im Wasser gelöst, das den Keimenden leicht macht.

Siehe, wir lieben nicht, wie die Blumen, aus einem
einzigen Jahr; uns steigt, wo wir lieben,
unvordenklicher Saft in die Arme. O Mädchen,
dies: daß wir liebten *in* uns, nicht Eines, ein Künftiges, sondern
das zahllos Brauende; nicht ein einzelnes Kind,
sondern die Väter, die wie Trümmer Gebirgs

There wasn't a creak that your smile could not explain,
as though you had long known just when the floor would do that . . .
And he listened and was soothed. So powerful was your presence
as you tenderly stood by the bed; his fate,
tall and cloaked, retreated behind the wardrobe, and his restless
future, delayed for a while, adapted to the folds of the curtain.

And he himself, as he lay there, relieved, with the sweetness
of the gentle world you had made for him dissolving beneath
his drowsy eyelids, into the foretaste of sleep—:
he *seemed* protected . . . But inside: who could ward off,
who could divert, the floods of origin inside him?
Ah, there *was* no trace of caution in that sleeper; sleeping,
yes but dreaming, but flushed with what fevers: how he threw himself in.
All at once new, trembling, how he was caught up
and entangled in the spreading tendrils of inner event
already twined into patterns, into strangling undergrowth, prowling
bestial shapes. How he submitted—. Loved.
Loved his interior world, his interior wilderness,
that primal forest inside him, where among decayed treetrunks
his heart stood, light-green. Loved. Left it, went through
his own roots and out, into the powerful source
where his little birth had already been outlived. Loving,
he waded down into more ancient blood, to ravines
where Horror lay, still glutted with his fathers. And every
Terror knew him, winked at him like an accomplice.
Yes, Atrocity smiled . . . Seldom
had you smiled so tenderly, mother. How could he help
loving what smiled at him. Even before he knew you,
he had loved it, for already while you carried him inside you, it
was dissolved in the water that makes the embryo weightless.

No, we don't accomplish our love in a single year
as the flowers do; an immemorial sap
flows up through our arms when we love. Dear girl,
this: that we loved, inside us, not One who would someday appear, but
seething multitudes; not just a single child,
but also the fathers lying in our depths

uns im Grunde beruhn; sondern das trockene Flußbett
einstiger Mütter—; sondern die ganze
lautlose Landschaft unter dem wolkigen oder
reinen Verhängnis—: *dies* kam dir, Mädchen, zuvor.

Und du selber, was weißt du—, du locktest
Vorzeit empor in dem Liebenden. Welche Gefühle
wühlten herauf aus entwandelten Wesen. Welche
Frauen haßten dich da. Wasfür finstere Männer
regtest du auf im Geäder des Jünglings? Tote
Kinder wollten zu dir . . . O leise, leise,
tu ein liebes vor ihm, ein verläßliches Tagwerk,—führ ihn
nah an den Garten heran, gieb ihm der Nächte
Übergewicht . . . . . .
                    Verhalt ihn. . . . . .

like fallen mountains; also the dried-up riverbeds
of ancient mothers—; also the whole
soundless landscape under the clouded or clear
sky of its destiny—: all this, my dear, preceded you.

And you yourself, how could you know
what primordial time you stirred in your lover. What passions
welled up inside him from departed beings. What
women hated you there. How many dark
sinister men you aroused in his young veins. Dead
children reached out to touch you . . . Oh gently, gently,
let him see you performing, with love, some confident daily task,—
lead him out close to the garden, give him what outweighs
the heaviest night . . . . . .
                    Restrain him . . . . . .

DIE VIERTE ELEGIE

O Bäume Lebens, o wann winterlich?
Wir sind nicht einig. Sind nicht wie die Zug-
vögel verständigt. Überholt und spät,
so drängen wir uns plötzlich Winden auf
und fallen ein auf teilnahmslosen Teich.
Blühn und verdorrn ist uns zugleich bewußt.
Und irgendwo gehn Löwen noch und wissen,
solang sie herrlich sind, von keiner Ohnmacht.

Uns aber, wo wir Eines meinen, ganz,
ist schon des andern Aufwand fühlbar. Feindschaft
ist uns das Nächste. Treten Liebende
nicht immerfort an Ränder, eins im andern,
die sich versprachen Weite, Jagd und Heimat.
    Da wird für eines Augenblickes Zeichnung
ein Grund von Gegenteil bereitet, mühsam,
daß wir sie sähen; denn man ist sehr deutlich
mit uns. Wir kennen den Kontur
des Fühlens nicht: nur, was ihn formt von außen.
    Wer saß nicht bang vor seines Herzens Vorhang?
Der schlug sich auf: die Szenerie war Abschied.
Leicht zu verstehen. Der bekannte Garten,
und schwankte leise: dann erst kam der Tänzer.
Nicht *der*. Genug! Und wenn er auch so leicht tut,
er ist verkleidet und er wird ein Bürger
und geht durch seine Küche in die Wohnung.
    Ich will nicht diese halbgefüllten Masken,
lieber die Puppe. Die ist voll. Ich will
den Balg aushalten und den Draht und ihr
Gesicht aus Aussehn. Hier. Ich bin davor.
Wenn auch die Lampen ausgehn, wenn mir auch
gesagt wird: Nichts mehr—, wenn auch von der Bühne
das Leere herkommt mit dem grauen Luftzug,
wenn auch von meinen stillen Vorfahrn keiner
mehr mit mir dasitzt, keine Frau, sogar
der Knabe nicht mehr mit dem braunen Schielaug:
Ich bleibe dennoch. Es giebt immer Zuschaun.

THE FOURTH ELEGY

O trees of life, when does your winter come?
We are not in harmony, our blood does not forewarn us
like migratory birds'. Late, overtaken,
we force ourselves abruptly onto the wind
and fall to earth at some iced-over lake.
Flowering and fading come to us both at once.
And somewhere lions still roam and never know,
in their majestic power, of any weakness.

But we, while we are intent upon one object,
already feel the pull of another. Conflict
is second nature to us. Aren't lovers
always arriving at each other's boundaries?—
although they promised vastness, hunting, home.
　　As when for some quick sketch, a wide background
of contrast is laboriously prepared
so that we can see more clearly: we never know
the actual, vital contour of our own
emotions—just what forms them from outside.
　　Who has not sat, afraid, before his heart's
curtain? It rose: the scenery of farewell.
Easy to recognize. The well-known garden,
which swayed a little. Then the dancer came.
Not *him*. Enough! However lightly he moves,
he's costumed, made up—an ordinary man
who hurries home and walks in through the kitchen.
　　I won't endure these half-filled human masks;
better, the puppet. It at least is full.
I'll put up with the stuffed skin, the wire, the face
that is nothing but appearance. Here. I'm waiting.
Even if the lights go out; even if someone
tells me "That's all"; even if emptiness
floats toward me in a gray draft from the stage;
even if not one of my silent ancestors
stays seated with me, not one woman, not
the boy with the immovable brown eye—
I'll sit here anyway. One can always watch.

Hab ich nicht recht? Du, der um mich so bitter
das Leben schmeckte, meines kostend, Vater,
den ersten trüben Aufguß meines Müssens,
da ich heranwuchs, immer wieder kostend
und, mit dem Nachgeschmack so fremder Zukunft
beschäftigt, prüftest mein beschlagnes Aufschaun,—
der du, mein Vater, seit du tot bist, oft
in meiner Hoffnung, innen in mir, Angst hast,
und Gleichmut, wie ihn Tote haben, Reiche
von Gleichmut, aufgiebst für mein bißchen Schicksal,
hab ich nicht recht? Und ihr, hab ich nicht recht,
die ihr mich liebtet für den kleinen Anfang
Liebe zu euch, von dem ich immer abkam,
weil mir der Raum in eurem Angesicht,
da ich ihn liebte, überging in Weltraum,
in dem ihr nicht mehr wart. . . . : wenn mir zumut ist,
zu warten vor der Puppenbühne, nein,
so völlig hinzuschaun, daß, um mein Schauen
am Ende aufzuwiegen, dort als Spieler
ein Engel hinmuß, der die Bälge hochreißt.
Engel und Puppe: dann ist endlich Schauspiel.
Dann kommt zusammen, was wir immerfort
entzwein, indem wir da sind. Dann entsteht
aus unsern Jahreszeiten erst der Umkreis
des ganzen Wandelns. Über uns hinüber
spielt dann der Engel. Sieh, die Sterbenden,
sollten sie nicht vermuten, wie voll Vorwand
das alles ist, was wir hier leisten. Alles
ist nicht es selbst. O Stunden in der Kindheit,
da hinter den Figuren mehr als nur
Vergangnes war und vor uns nicht die Zukunft.
Wir wuchsen freilich und wir drängten manchmal,
bald groß zu werden, denen halb zulieb,
die andres nicht mehr hatten, als das Großsein.
Und waren doch, in unserem Alleingehn,

Am I not right? You, to whom life tasted
so bitter after you took a sip of mine,
the first, gritty infusion of my will,
Father—who, as I grew up, kept on tasting
and, troubled by the aftertaste of so
strange a future, searched my unfocused gaze—
you who, so often since you died, have trembled
for my well-being, within my deepest hope,
relinquishing that calmness which the dead
feel as their very essence, countless realms
of equanimity, for my scrap of life—
tell me, am I not right? And you, dear women
who must have loved me for my small beginning
of love toward you, which I always turned away from
because the space in your features grew, changed,
even while I loved it, into cosmic space,
where you no longer were—: am I not right
to feel as if I *must* stay seated, must
wait before the puppet stage, or, rather,
gaze at it so intensely that at last,
to balance my gaze, an angel has to come and
make the stuffed skins startle into life.
Angel and puppet: a real play, finally.
Then what we separate by our very presence
can come together. And only then, the whole
cycle of transformation will arise,
out of our own life-seasons. Above, beyond us,
the angel plays. If no one else, the dying
must notice how unreal, how full of pretense,
is all that we accomplish here, where nothing
is allowed to be itself. Oh hours of childhood,
when behind each shape more than the past appeared
and what streamed out before us was not the future.
We felt our bodies growing and were at times
impatient to *be* grown up, half for the sake
of those with nothing left but their grownupness.
Yet were, when playing by ourselves, enchanted

mit Dauerndem vergnügt und standen da
im Zwischenraume zwischen Welt und Spielzeug,
an einer Stelle, die seit Anbeginn
gegründet war für einen reinen Vorgang.

Wer zeigt ein Kind, so wie es steht? Wer stellt
es ins Gestirn und giebt das Maß des Abstands
ihm in die Hand? Wer macht den Kindertod
aus grauem Brot, das hart wird,—oder läßt
ihn drin im runden Mund, so wie den Gröps
von einem schönen Apfel? . . . . . . Mörder sind
leicht einzusehen. Aber dies: den Tod,
den ganzen Tod, noch *vor* dem Leben so
sanft zu enthalten und nicht bös zu sein,
ist unbeschreiblich.

with what alone endures; and we would stand there
in the infinite, blissful space between world and toy,
at a point which, from the earliest beginning,
had been established for a pure event.

Who shows a child as he really is? Who sets him
in his constellation and puts the measuring-rod
of distance in his hand? Who makes his death
out of gray bread, which hardens—or leaves it there
inside his round mouth, jagged as the core
of a sweet apple? . . . . . . Murderers are easy
to understand. But this: that one can contain
death, the whole of death, even before
life has begun, can hold it to one's heart
gently, and not refuse to go on living,
is inexpressible.

DIE FÜNFTE ELEGIE

Frau Hertha Koenig zugeeignet

Wer aber *sind* sie, sag mir, die Fahrenden, diese ein wenig
Flüchtigern noch als wir selbst, die dringend von früh an
wringt ein *wem, wem* zu Liebe
niemals zufriedener Wille? Sondern er wringt sie,
biegt sie, schlingt sie und schwingt sie,
wirft sie und fängt sie zurück; wie aus geölter,
glatterer Luft kommen sie nieder
auf dem verzehrten, von ihrem ewigen
Aufsprung dünneren Teppich, diesem verlorenen
Teppich im Weltall.
Aufgelegt wie ein Pflaster, als hätte der Vorstadt-
Himmel der Erde dort wehe getan.
                          Und kaum dort,
aufrecht, da und gezeigt: des Dastehns
großer Anfangsbuchstab . . . , schon auch, die stärksten
Männer, rollt sie wieder, zum Scherz, der immer
kommende Griff, wie August der Starke bei Tisch
einen zinnenen Teller.

Ach und um diese
Mitte, die Rose des Zuschauns:
blüht und entblättert. Um diesen
Stampfer, den Stempel, den von dem eignen
blühenden Staub getroffnen, zur Scheinfrucht
wieder der Unlust befruchteten, ihrer
niemals bewußten,—glänzend mit dünnster
Oberfläche leicht scheinlächelnden Unlust.

Da: der welke, faltige Stemmer,
der alte, der nur noch trommelt,
eingegangen in seiner gewaltigen Haut, als hätte sie früher
zwei Männer enthalten, und einer
läge nun schon auf dem Kirchhof, und er überlebte den andern,

THE FIFTH ELEGY

Dedicated to Frau Hertha Koenig

But tell me, who *are* they, these wanderers, even more
transient than we ourselves, who from their earliest days
are savagely wrung out
by a never-satisfied will (for *whose* sake)? Yet it wrings them,
bends them, twists them, swings them and flings them
and catches them again; and falling as if through oiled
slippery air, they land
on the threadbare carpet, worn constantly thinner
by their perpetual leaping, this carpet that is lost
in infinite space.
Stuck on like a bandage, as if the suburban sky
had wounded the earth.
                    And hardly has it appeared
when, standing there, upright, is: the large capital D
that begins Duration . . . , and the always-approaching grip
takes them again, as a joke, even the strongest
men, and crushes them, the way King Augustus the Strong
would crush a pewter plate.

Ah and around this
center: the rose of Onlooking
blooms and unblossoms. Around this
pestle pounding the carpet,
this pistil, fertilized by the pollen
of its own dust, and producing in turn
the specious fruit of displeasure: the unconscious
gaping faces, their thin
surfaces glossy with boredom's specious half-smile.

There: the shriveled-up, wrinkled weight-lifter,
an old man who only drums now,
shrunk in his enormous skin, which looks as if it had once
contained *two* men, and the other
were already lying in the graveyard, while this one lived on without him,

taub und manchmal ein wenig
wirr, in der verwitweten Haut

Aber der junge, der Mann, als wär er der Sohn eines Nackens
und einer Nonne: prall und strammig erfüllt
mit Muskeln und Einfalt.

Oh ihr,
die ein Leid, das noch klein war,
einst als Spielzeug bekam, in einer seiner
langen Genesungen . . . .

Du, der mit dem Aufschlag,
wie nur Früchte ihn kennen, unreif,
täglich hundertmal abfällt vom Baum der gemeinsam
erbauten Bewegung (der, rascher als Wasser, in wenig
Minuten Lenz, Sommer und Herbst hat)—
abfällt und anprallt ans Grab:
manchmal, in halber Pause, will dir ein liebes
Antlitz entstehn hinüber zu deiner selten
zärtlichen Mutter; doch an deinen Körper verliert sich,
der es flächig verbraucht, das schüchtern
kaum versuchte Gesicht . . . Und wieder
klatscht der Mann in die Hand zu dem Ansprung, und eh dir
jemals ein Schmerz deutlicher wird in der Nähe des immer
trabenden Herzens, kommt das Brennen der Fußsohln
ihm, seinem Ursprung, zuvor mit ein paar dir
rasch in die Augen gejagten leiblichen Tränen.
Und dennoch, blindlings,
das Lächeln . . . . .

Engel! o nimms, pflücks, das kleinblütige Heilkraut.
Schaff eine Vase, verwahrs! Stells unter jene, uns *noch* nicht
offenen Freuden; in lieblicher Urne
rühms mit blumiger schwungiger Aufschrift:
›Subrisio Saltat.‹.

Du dann, Liebliche,
du, von den reizendsten Freuden

deaf and sometimes a little
confused, in the widowed skin.

And the young one over there, the man, who might be the son of a neck
and a nun: firm and vigorously filled
with muscles and innocence.

Children,
whom a grief that was still quite small
once received as a toy, during one of its
long convalescences . . . .

You, little boy, who fall down
a hundred times daily, with the thud
that only unripe fruits know, from the tree of mutually
constructed motion (which more quickly than water, in a few
minutes, has its spring, summer, and autumn)—
fall down hard on the grave:
sometimes, during brief pauses, a loving look
toward your seldom affectionate mother tries to be born
in your expression; but it gets lost along the way,
your body consumes it, that timid
scarcely-attempted face . . . And again
the man is clapping his hands for your leap, and before
a pain can become more distinct near your constantly racing
heart, the stinging in your soles rushes ahead of
that other pain, chasing a pair
of physical tears quickly into your eyes.
And nevertheless, blindly,
the smile . . . . .

Oh gather it, Angel, that small-flowered herb of healing.
Create a vase and preserve it. Set it among those joys
not *yet* open to us; on that lovely urn
praise it with the ornately flowing inscription:
                              "Subrisio Saltat."

    And you then, my lovely darling,
you whom the most tempting joys

stumm Übersprungne. Vielleicht sind
deine Fransen glücklich für dich—,
oder über den jungen
prallen Brüsten die grüne metallene Seide
fühlt sich unendlich verwöhnt und entbehrt nichts.
Du,
immerfort anders auf alle des Gleichgewichts schwankende Waagen
hingelegte Marktfrucht des Gleichmuts,
öffentlich unter den Schultern.

Wo, o *wo* ist der Ort—ich trag ihn im Herzen—,
wo sie noch lange nicht *konnten,* noch von einander
abfieln, wie sich bespringende, nicht recht
paarige Tiere;—
wo die Gewichte noch schwer sind;
wo noch von ihren vergeblich
wirbelnden Stäben die Teller
torkeln . . . . .

Und plötzlich in diesem mühsamen Nirgends, plötzlich
die unsägliche Stelle, wo sich das reine Zuwenig
unbegreiflich verwandelt—, umspringt
in jenes leere Zuviel.
Wo die vielstellige Rechnung
zahlenlos aufgeht.

Plätze, o Platz in Paris, unendlicher Schauplatz,
wo die Modistin, Madame Lamort,
die ruhlosen Wege der Erde, endlose Bänder,
schlingt und windet und neue aus ihnen
Schleifen erfindet, Rüschen, Blumen, Kokarden, künstliche Früchte—, alle
unwahr gefärbt,—für die billigen
Winterhüte des Schicksals.
. . . .

Engel!: Es wäre ein Platz, den wir nicht wissen, und dorten,
auf unsäglichem Teppich, zeigten die Liebenden, die's hier

have mutely leapt over. Perhaps
your fringes are happy *for* you—,
or perhaps the green
metallic silk stretched over your firm young breasts
feels itself endlessly indulged and in need of nothing.
You
display-fruit of equanimity,
set out in front of the public, in continual variations
on all the swaying scales of equipoise,
lifted among the shoulders.

Oh *where* is the place—I carry it in my heart—,
where they still were far from mastery, still fell apart
from each other, like mating cattle that someone
has badly paired;—
where the weights are still heavy; where
from their vainly twirling sticks
the plates still wobble
and drop . . . . .

And suddenly in this laborious nowhere, suddenly
the unsayable spot where the pure Too-little is transformed
incomprehensibly—, leaps around and changes
into that empty Too-much;
where the difficult calculation
becomes numberless and resolved.

Squares, oh square in Paris, infinite showplace
where the milliner Madame Lamort
twists and winds the restless paths of the earth,
those endless ribbons, and, from them, designs
new bows, frills, flowers, ruffles, artificial fruits—, all
falsely colored,—for the cheap
winter bonnets of Fate.

. . . .

Angel!: If there were a place that we didn't know of, and there,
on some unsayable carpet, lovers displayed

bis zum Können nie bringen, ihre kühnen
hohen Figuren des Herzschwungs,
ihre Türme aus Lust, ihre
längst, wo Boden nie war, nur an einander
lehnenden Leitern, bebend,—und *könntens,*
vor den Zuschauern rings, unzähligen lautlosen Toten:
    Würfen die dann ihre letzten, immer ersparten,
immer verborgenen, die wir nicht kennen, ewig
gültigen Münzen des Glücks vor das endlich
wahrhaft lächelnde Paar auf gestilltem
Teppich?

what they never could bring to mastery here—the bold
exploits of their high-flying hearts,
their towers of pleasure, their ladders
that have long since been standing where there was no ground, leaning
just on each other, trembling,—and could *master* all this,
before the surrounding spectators, the innumerable soundless dead:
    Would these, then, throw down their final, forever saved-up,
forever hidden, unknown to us, eternally valid
coins of happiness before the at last
genuinely smiling pair on the gratified
carpet?

DIE SECHSTE ELEGIE

Feigenbaum, seit wie lange schon ists mir bedeutend,
wie du die Blüte beinah ganz überschlägst
und hinein in die zeitig entschlossene Frucht,
ungerühmt, drängst dein reines Geheimnis.
Wie der Fontäne Rohr treibt dein gebognes Gezweig
abwärts den Saft und hinan: und er springt aus dem Schlaf,
fast nicht erwachend, ins Glück seiner süßesten Leistung.
Sieh: wie der Gott in den Schwan.
. . . . . .Wir aber verweilen,
ach, uns rühmt es zu blühn, und ins verspätete Innre
unserer endlichen Frucht gehn wir verraten hinein.
Wenigen steigt so stark der Andrang des Handelns,
daß sie schon anstehn und glühn in der Fülle des Herzens,
wenn die Verführung zum Blühn wie gelinderte Nachtluft
ihnen die Jugend des Munds, ihnen die Lider berührt:
Helden vielleicht und den frühe Hinüberbestimmten,
denen der gärtnernde Tod anders die Adern verbiegt.
Diese stürzen dahin: dem eigenen Lächeln
sind sie voran, wie das Rossegespann in den milden
muldigen Bildern von Karnak dem siegenden König.

Wunderlich nah ist der Held doch den jugendlich Toten. Dauern
ficht ihn nicht an. Sein Aufgang ist Dasein; beständig
nimmt er sich fort und tritt ins veränderte Sternbild
seiner steten Gefahr. Dort fänden ihn wenige. Aber,
das uns finster verschweigt, das plötzlich begeisterte Schicksal
singt ihn hinein in den Sturm seiner aufrauschenden Welt.
Hör ich doch keinen wie *ihn.* Auf einmal durchgeht mich
mit der strömenden Luft sein verdunkelter Ton.

Dann, wie verbärg ich mich gern vor der Sehnsucht: O wär ich,
wär ich ein Knabe und dürft es noch werden und säße
in die künftigen Arme gestützt und läse von Simson,
wie seine Mutter erst nichts und dann alles gebar.

War er nicht Held schon in dir, o Mutter, begann nicht
dort schon, in dir, seine herrische Auswahl?

THE SIXTH ELEGY

Fig-tree, for such a long time I have found meaning
in the way you almost completely omit your blossoms
and urge your pure mystery, unproclaimed,
into the early ripening fruit.
Like the curved pipe of a fountain, your arching boughs drive the sap
downward and up again: and almost without awakening
it bursts out of sleep, into its sweetest achievement.
Like the god stepping into the swan.
      . . . . . . But *we* still linger, alas,
we, whose pride is in blossoming; we enter the overdue
interior of our final fruit and are already betrayed.
In only a few does the urge to action rise up
so powerfully that they stop, glowing in their heart's abundance,
while, like the soft night air, the temptation to blossom
touches their tender mouths, touches their eyelids, softly:
heroes perhaps, and those chosen to disappear early,
whose veins Death the gardener twists into a different pattern.
These plunge on ahead: in advance of their own smile
like the team of galloping horses before the triumphant
pharaoh in the mildly hollowed reliefs at Karnak.

The hero is strangely close to those who died young. Permanence
does not concern him. He lives in continual ascent,
moving on into the ever-changed constellation
of perpetual danger. Few could find him there. But
Fate, which is silent about us, suddenly grows inspired
and sings him into the storm of his onrushing world.
I hear no one like *him*. All at once I am pierced
by his darkened voice, carried on the streaming air.

Then how gladly I would hide from the longing to be once again
oh a boy once again, with my life before me, to sit
leaning on future arms and reading of Samson,
how from his mother first nothing, then everything, was born.

Wasn't he a hero inside you, mother? didn't
his imperious choosing already begin there, in you?

Tausende brauten im Schooß und wollten *er* sein,
aber sieh: er ergriff und ließ aus—, wählte und konnte.
Und wenn er Säulen zerstieß, so wars, da er ausbrach
aus der Welt deines Leibs in die engere Welt, wo er weiter
wählte und konnte. O Mütter der Helden, o Ursprung
reißender Ströme! Ihr Schluchten, in die sich
hoch von dem Herzrand, klagend,
schon die Mädchen gestürzt, künftig die Opfer dem Sohn.

Denn hinstürmte der Held durch Aufenthalte der Liebe,
jeder hob ihn hinaus, jeder ihn meinende Herzschlag,
abgewendet schon, stand er am Ende der Lächeln,—anders.

Thousands seethed in your womb, wanting to be *him,*
but look: he grasped and excluded—, chose and prevailed.
And if he demolished pillars, it was when he burst
from the world of your body into the narrower world, where again
he chose and prevailed. O mothers of heroes, O sources
of ravaging floods! You ravines into which
virgins have plunged, lamenting,
from the highest rim of the heart, sacrifices to the son.

   For whenever the hero stormed through the stations of love,
each heartbeat intended for him lifted him up, beyond it;
and, turning away, he stood there, at the end of all smiles,—transfigured.

DIE SIEBENTE ELEGIE

Werbung nicht mehr, nicht Werbung, entwachsene Stimme,
sei deines Schreies Natur; zwar schrieest du rein wie der Vogel,
wenn ihn die Jahreszeit aufhebt, die steigende, beinah vergessend,
daß er ein kümmerndes Tier und nicht nur ein einzelnes Herz sei,
das sie ins Heitere wirft, in die innigen Himmel. Wie er, so
würbest du wohl, nicht minder—, daß, noch unsichtbar,
dich die Freundin erführ, die stille, in der eine Antwort
langsam erwacht und über dem Hören sich anwärmt,—
deinem erkühnten Gefühl die erglühte Gefühlin.

O und der Frühling begriffe—, da ist keine Stelle,
die nicht trüge den Ton der Verkündigung. Erst jenen kleinen
fragenden Auflaut, den, mit steigernder Stille,
weithin umschweigt ein reiner bejahender Tag.
Dann die Stufen hinan, Ruf-Stufen hinan, zum geträumten
Tempel der Zukunft—; dann den Triller, Fontäne,
die zu dem drängenden Strahl schon das Fallen zuvornimmt
im versprechlichen Spiel. . . . Und vor sich, den Sommer.
   Nicht nur die Morgen alle des Sommers—, nicht nur
wie sie sich wandeln in Tag und strahlen vor Anfang.
Nicht nur die Tage, die zart sind um Blumen, und oben,
um die gestalteten Bäume, stark und gewaltig.
Nicht nur die Andacht dieser entfalteten Kräfte,
nicht nur die Wege, nicht nur die Wiesen im Abend,
nicht nur, nach spätem Gewitter, das atmende Klarsein,
nicht nur der nahende Schlaf und ein Ahnen, abends . . .
sondern die Nächte! Sondern die hohen, des Sommers,
Nächte, sondern die Sterne, die Sterne der Erde.
O einst tot sein und sie wissen unendlich,
alle die Sterne: denn wie, wie, wie sie vergessen!

Siehe, da rief ich die Liebende. Aber nicht *sie* nur
käme . . . Es kämen aus schwächlichen Gräbern
Mädchen und ständen . . . Denn, wie beschränk ich,
wie, den gerufenen Ruf? Die Versunkenen suchen
immer noch Erde.—Ihr Kinder, ein hiesig

THE SEVENTH ELEGY

Not wooing, no longer shall wooing, voice that has outgrown it,
be the nature of your cry; but instead, you would cry out as purely as a bird
when the quickly ascending season lifts him up, nearly forgetting
that he is a suffering creature and not just a single heart
being flung into brightness, into the intimate skies. Just like him
you would be wooing, not any less purely—, so that, still
unseen, she would sense you, the silent lover in whom a reply
slowly awakens and, as she hears you, grows warm,—
the ardent companion to your own most daring emotion.

Oh and springtime would hold it—, everywhere it would echo
the song of annunciation. First the small
questioning notes intensified all around
by the sheltering silence of a pure, affirmative day.
Then up the stairs, up the stairway of calls, to the dreamed-of
temple of the future—; and then the trill, like a fountain
which, in its rising jet, already anticipates its fall
in a game of promises. . . . And still ahead: summer.
    Not only all the dawns of summer—, not only
how they change themselves into day and shine with beginning.
Not only the days, so tender around flowers and, above,
around the patterned treetops, so strong, so intense.
Not only the reverence of all these unfolded powers,
not only the pathways, not only the meadows at sunset,
not only, after a late storm, the deep-breathing freshness,
not only approaching sleep, and a premonition . . .
but also the nights! But also the lofty summer
nights, and the stars as well, the stars of the earth.
Oh to be dead at last and know them endlessly,
all the stars: for how, how could we ever forget them!

Look, I was calling for my lover. But not just *she*
would come . . . Out of their fragile graves
girls would arise and gather . . . For how could I limit
the call, once I called it? These unripe spirits keep seeking
the earth.—Children, one earthly Thing

einmal ergriffenes Ding gälte für viele.
Glaubt nicht, Schicksal sei mehr, als das Dichte der Kindheit;
wie überholtet ihr oft den Geliebten, atmend,
atmend nach seligem Lauf, auf nichts zu, ins Freie.

Hiersein ist herrlich. Ihr wußtet es, Mädchen, *ihr* auch,
die ihr scheinbar entbehrtet, versankt—, ihr, in den ärgsten
Gassen der Städte, Schwärende, oder dem Abfall
Offene. Denn eine Stunde war jeder, vielleicht nicht
ganz eine Stunde, ein mit den Maßen der Zeit kaum
Meßliches zwischen zwei Weilen—, da sie ein Dasein
hatte. Alles. Die Adern voll Dasein.
Nur, wir vergessen so leicht, was der lachende Nachbar
uns nicht bestätigt oder beneidet. Sichtbar
wollen wirs heben, wo doch das sichtbarste Glück uns
erst zu erkennen sich giebt, wenn wir es innen verwandeln.

Nirgends, Geliebte, wird Welt sein, als innen. Unser
Leben geht hin mit Verwandlung. Und immer geringer
schwindet das Außen. Wo einmal ein dauerndes Haus war,
schlägt sich erdachtes Gebild vor, quer, zu Erdenklichem
völlig gehörig, als ständ es noch ganz im Gehirne.
Weite Speicher der Kraft schafft sich der Zeitgeist, gestaltlos
wie der spannende Drang, den er aus allem gewinnt.
Tempel kennt er nicht mehr. Diese, des Herzens, Verschwendung
sparen wir heimlicher ein. Ja, wo noch eins übersteht,
ein einst gebetetes Ding, ein gedientes, gekknietes—,
hält es sich, so wie es ist, schon ins Unsichtbare hin.
Viele gewahrens nicht mehr, doch ohne den Vorteil,
daß sie's nun *innerlich* baun, mit Pfeilern und Statuen, größer!

Jede dumpfe Umkehr der Welt hat solche Enterbte,
denen das Frühere nicht und noch nicht das Nächste gehört.
Denn auch das Nächste ist weit für die Menschen. *Uns* soll
dies nicht verwirren; es stärke in uns die Bewahrung
der noch erkannten Gestalt.—Dies *stand* einmal unter Menschen,
mitten im Schicksal stands, im vernichtenden, mitten
im Nichtwissen-Wohin stand es, wie seiend, und bog
Sterne zu sich aus gesicherten Himmeln. Engel,

truly experienced, even once, is enough for a lifetime.
Don't think that fate is more than the density of childhood;
how often you outdistanced the man you loved, breathing, breathing
after the blissful chase, and passed on into freedom.

Truly being here is glorious. Even *you* knew it,
you girls who seemed to be lost, to go under—, in the filthiest
streets of the city, festering there, or wide open
for garbage. For each of you had an hour, or perhaps
not even an hour, a barely measurable time
between two moments—, when you were granted a sense
of being. Everything. Your veins flowed with being.
But we can so easily forget what our laughing neighbor
neither confirms nor envies. We want to display it,
to make it visible, though even the most visible happiness
can't reveal itself to us until we transform it, within.

Nowhere, Beloved, will world be but within us. Our life
passes in transformation. And the external
shrinks into less and less. Where once an enduring house was,
now a cerebral structure crosses our path, completely
belonging to the realm of concepts, as though it still stood in the brain.
Our age has built itself vast reservoirs of power,
formless as the straining energy that it wrests from the earth.
Temples are no longer known. It is we who secretly save up
these extravagances of the heart. Where one of them still survives,
a Thing that was formerly prayed to, worshipped, knelt before—
just as it is, it passes into the invisible world.
Many no longer perceive it, yet miss the chance
to build it *inside* themselves now, with pillars and statues: greater.

Each torpid turn of the world has such disinherited ones,
to whom neither the past belongs, nor yet what has nearly arrived.
For even the nearest moment is far from mankind. Though *we*
should not be confused by this, but strengthened in our task of preserving
the still-recognizable form.— This once *stood* among mankind,
in the midst of Fate the annihilator, in the midst
of Not-Knowing-Whither, it stood as if enduring, and bent
stars down to it from their safeguarded heavens. Angel,

dir noch zeig ich es, *da!* in deinem Anschaun
steh es gerettet zuletzt, nun endlich aufrecht.
Säulen, Pylone, der Sphinx, das strebende Stemmen,
grau aus vergehender Stadt oder aus fremder, des Doms.

War es nicht Wunder? O staune, Engel, denn *wir* sinds,
wir, o du Großer, erzähls, daß wir solches vermochten, mein Atem
reicht für die Rühmung nicht aus. So haben wir dennoch
nicht die Räume versäumt, diese gewährenden, diese
unseren Räume. (Was müssen sie fürchterlich groß sein,
da sie Jahrtausende nicht unseres Fühlns überfülln.)
Aber ein Turm war groß, nicht wahr? O Engel, er war es,—
groß, auch noch neben dir? Chartres war groß—, und Musik
reichte noch weiter hinan und überstieg uns. Doch selbst nur
eine Liebende—, oh, allein am nächtlichen Fenster. . . .
reichte sie dir nicht ans Knie—?
                              Glaub *nicht,* daß ich werbe.
Engel, und würb ich dich auch! Du kommst nicht. Denn mein
Anruf ist immer voll Hinweg; wider so starke
Strömung kannst du nicht schreiten. Wie ein gestreckter
Arm ist mein Rufen. Und seine zum Greifen
oben offene Hand bleibt vor dir
offen, wie Abwehr und Warnung,
Unfaßlicher, weitauf.

to *you* I will show it, *there!* in your endless vision
it shall stand, now finally upright, rescued at last.
Pillars, pylons, the Sphinx, the striving thrust
of the cathedral, gray, from a fading or alien city.

Wasn't all this a miracle? Be astonished, Angel, for we
are this, O Great One; proclaim that we could achieve this, my breath
is too short for such praise. So, after all, we have not
failed to make use of these generous spaces, these
spaces of *ours*. (How frighteningly great they must be,
since thousands of years have not made them overflow with our feelings.)
But a tower was great, wasn't it? Oh Angel, it was—
even when placed beside you? Chartres was great—, and music
reached still higher and passed far beyond us. But even
a woman in love—, oh alone at night by her window. . . .
didn't she reach your knee—?
                                        Don't think that I'm wooing.
Angel, and even if I were, you would not come. For my call
is always filled with departure; against such a powerful
current you cannot move. Like an outstretched arm
is my call. And its hand, held open and reaching up
to seize, remains in front of you, open
as if in defense and warning,
Ungraspable One, far above.

DIE ACHTE ELEGIE

Rudolf Kassner zugeeignet

Mit allen Augen sieht die Kreatur
das Offene. Nur unsre Augen sind
wie umgekehrt und ganz um sie gestellt
als Fallen, rings um ihren freien Ausgang.
Was draußen *ist,* wir wissens aus des Tiers
Antlitz allein; denn schon das frühe Kind
wenden wir um und zwingens, daß es rückwärts
Gestaltung sehe, nicht das Offne, das
im Tiergesicht so tief ist. Frei von Tod.
Ihn sehen wir allein; das freie Tier
hat seinen Untergang stets hinter sich
und vor sich Gott, und wenn es geht, so gehts
in Ewigkeit, so wie die Brunnen gehen.

Wir haben nie, nicht einen einzigen Tag,
den reinen Raum vor uns, in den die Blumen
unendlich aufgehn. Immer ist es Welt
und niemals Nirgends ohne Nicht: das Reine,
Unüberwachte, das man atmet und
unendlich *weiß* und nicht begehrt. Als Kind
verliert sich eins im Stilln an dies und wird
gerüttelt. Oder jener stirbt und ists.
Denn nah am Tod sieht man den Tod nicht mehr
und starrt *hinaus,* vielleicht mit großem Tierblick.
Liebende, wäre nicht der andre, der
die Sicht verstellt, sind nah daran und staunen . . .
Wie aus Versehn ist ihnen aufgetan
hinter dem andern . . . Aber über ihn
kommt keiner fort, und wieder wird ihm Welt.
Der Schöpfung immer zugewendet, sehn
wir nur auf ihr die Spiegelung des Frein,
von uns verdunkelt. Oder daß ein Tier,
ein stummes, aufschaut, ruhig durch uns durch.
Dieses heißt Schicksal: gegenüber sein
und nichts als das und immer gegenüber.

THE EIGHTH ELEGY

Dedicated to Rudolf Kassner

With all its eyes the natural world looks out
into the Open. Only *our* eyes are turned
backward, and surround plant, animal, child
like traps, as they emerge into their freedom.
We know what is really out there only from
the animal's gaze; for we take the very young
child and force it around, so that it sees
objects—not the Open, which is so
deep in animals' faces. Free from death.
We, only, can see death; the free animal
has its decline in back of it, forever,
and God in front, and when it moves, it moves
already in eternity, like a fountain.

Never, not for a single day, do *we* have
before us that pure space into which flowers
endlessly open. Always there is World
and never Nowhere without the No: that pure
unseparated element which one breathes
without desire and endlessly *knows.* A child
may wander there for hours, through the timeless
stillness, may get lost in it and be
shaken back. Or someone dies and *is* it.
For, nearing death, one doesn't see death; but stares
beyond, perhaps with an animal's vast gaze.
Lovers, if the beloved were not there
blocking the view, are close to it, and marvel . . .
As if by some mistake, it opens for them
behind each other . . . But neither can move past
the other, and it changes back to World.
Forever turned toward objects, we see in them
the mere reflection of the realm of freedom,
which we have dimmed. Or when some animal
mutely, serenely, looks us through and through.
That is what fate means: to be opposite,
to be opposite and nothing else, forever.

Wäre Bewußtheit unsrer Art in dem
sicheren Tier, das uns entgegenzieht
in anderer Richtung—, riß es uns herum
mit seinem Wandel. Doch sein Sein ist ihm
unendlich, ungefaßt und ohne Blick
auf seinen Zustand, rein, so wie sein Ausblick.
Und wo wir Zukunft sehn, dort sieht es Alles
und sich in Allem und geheilt für immer.

Und doch ist in dem wachsam warmen Tier
Gewicht und Sorge einer großen Schwermut.
Denn ihm auch haftet immer an, was uns
oft überwältigt,—die Erinnerung,
als sei schon einmal das, wonach man drängt,
näher gewesen, treuer und sein Anschluß
unendlich zärtlich. Hier ist alles Abstand,
und dort wars Atem. Nach der ersten Heimat
ist ihm die zweite zwitterig und windig.
    O Seligkeit der *kleinen* Kreatur,
die immer *bleibt* im Schooße, der sie austrug;
o Glück der Mücke, die noch *innen* hüpft,
selbst wenn sie Hochzeit hat: denn Schooß ist Alles.
Und sieh die halbe Sicherheit des Vogels,
der beinah beides weiß aus seinem Ursprung,
als wär er eine Seele der Etrusker,
aus einem Toten, den ein Raum empfing,
doch mit der ruhenden Figur als Deckel.
Und wie bestürzt ist eins, das fliegen muß
und stammt aus einem Schooß. Wie vor sich selbst
erschreckt, durchzuckts die Luft, wie wenn ein Sprung
durch eine Tasse geht. So reißt die Spur
der Fledermaus durchs Porzellan des Abends.

Und wir: Zuschauer, immer, überall,
dem allen zugewandt und nie hinaus!
Uns überfüllts. Wir ordnens. Es zerfällt.
Wir ordnens wieder und zerfallen selbst.

If the animal moving toward us so securely
in a different direction had our kind of
consciousness—, it would wrench us around and drag us
along its path. But it feels its life as boundless,
unfathomable, and without regard
to its own condition: pure, like its outward gaze.
And where we see the future, it sees all time
and itself within all time, forever healed.

Yet in the alert, warm animal there lies
the pain and burden of an enormous sadness.
For it too feels the presence of what often
overwhelms us: a memory, as if
the element we keep pressing toward was once
more intimate, more true, and our communion
infinitely tender. Here all is distance;
there it was breath. After that first home,
the second seems ambiguous and drafty.
    Oh bliss of the *tiny* creature which remains
forever inside the womb that was its shelter;
joy of the gnat which, still *within,* leaps up
even at its marriage: for everything is womb.
And look at the half-assurance of the bird,
which knows both inner and outer, from its source,
as if it were the soul of an Etruscan,
flown out of a dead man received inside a space,
but with his reclining image as the lid.
And how bewildered is any womb-born creature
that has to fly. As if terrified and fleeing
from itself, it zigzags through the air, the way
a crack runs through a teacup. So the bat
quivers across the porcelain of evening.

And we: spectators, always, everywhere,
turned toward the world of objects, never outward.
It fills us. We arrange it. It breaks down.
We rearrange it, then break down ourselves.

Wer hat uns also umgedreht, daß wir,
was wir auch tun, in jener Haltung sind
von einem, welcher fortgeht? Wie er auf
dem letzten Hügel, der ihm ganz sein Tal
noch einmal zeigt, sich wendet, anhält, weilt—,
so leben wir und nehmen immer Abschied.

Who has twisted us around like this, so that
no matter what we do, we are in the posture
of someone going away? Just as, upon
the farthest hill, which shows him his whole valley
one last time, he turns, stops, lingers—,
so we live here, forever taking leave.

DIE NEUNTE ELEGIE

Warum, wenn es angeht, also die Frist des Daseins
hinzubringen, als Lorbeer, ein wenig dunkler als alle
andere Grün, mit kleinen Wellen an jedem
Blattrand (wie eines Windes Lächeln)—: warum dann
Menschliches müssen—und, Schicksal vermeidend,
sich sehnen nach Schicksal? . . .

                             Oh, *nicht*, weil Glück *ist*,
dieser voreilige Vorteil eines nahen Verlusts.
Nicht aus Neugier, oder zur Übung des Herzens,
das auch im Lorbeer *wäre*. . . . .

Aber weil Hiersein viel ist, und weil uns scheinbar
alles das Hiesige braucht, dieses Schwindende, das
seltsam uns angeht. Uns, die Schwindendsten. *Ein* Mal
jedes, nur *ein* Mal. *Ein* Mal und nichtmehr. Und wir auch
ein Mal. Nie wieder. Aber dieses
ein Mal gewesen zu sein, wenn auch nur *ein* Mal:
irdisch gewesen zu sein, scheint nicht widerrufbar.

Und so drängen wir uns und wollen es leisten,
wollens enthalten in unsern einfachen Händen,
im überfüllteren Blick und im sprachlosen Herzen.
Wollen es werden.—Wem es geben? Am liebsten
alles behalten für immer . . . Ach, in den andern Bezug,
wehe, was nimmt man hinüber? Nicht das Anschaun, das hier
langsam erlernte, und kein hier Ereignetes. Keins.
Also die Schmerzen. Also vor allem das Schwersein,
also der Liebe lange Erfahrung,—also
lauter Unsägliches. Aber später,
unter den Sternen, was solls: *die* sind *besser* unsäglich.
Bringt doch der Wanderer auch vom Hange des Bergrands
nicht eine Hand voll Erde ins Tal, die Allen unsägliche, sondern
ein erworbenes Wort, reines, den gelben und blaun
Enzian. Sind wir vielleicht *hier*, um zu sagen: Haus,
Brücke, Brunnen, Tor, Krug, Obstbaum, Fenster,—

THE NINTH ELEGY

Why, if this interval of being can be spent serenely
in the form of a laurel, slightly darker than all
other green, with tiny waves on the edges
of every leaf (like the smile of a breeze)—: why then
have to be human—and, escaping from fate,
keep longing for fate? . . .

                           Oh *not* because happiness *exists,*
that too-hasty profit snatched from approaching loss.
Not out of curiosity, not as practice for the heart, which
would exist in the laurel too. . . . . .

But because *truly* being here is so much; because everything here
apparently needs us, this fleeting world, which in some strange way
keeps calling to us. Us, the most fleeting of all.
Once for each thing. Just once; no more. And we too,
just once. And never again. But to have been
this once, completely, even if only once:
to have been at one with the earth, seems beyond undoing.

And so we keep pressing on, trying to achieve it,
trying to hold it firmly in our simple hands,
in our overcrowded gaze, in our speechless heart.
Trying to become it.—Whom can we give it to? We would
hold on to it all, forever . . . Ah, but what can we take along
into that other realm? Not the art of looking,
which is learned so slowly, and nothing that happened here. Nothing.
The sufferings, then. And, above all, the heaviness,
and the long experience of love,— just what is wholly
unsayable. But later, among the stars,
what good is it—*they* are *better* as they are: unsayable.
For when the traveler returns from the mountain-slopes into the valley,
he brings, not a handful of earth, unsayable to others, but instead
some word he has gained, some pure word, the yellow and blue
gentian. Perhaps we are *here* in order to say: house,
bridge, fountain, gate, pitcher, fruit-tree, window—

höchstens: Säule, Turm . . . . aber zu *sagen,* verstehs,
oh zu sagen *so,* wie selber die Dinge niemals
innig meinten zu sein. Ist nicht die heimliche List
dieser verschwiegenen Erde, wenn sie die Liebenden drängt,
daß sich in ihrem Gefühl jedes und jedes entzückt?
Schwelle: was ists für zwei
Liebende, daß sie die eigne ältere Schwelle der Tür
ein wenig verbrauchen, auch sie, nach den vielen vorher
und vor den Künftigen . . . . , leicht.

Hier ist des *Säglichen* Zeit, *hier* seine Heimat.
Sprich und bekenn. Mehr als je
fallen die Dinge dahin, die erlebbaren, denn,
was sie verdrängend ersetzt, ist ein Tun ohne Bild.
Tun unter Krusten, die willig zerspringen, sobald
innen das Handeln entwächst und sich anders begrenzt.
Zwischen den Hämmern besteht
unser Herz, wie die Zunge
zwischen den Zähnen, die doch,
dennoch, die preisende bleibt.

Preise dem Engel die Welt, nicht die unsägliche, *ihm*
kannst du nicht großtun mit herrlich Erfühltem; im Weltall,
wo er fühlender fühlt, bist du ein Neuling. Drum zeig
ihm das Einfache, das, von Geschlecht zu Geschlechtern gestaltet,
als ein Unsriges lebt, neben der Hand und im Blick.
Sag ihm die Dinge. Er wird staunender stehn; wie du standest
bei dem Seiler in Rom, oder beim Töpfer am Nil.
Zeig ihm, wie glücklich ein Ding sein kann, wie schuldlos und unser,
wie selbst das klagende Leid rein zur Gestalt sich entschließt,
dient als ein Ding, oder stirbt in ein Ding—, und jenseits
selig der Geige entgeht.—Und diese, von Hingang
lebenden Dinge verstehn, daß du sie rühmst; vergänglich,
traun sie ein Rettendes uns, den Vergänglichsten, zu.
Wollen, wir sollen sie ganz im unsichtbarn Herzen verwandeln
in—o unendlich—in uns! Wer wir am Ende auch seien.

Erde, ist es nicht dies, was du willst: *unsichtbar*
in uns erstehn?—Ist es dein Traum nicht,

at most: column, tower. . . . But to *say* them, you must understand,
oh to say them *more* intensely than the Things themselves
ever dreamed of existing. Isn't the secret intent
of this taciturn earth, when it forces lovers together,
that inside their boundless emotion all things may shudder with joy?
Threshold: what it means for two lovers
to be wearing down, imperceptibly, the ancient threshold of their door—
they too, after the many who came before them
and before those to come. . . . , lightly.

Here is the time for the *sayable, here* is its homeland.
Speak and bear witness. More than ever
the Things that we might experience are vanishing, for
what crowds them out and replaces them is an imageless act.
An act under a shell, which easily cracks open as soon as
the business inside outgrows it and seeks new limits.
Between the hammers our heart
endures, just as the tongue does
between the teeth and, despite that,
still is able to praise.

Praise this world to the angel, not the unsayable one,
you can't impress *him* with glorious emotion; in the universe
where he feels more powerfully, you are a novice. So show him
something simple which, formed over generations,
lives as our own, near our hand and within our gaze.
Tell him of Things. He will stand astonished; as *you* stood
by the rope-maker in Rome or the potter along the Nile.
Show him how happy a Thing can be, how innocent and ours,
how even lamenting grief purely decides to take form,
serves as a Thing, or dies into a Thing—, and blissfully
escapes far beyond the violin.—And these Things,
which live by perishing, know you are praising them; transient,
they look to us for deliverance: us, the most transient of all.
They want us to change them, utterly, in our invisible heart,
within—oh endlessly—within us! Whoever we may be at last.

Earth, isn't this what you want: to arise within us,
invisible? Isn't it your dream

einmal unsichtbar zu sein?—Erde! unsichtbar!
Was, wenn Verwandlung nicht, ist dein drängender Auftrag?
Erde, du liebe, ich will. Oh glaub, es bedürfte
nicht deiner Frühlinge mehr, mich dir zu gewinnen—, *einer,*
ach, ein einziger ist schon dem Blute zu viel.
Namenlos bin ich zu dir entschlossen, von weit her.
Immer warst du im Recht, und dein heiliger Einfall
ist der vertrauliche Tod.

Siehe, ich lebe. Woraus? Weder Kindheit noch Zukunft
werden weniger. . . . . Überzähliges Dasein
entspringt mir im Herzen.

to be wholly invisible someday?—O Earth: invisible!
What, if not transformation, is your urgent command?
Earth, my dearest, I will. Oh believe me, you no longer
need your springtimes to win me over—one of them,
ah, even one, is already too much for my blood.
Unspeakably I have belonged to you, from the first.
You were always right, and your holiest inspiration
is our intimate companion, Death.

Look, I am living. On what? Neither childhood nor future
grows any smaller . . . . . Superabundant being
wells up in my heart.

DIE ZEHNTE ELEGIE

Daß ich dereinst, an dem Ausgang der grimmigen Einsicht,
Jubel und Ruhm aufsinge zustimmenden Engeln.
Daß von den klar geschlagenen Hämmern des Herzens
keiner versage an weichen, zweifelnden oder
reißenden Saiten. Daß mich mein strömendes Antlitz
glänzender mache; daß das unscheinbare Weinen
blühe. O wie werdet ihr dann, Nächte, mir lieb sein,
gehärmte. Daß ich euch knieender nicht, untröstliche Schwestern,
hinnahm, nicht in euer gelöstes
Haar mich gelöster ergab. Wir, Vergeuder der Schmerzen.
Wie wir sie absehn voraus, in die traurige Dauer,
ob sie nicht enden vielleicht. Sie aber sind ja
unser winterwähriges Laub, unser dunkeles Sinngrün,
eine der Zeiten des heimlichen Jahres—, nicht nur
Zeit—, sind Stelle, Siedelung, Lager, Boden, Wohnort.

Freilich, wehe, wie fremd sind die Gassen der Leid-Stadt,
wo in der falschen, aus Übertönung gemachten
Stille, stark, aus der Gußform des Leeren der Ausguß
prahlt: der vergoldete Lärm, das platzende Denkmal.
O, wie spurlos zerträte ein Engel ihnen den Trostmarkt,
den die Kirche begrenzt, ihre fertig gekaufte:
reinlich und zu und enttäuscht wie ein Postamt am Sonntag.
Draußen aber kräuseln sich immer die Ränder von Jahrmarkt.
Schaukeln der Freiheit! Taucher und Gaukler des Eifers!
Und des behübschten Glücks figürliche Schießstatt,
wo es zappelt von Ziel und sich blechern benimmt,
wenn ein Geschickterer trifft. Von Beifall zu Zufall
taumelt er weiter; denn Buden jeglicher Neugier
werben, trommeln und plärrn. Für Erwachsene aber
ist noch besonders zu sehn, wie das Geld sich vermehrt, anatomisch,
nicht zur Belustigung nur: der Geschlechtsteil des Gelds,
alles, das Ganze, der Vorgang—, das unterrichtet und macht
fruchtbar . . . .
. . . . Oh aber gleich darüber hinaus,
hinter der letzten Planke, beklebt mit Plakaten des ›Todlos‹,

THE TENTH ELEGY

Someday, emerging at last from the violent insight,
let me sing out jubilation and praise to assenting angels.
Let not even one of the clearly-struck hammers of my heart
fail to sound because of a slack, a doubtful,
or a broken string. Let my joyfully streaming face
make me more radiant; let my hidden weeping arise
and blossom. How dear you will be to me then, you nights
of anguish. Why didn't I kneel more deeply to accept you,
inconsolable sisters, and, surrendering, lose myself
in your loosened hair. How we squander our hours of pain.
How we gaze beyond them into the bitter duration
to see if they have an end. Though they are really
our winter-enduring foliage, our dark evergreen,
one season in our inner year—, not only a season
in time—, but are place and settlement, foundation and soil and home.

But how alien, alas, are the streets of the city of grief,
where, in the false silence formed of continual uproar,
the figure cast from the mold of emptiness stoutly
swaggers: the gilded noise, the bursting memorial.
Oh how completely an angel would stamp out their market of solace,
bounded by the church with its ready-made consolations:
clean and disenchanted and shut as a post-office on Sunday.
Farther out, though, the city's edges are curling with carnival.
Swings of freedom! Divers and jugglers of zeal!
And the shooting-gallery's targets of prettified happiness,
which jump and kick back with a tinny sound
when hit by some better marksman. From cheers to chance
he goes staggering on, as booths with all sorts of attractions
are wooing, drumming, and bawling. For adults only
there is something special to see: how money multiplies, naked,
right there on stage, money's genitals, nothing concealed,
the whole action—, educational, and guaranteed
to increase your potency . . . .
. . . . Oh, but a little farther,
beyond the last of the billboards, plastered with signs for "Deathless,"

jenes bitteren Biers, das den Trinkenden süß scheint,
wenn sie immer dazu frische Zerstreuungen kaun . . . ,
gleich im Rücken der Planke, gleich dahinter, ists *wirklich*.
Kinder spielen, und Liebende halten einander,—abseits,
ernst, im ärmlichen Gras, und Hunde haben Natur.
Weiter noch zieht es den Jüngling; vielleicht, daß er eine junge
Klage liebt. . . . . . Hinter ihr her kommt er in Wiesen. Sie sagt:
—Weit. Wir wohnen dort draußen . . . .

                           Wo? Und der Jüngling
folgt. Ihn rührt ihre Haltung. Die Schulter, der Hals—, vielleicht
ist sie von herrlicher Herkunft. Aber er läßt sie, kehrt um,
wendet sich, winkt . . . Was solls? Sie ist eine Klage.

Nur die jungen Toten, im ersten Zustand
zeitlosen Gleichmuts, dem der Entwöhnung,
folgen ihr liebend. Mädchen
wartet sie ab und befreundet sie. Zeigt ihnen leise,
was sie an sich hat. Perlen des Leids und die feinen
Schleier der Duldung.—Mit Jünglingen geht sie
schweigend.

Aber dort, wo sie wohnen, im Tal, der Älteren eine, der Klagen,
nimmt sich des Jünglinges an, wenn er fragt:—Wir waren,
sagt sie, ein Großes Geschlecht, einmal, wir Klagen. Die Väter
trieben den Bergbau dort in dem großen Gebirg; bei Menschen
findest du manchmal ein Stück geschliffenes Ur-Leid
oder, aus altem Vulkan, schlackig versteinerten Zorn.
Ja, das stammte von dort. Einst waren wir reich.—

Und sie leitet ihn leicht durch die weite Landschaft der Klagen,
zeigt ihm die Säulen der Tempel oder die Trümmer
jener Burgen, von wo Klage-Fürsten das Land
einstens weise beherrscht. Zeigt ihm die hohen
Tränenbäume und Felder blühender Wehmut,
(Lebendige kennen sie nur als sauftes Blattwerk);
zeigt ihm die Tiere der Trauer, weidend,—und manchmal
schreckt ein Vogel und zieht, flach ihnen fliegend durchs Aufschaun,

that bitter beer which seems so sweet to its drinkers
as long as they chew fresh distractions in between sips . . . ,
just in back of the billboard, just behind, the view becomes *real*.
Children are playing, and lovers are holding hands, to the side,
solemnly in the meager grass, and dogs are doing what is natural.
The young man is drawn on, farther; perhaps he is in love with a young
Lament . . . . . He comes out behind her, into the meadows. She says:
—It's a long walk. We live way out there . . . .
                                        Where? And the youth
follows. He is touched by her manner. Her shoulders, her neck—, perhaps
she is of noble descent. But he leaves her, turns around,
looks back, waves . . . What's the use? She is a Lament.

Only those who died young, in their first condition
of timeless equanimity, while they are being weaned,
follow her lovingly. She waits
for girls and befriends them. Shows them, gently,
what she is wearing. Pearls of grief and the fine-spun
veils of patience.—With young men she walks
in silence.

But there, in the valley, where they live, one of the elder Laments
answers the youth when he questions her:—Long ago,
she says, we Laments were a powerful race. Our forefathers worked
the mines, up there in the mountain-range; sometimes even
among men you can find a polished nugget of primal grief
or a chunk of petrified rage from the slag of an ancient volcano.
Yes, that came from up there. We used to be rich.—

And gently she guides him through the vast landscape of Lament,
shows him the pillars of the temples, and the ruined walls
of those castles from which, long ago, the princes of Lament
wisely ruled the land. Shows him the tall
trees of tears and the fields of blossoming grief
(the living know it just as a mild green shrub);
shows him the herds of sorrow, grazing,—and sometimes
a startled bird, flying low through their upward gaze,

weithin das schriftliche Bild seines vereinsamten Schreis.—
Abends führt sie ihn hin zu den Gräbern der Alten
aus dem Klage-Geschlecht, den Sibyllen und Warn-Herrn.
Naht aber Nacht, so wandeln sie leiser, und bald
mondets empor, das über Alles
wachende Grab-Mal. Brüderlich jenem am Nil,
der erhabene Sphinx—: der verschwiegenen Kammer
Antlitz.
Und sie staunen dem krönlichen Haupt, das für immer,
schweigend, der Menschen Gesicht
auf die Waage der Sterne gelegt.

Nicht erfaßt es sein Blick, im Frühtod
schwindelnd. Aber ihr Schaun,
hinter dem Pschent-Rand hervor, scheucht es die Eule. Und sie,
streifend im langsamen Abstrich die Wange entlang,
jene der reifesten Rundung,
zeichnet weich in das neue
Totengehör, über ein doppelt
aufgeschlagenes Blatt, den unbeschreiblichen Umriß.

Und höher, die Sterne. Neue. Die Sterne des Leidlands.
Langsam nennt sie die Klage:—Hier,
siehe: den *Reiter,* den *Stab,* und das vollere Sternbild
nennen sie: *Fruchtkranz.* Dann, weiter, dem Pol zu:
Wiege; Weg; Das Brennende Buch; Puppe; Fenster.
Aber im südlichen Himmel, rein wie im Innern
einer gesegneten Hand, das klar erglänzende *M,*
das die Mütter bedeutet . . . . . . —

Doch der Tote muß fort, und schweigend bringt ihn die ältere
Klage bis an die Talschlucht,
wo es schimmert im Mondschein:
die Quelle der Freude. In Ehrfurcht
nennt sie sie, sagt:—Bei den Menschen
ist sie ein tragender Strom.—

Stehn am Fuß des Gebirgs.
Und da umarmt sie ihn, weinend.

far away traces the image of its solitary cry.—
In the twilight she leads him out to the graves of the elders
who gave warning to the race of Laments, the sibyls and prophets.
But as night approaches, they move more softly, and soon
the sepulchre rises up
like a moon, watching over everything. Brother to the one on the Nile,
the lofty Sphinx—: the taciturn chamber's
countenance.
And they look in wonder at the regal head that has silently
lifted the human face
to the scale of the stars, forever.

Still dizzy from recent death, his sight
cannot grasp it. But her gaze
frightens an owl from behind the rim of the crown. And the bird,
with slow downstrokes, brushes along the cheek,
the one with the fuller curve,
and faintly, in the dead youth's new
sense of hearing, as upon a double
unfolded page, it sketches the indescribable outline.

And higher, the stars. The new stars of the land of grief.
Slowly the Lament names them:—Look, there:
the *Rider,* the *Staff,* and the larger constellation
called *Garland of Fruit.* Then, farther up toward the Pole:
Cradle; Path; The Burning Book; Puppet; Window.
But there, in the southern sky, pure as the lines
on the palm of a blessed hand, the clear sparkling *M*
that stands for Mothers . . . . . . —

But the dead youth must go on by himself, and silently the elder Lament
takes him as far as the ravine,
where shimmering in the moonlight
is the fountainhead of joy. With reverence
she names it and says: —Among men
it is a mighty stream.—

They stand at the foot of the mountain-range.
And she embraces him, weeping.

Einsam steigt er dahin, in die Berge des Ur-Leids.
Und nicht einmal sein Schritt klingt aus dem tonlosen Los.

*

Aber erweckten sie uns, die unendlich Toten, ein Gleichnis,
siehe, sie zeigten vielleicht auf die Kätzchen der leeren
Hasel, die hängenden, oder
meinten den Regen, der fällt auf dunkles Erdreich im Frühjahr.—

Und wir, die an *steigendes* Glück
denken, empfänden die Rührung,
die uns beinah bestürzt,
wenn ein Glückliches *fällt*.

Alone, he climbs on, up the mountains of primal grief.
And not once do his footsteps echo from the soundless path.

*

But if the endlessly dead awakened a symbol in us,
perhaps they would point to the catkins hanging from the bare
branches of the hazel-trees, or
would evoke the raindrops that fall onto the dark earth in springtime.—

And we, who have always thought
of happiness as *rising,* would feel
the emotion that almost overwhelms us
whenever a happy thing *falls.*

APPENDIX TO

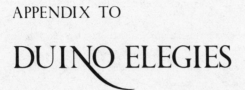

DUINO ELEGIES

[FRAGMENT EINER ELEGIE]

Soll ich die Städte rühmen, die überlebenden
(die ich anstaunte) großen Sternbilder der Erde.
Denn nur zum Rühmen noch steht mir das Herz, so gewaltig
weiß ich die Welt. Und selbst meine Klage
wird mir zur Preisung dicht vor dem stöhnenden Herzen.
Sage mir keiner, daß ich die Gegenwart nicht
liebe; ich schwinge in ihr; sie trägt mich, sie giebt mir
diesen geräumigen Tag, den uralten Werktag
daß ich ihn brauche, und wirft in gewährender Großmut
über mein Dasein niegewesene Nächte.
Ihre Hand ist stark über mir und wenn sie im Schicksal
unten mich hielte, vertaucht, ich müßte versuchen
unten zu atmen. Auch bei dem leisesten Auftrag
säng ich sie gerne. Doch vermut ich, sie will nur,
daß ich vibriere wie sie. Einst tönte der Dichter
über die Feldschlacht hinaus; was will eine Stimme
neben dem neuen Gedröhn der metallenen Handlung
drin diese Zeit sich verringt mit anstürmender Zukunft.
Auch bedarf sie des Anrufes kaum, ihr eigener Schlachtlärm
übertönt sich zum Lied. So laßt mich solange
vor Vergehendem stehn; anklagend nicht, aber
noch einmal bewundernd. Und wo mich eines
das mir vor Augen versinkt, etwa zur Klage bewegt
sei es kein Vorwurf für euch. Was sollen jüngere Völker
nicht fortstürmen von dem was der morschen oft
ruhmloser Abbruch begrub. Sehet, es wäre
arg um das Große bestellt, wenn es irgend der Schonung
bedürfte. Wem die Paläste oder der Gärten
Kühnheit nicht mehr, wem Aufstieg und Rückfall
alter Fontänen nicht mehr, wem das Verhaltene
in den Bildern oder der Statuen ewiges Dastehn
nicht mehr die Seele erschreckt und verwandelt, der gehe
diesem hinaus und tue sein Tagwerk; wo anders
lauert das Große auf ihn und wird ihn wo anders
anfalln, daß er sich wehrt.

[FRAGMENT OF AN ELEGY]

Now shall I praise the cities, those long-surviving
(I watched them in awe) great constellations of earth.
For only in praising is my heart still mine, so violently
do I know the world. And even my lament
turns into a paean before my disconsolate heart.
Let no one say that I don't love life, the eternal
presence: I pulsate in her; she bears me, she gives me
the spaciousness of this day, the primeval workday
for me to make use of, and over my existence flings,
in her magnanimity, nights that have never been.
Her strong hand is above me, and if she should hold me under,
submerged in fate, I would have to learn how to breathe
down there. Even her most lightly-entrusted mission
would fill me with songs of her; although I suspect
that all she wants is for me to be vibrant as she is.
Once poets resounded over the battlefield; what voice
can outshout the rattle of this metallic age
that is struggling on toward its careening future?
And indeed it hardly requires the call, its own battle-din
roars into song. So let me stand for a while
in front of the transient: not accusing, but once again
admiring, marveling. And if perhaps something founders
before my eyes and stirs me into lament,
it is not a reproach. Why shouldn't more youthful nations
rush past the graveyard of cultures long ago rotten?
How pitiful it would be if greatness needed the slightest
indulgence. Let him whose soul is no longer startled
and transformed by palaces, by gardens' boldness, by the rising
and falling of ancient fountains, by everything held back
in paintings or by the infinite thereness of statues—
let such a person go out to his daily work, where
greatness is lying in ambush and someday, at some turn,
will leap upon him and force him to fight for his life.

[URSPRÜNGLICHE FASSUNG DER ZEHNTEN ELEGIE]

[Fragmentarisch]

Daß ich dereinst, an dem Ausgang der grimmigen Einsicht
Jubel und Ruhm aufsinge zustimmenden Engeln.
Daß von den klar geschlagenen Hämmern des Herzens
keiner versage an weichen, zweifelnden oder
jähzornigen Saiten. Daß mich mein strömendes Antlitz
glänzender mache; daß das unscheinbare Weinen
blühe. O wie werdet ihr dann, Nächte, mir lieb sein,
gehärmte. Daß ich euch knieender nicht, untröstliche Schwestern,
hinnahm, nicht in euer gelöstes
Haar mich gelöster ergab. Wir Vergeuder der Schmerzen.
Wie wir sie absehn voraus in die traurige Dauer,
ob sie nicht enden vielleicht. Sie aber sind ja
Zeiten von uns, unser winter-
währiges Laubwerk, Wiesen, Teiche, angeborene Landschaft,
von Geschöpfen im Schilf und von Vögeln bewohnt.

*

Oben, der hohen, steht nicht die Hälfte der Himmel
über der Wehmut in uns, der bemühten Natur?
Denk, du beträtest nicht mehr dein verwildertes Leidtum,
sähest die Sterne nicht mehr durch das herbere Blättern
schwärzlichen Schmerzlaubs, und die Trümmer von Schicksal
böte dir höher nicht mehr der vergrößernde Mondschein,
daß du an ihnen dich fühlst wie ein einstiges Volk?
Lächeln auch wäre nicht mehr, das zehrende derer,
die du hinüberverlorest—, so wenig gewaltsam,
eben an dir nur vorbei, traten sie rein in dein Leid.
(Fast wie das Mädchen, das grade dem Freier sich zusprach,
der sie seit Wochen bedrängt, und sie bringt ihn erschrocken
an das Gitter des Gartens, den Mann, der frohlockt und ungern
fortgeht: da stört sie ein Schritt in dem neueren Abschied,
und sie wartet und steht und da trifft ihr vollzähliges Aufschaun
ganz in das Aufschaun des Fremden, das Aufschaun der Jungfrau,
die ihn unendlich begreift, den draußen, der ihr bestimmt war,

[ORIGINAL VERSION OF THE TENTH ELEGY]

[Fragmentary]

Someday, emerging at last from the violent insight,
let me sing out jubilation and praise to assenting angels.
Let not even one of the clearly-struck hammers of my heart
fail to sound because of a slack, a doubtful,
or an ill-tempered string. Let my joyfully streaming face
make me more radiant; let my hidden weeping arise
and blossom. How dear you will be to me then, you nights
of anguish. Why didn't I kneel more deeply to accept you,
inconsolable sisters, and, surrendering, lose myself
in your loosened hair. How we squander our hours of pain.
How we gaze beyond them into the bitter duration
to see if they have an end. Though they are really
seasons of us, our winter-
enduring foliage, ponds, meadows, our inborn landscape,
where birds and reed-dwelling creatures are at home.

High overhead, isn't half of the night sky standing
above the sorrow in us, the disquieted garden?
Imagine that you no longer walked through your grief grown wild,
no longer looked at the stars through the jagged leaves
of the dark tree of pain, and the enlarging moonlight
no longer exalted fate's ruins so high
that among them you felt like the last of some ancient race.
Nor would smiles any longer exist, the consuming smiles
of those you lost over there—with so little violence,
once they were past, did they purely enter your grief.
(Almost like the girl who has just said yes to the lover
who begged her, so many weeks, and she brings him astonished
to the garden gate and, reluctant, he walks away,
giddy with joy; and then, amid this new parting,
a step disturbs her; she waits; and her glance in its fullness
sinks totally into a stranger's: her virgin glance
that endlessly comprehends him, the outsider, who was meant for her;

draußen den wandernden Andern, der ihr ewig bestimmt war.
Hallend geht er vorbei.) So immer verlorst du;
als ein Besitzender nicht: wie sterbend einer,
vorgebeugt in die feucht herwehende Märznacht,
ach, den Frühling verliert in die Kehlen der Vögel.

Viel zu weit gehörst du in's Leiden. Vergäßest
du die geringste der maßlos erschmerzten Gestalten,
riefst du, schrieest, hoffend auf frühere Neugier,
einen der Engel herbei, der mühsam verdunkelten Ausdrucks
leidunmächtig, immer wieder versuchend,
dir dein Schluchzen damals, um jene, beschriebe.
Engel wie wars? Und er ahmte dir nach und verstünde
nicht daß es Schmerz sei, wie man dem rufenden Vogel
nachformt, die ihn erfüllt, die schuldlose Stimme.

the wandering other, who eternally was meant for her.
Echoing, he walks by.) That is how, always, you lost:
never as one who possesses, but like someone dying
who, bending into the moist breeze of an evening in March,
loses the springtime, alas, in the throats of the birds.

Far too much you belong to grief. If you could forget her—
even the least of these figures so infinitely pained—
you would call down, shout down, hoping they might still be curious,
one of the angels (those beings unmighty in grief)
who, as his face darkened, would try again and again
to describe the way you kept sobbing, long ago, for her.
Angel, what was it like? And he would imitate you and never
understand that it was pain, as after a calling bird
one tries to repeat the innocent voice it is filled with.

GEGEN-STROPHEN

Oh, daß ihr hier, Frauen, einhergeht,
hier unter uns, leidvoll,
nicht geschonter als wir und dennoch imstande,
selig zu machen wie Selige.

Woher,
wenn der Geliebte erscheint,
nehmt ihr die Zukunft?
Mehr, als je sein wird.
Wer die Entfernungen weiß
bis zum äußersten Fixstern,
staunt, wenn er diesen gewahrt,
euern herrlichen Herzraum.
Wie, im Gedräng, spart ihr ihn aus?
Ihr, voll Quellen und Nacht.

Seid ihr wirklich die gleichen,
die, da ihr Kind wart,
unwirsch im Schulgang
anstieß der ältere Bruder?
Ihr Heilen.

    Wo wir als Kinder uns schon
    häßlich für immer verzerrn,
    wart ihr wie Brot vor der Wandlung.

Abbruch der Kindheit
war euch nicht Schaden. Auf einmal
standet ihr da, wie im Gott
plötzlich zum Wunder ergänzt.

    Wir, wie gebrochen vom Berg,
    oft schon als Knaben scharf
    an den Rändern, vielleicht
    manchmal glücklich behaun;
    wir, wie Stücke Gesteins,
    über Blumen gestürzt.

ANTISTROPHES

Ah, Women, that you should be moving
here, among us, grief-filled,
no more protected than we, and nevertheless
able to bless like the blessed.

From what realm,
when your beloved appears,
do you take the future?
More than will ever be.
One who knows distances
out to the outermost star
is astonished when he discovers
the magnificent space in your hearts.
. How, in the crowd, can you spare it?
You, full of sources and night.

Are you really the same
as those children who
on the way to school were rudely
shoved by an older brother?
Unharmed by it.

    While we, even as children,
    disfigured ourselves forever,
    you were like bread on the altar
    before it is changed.

The breaking away of childhood
left you intact. In a moment,
you stood there, as if completed
in a miracle, all at once.

    We, as if broken from crags,
    even as boys, too sharp
    at the edges, although perhaps
    sometimes skillfully cut;
    we, like pieces of rock
    that have fallen on flowers.

Blumen des tieferen Erdreichs,
von allen Wurzeln geliebte,
ihr, der Eurydike Schwestern,
immer voll heiliger Umkehr
hinter dem steigenden Mann.

    Wir, von uns selber gekränkt,
    Kränkende gern und gern
    Wiedergekränkte aus Not.
    Wir, wie Waffen, dem Zorn
    neben den Schlaf gelegt.

Ihr, die ihr beinah Schutz seid, wo niemand
schützt. Wie ein schattiger Schlafbaum
ist der Gedanke an euch
für die Schwärme des Einsamen.

Flowers of the deeper soil,
loved by all roots,
you, Eurydice's sisters,
full of holy return
behind the ascending man.

We, afflicted by ourselves,
gladly afflicting, gladly
needing to be afflicted.
We, who sleep with our anger
laid beside us like a knife.

You, who are almost protection
where no one protects. The thought of you
is a shade-giving tree of sleep for the restless
creatures of a solitary man.

FROM ·

THE SONNETS
TO ORPHEUS

(1923)

*Written as a monument
for Vera Ouckama Knoop*

Château de Muzot, February 1922

I, 1

Da stieg ein Baum. O reine Übersteigung!
O Orpheus singt! O hoher Baum im Ohr!
Und alles schwieg. Doch selbst in der Verschweigung
ging neuer Anfang, Wink und Wandlung vor.

Tiere aus Stille drangen aus dem klaren
gelösten Wald von Lager und Genist;
und da ergab sich, daß sie nicht aus List
und nicht aus Angst in sich so leise waren,

sondern aus Hören. Brüllen, Schrei, Geröhr
schien klein in ihren Herzen. Und wo eben
kaum eine Hütte war, dies zu empfangen,

ein Unterschlupf aus dunkelstem Verlangen
mit einem Zugang, dessen Pfosten beben,—
da schufst du ihnen Tempel im Gehör.

I, 1

A tree ascended there. Oh pure transcendence!
Oh Orpheus sings! Oh tall tree in the ear!
And all things hushed. Yet even in that silence
a new beginning, beckoning, change appeared.

Creatures of stillness crowded from the bright
unbound forest, out of their lairs and nests;
and it was not from any dullness, not
from fear, that they were so quiet in themselves,

but from simply listening. Bellow, roar, shriek
seemed small inside their hearts. And where there had been
just a makeshift hut to receive the music,

a shelter nailed up out of their darkest longing,
with an entryway that shuddered in the wind—
you built a temple deep inside their hearing.

I, 2

Und fast ein Mädchen wars und ging hervor
aus diesem einigen Glück von Sang und Leier
und glänzte klar durch ihre Frühlingsschleier
und machte sich ein Bett in meinem Ohr.

Und schlief in mir. Und alles war ihr Schlaf.
Die Bäume, die ich je bewundert, diese
fühlbare Ferne, die gefühlte Wiese
und jedes Staunen, das mich selbst betraf.

Sie schlief die Welt. Singender Gott, wie hast
du sie vollendet, daß sie nicht begehrte,
erst wach zu sein? Sieh, sie erstand und schlief.

Wo ist ihr Tod? O, wirst du dies Motiv
erfinden noch, eh sich dein Lied verzehrte?—
Wo sinkt sie hin aus mir? . . . Ein Mädchen fast . . . .

I, 2

And it was almost a girl who, stepping from
this single harmony of song and lyre,
appeared to me through her diaphanous form
and made herself a bed inside my ear.

And slept in me. Her sleep was everything:
the awesome trees, the distances I had felt
so deeply that I could touch them, meadows in spring:
all wonders that had ever seized my heart.

She slept the world. Singing god, how was that first
sleep so perfect that she had no desire
ever to wake? See: she arose and slept.

Where is her death now? Ah, will you discover
this theme before your song consumes itself?—
Where is she vanishing? . . . A girl, almost . . . .

I, 3

Ein Gott vermags. Wie aber, sag mir, soll
ein Mann ihm folgen durch die schmale Leier?
Sein Sinn ist Zwiespalt. An der Kreuzung zweier
Herzwege steht kein Tempel für Apoll.

Gesang, wie du ihn lehrst, ist nicht Begehr,
nicht Werbung um ein endlich noch Erreichtes;
Gesang ist Dasein. Für den Gott ein Leichtes.
Wann aber *sind* wir? Und wann wendet *er*

an unser Sein die Erde und die Sterne?
Dies *ists* nicht, Jüngling, daß du liebst, wenn auch
die Stimme dann den Mund dir aufstößt,—lerne

vergessen, daß du aufsangst. Das verrinnt.
In Wahrheit singen, ist ein andrer Hauch.
Ein Hauch um nichts. Ein Wehn im Gott. Ein Wind.

I, 3

A god can do it. But will you tell me how
a man can penetrate through the lyre's strings?
Our mind is split. And at the shadowed crossing
of heart-roads, there is no temple for Apollo.

Song, as you have taught it, is not desire,
not wooing any grace that can be achieved;
song is reality. Simple, for a god.
But when can *we* be real? When does he pour

the earth, the stars, into us? Young man,
it is not your loving, even if your mouth
was forced wide open by your own voice—learn

to forget that passionate music. It will end.
True singing is a different breath, about
nothing. A gust inside the god. A wind.

I, 5

Errichtet keinen Denkstein. Laßt die Rose
nur jedes Jahr zu seinen Gunsten blühn.
Denn Orpheus ists. Seine Metamorphose
in dem und dem. Wir sollen uns nicht mühn

um andre Namen. Ein für alle Male
ists Orpheus, wenn es singt. Er kommt und geht.
Ists nicht schon viel, wenn er die Rosenschale
um ein paar Tage manchmal übersteht?

O wie er schwinden muß, daß ihrs begrifft!
Und wenn ihm selbst auch bangte, daß er schwände.
Indem sein Wort das Hiersein übertrifft,

ist er schon dort, wohin ihrs nicht begleitet.
Der Leier Gitter zwängt ihm nicht die Hände.
Und er gehorcht, indem er überschreitet.

I, 5

Erect no gravestone to his memory; just
let the rose blossom each year for his sake.
For it *is* Orpheus. Wherever he has passed
through this or that. We do not need to look

for other names. When there is poetry,
it is Orpheus singing. He lightly comes and goes.
Isn't it enough if sometimes he can stay
with us a few days longer than a rose?

Though he himself is afraid to disappear,
he *has* to vanish: don't you understand?
The moment his word steps out beyond our life here,

he moves where you will never find his trace.
The lyre's strings do not constrict his hands.
And it is in overstepping that he obeys.

I, 7

Rühmen, das ists! Ein zum Rühmen Bestellter,
ging er hervor wie das Erz aus des Steins
Schweigen. Sein Herz, o vergängliche Kelter
eines den Menschen unendlichen Weins.

Nie versagt ihm die Stimme am Staube,
wenn ihn das göttliche Beispiel ergreift.
Alles wird Weinberg, alles wird Traube,
in seinem fühlenden Süden gereift.

Nicht in den Grüften der Könige Moder
straft ihm die Rühmung lügen, oder
daß von den Göttern ein Schatten fällt.

Er ist einer der bleibenden Boten,
der noch weit in die Türen der Toten
Schalen mit rühmlichen Früchten hält.

I, 7

Praising is what matters! He was summoned for that,
and came to us like the ore from a stone's
silence. His mortal heart presses out
a deathless, inexhaustible wine.

Whenever he feels the god's paradigm grip
his throat, the voice does not die in his mouth.
All becomes vineyard, all becomes grape,
ripened on the hills of his sensuous South.

Neither decay in the sepulchre of kings
nor any shadow that has fallen from the gods
can ever detract from his glorious praising.

For he is a herald who is with us always,
holding far into the doors of the dead
a bowl with ripe fruit worthy of praise.

I, 8

Nur im Raum der Rühmung darf die Klage
gehn, die Nymphe des geweinten Quells,
wachend über unserm Niederschlage,
daß er klar sei an demselben Fels,

der die Tore trägt und die Altäre.—
Sieh, um ihre stillen Schultern früht
das Gefühl, daß sie die jüngste wäre
unter den Geschwistern im Gemüt.

Jubel *weiß*, und Sehnsucht ist geständig,—
nur die Klage lernt noch; mädchenhändig
zählt sie nächtelang das alte Schlimme.

Aber plötzlich, schräg und ungeübt,
hält sie doch ein Sternbild unsrer Stimme
in den Himmel, den ihr Hauch nicht trübt.

I, 8

Only in the realm of Praising should Lament
walk, the naiad of the wept-for fountain,
watching over the stream of our complaint,
that it be clear upon the very stone

that bears the arch of triumph and the altar.—
Look: around her shoulders dawns the bright
sense that she may be the youngest sister
among the deities hidden in our heart.

Joy *knows,* and Longing has accepted,—
only Lament still learns; upon her beads,
night after night, she counts the ancient curse.

Yet awkward as she is, she suddenly
lifts a constellation of our voice,
glittering, into the pure nocturnal sky.

I, 25

Dich aber will ich nun, *Dich,* die ich kannte
wie eine Blume, von der ich den Namen nicht weiß,
noch *ein* Mal erinnern und ihnen zeigen, Entwandte,
schöne Gespielin des unüberwindlichen Schrei's.

Tänzerin erst, die plötzlich, den Körper voll Zögern,
anhielt, als göß man ihr Jungsein in Erz;
trauernd und lauschend—. Da, von den hohen Vermögern
fiel ihr Musik in das veränderte Herz.

Nah war die Krankheit. Schon von den Schatten bemächtigt,
drängte verdunkelt das Blut, doch, wie flüchtig verdächtigt,
trieb es in seinen natürlichen Frühling hervor.

Wieder und wieder, von Dunkel und Sturz unterbrochen,
glänzte es irdisch. Bis es nach schrecklichem Pochen
trat in das trostlos offene Tor.

I, 25

But you now, dear girl, whom I loved like a flower whose name
I didn't know, you who so early were taken away:
I will once more call up your image and show it to them,
beautiful companion of the unsubduable cry.

Dancer whose body filled with your hesitant fate,
pausing, as though your young flesh had been cast in bronze;
grieving and listening——. Then, from the high dominions,
unearthly music fell into your altered heart.

Already possessed by shadows, with illness near,
your blood flowed darkly; yet though for a moment suspicious,
it burst out into the natural pulses of spring.

Again and again interrupted by downfall and darkness,
earthly, it gleamed. Till, after a terrible pounding,
it entered the inconsolably open door.

II, 4

O dieses ist das Tier, das es nicht giebt.
Sie wußtens nicht und habens jeden Falls
—sein Wandeln, seine Haltung, seinen Hals,
bis in des stillen Blickes Licht—geliebt.

Zwar *war* es nicht. Doch weil sie's liebten, ward
ein reines Tier. Sie ließen immer Raum.
Und in dem Raume, klar und ausgespart,
erhob es leicht sein Haupt und brauchte kaum

zu sein. Sie nährten es mit keinem Korn,
nur immer mit der Möglichkeit, es sei.
Und die gab solche Stärke an das Tier,

daß es aus sich ein Stirnhorn trieb. Ein Horn.
Zu einer Jungfrau kam es weiß herbei—
und war im Silber-Spiegel und in ihr.

II, 4

Oh this is the animal that never was.
They hadn't seen one; but just the same, they loved
its graceful movements, and the way it stood
looking at them calmly, with clear eyes.

It had not *been*. But for them, it appeared
in all its purity. They left space enough.
And in the space hollowed out by their love
it stood up all at once and didn't need

existence. They nourished it, not with grain,
but with the mere possibility of being.
And finally this gave it so much power

that from its forehead a horn grew. One horn.
It drew near to a virgin, white, gleaming—
and was, inside the mirror and in her.

II, 8

Wenige ihr, der einstigen Kindheit Gespielen
in den zerstreuten Gärten der Stadt:
wie wir uns fanden und uns zögernd gefielen
und, wie das Lamm mit dem redenden Blatt,

sprachen als Schweigende. Wenn wir uns einmal freuten,
keinem gehörte es. Wessen wars?
Und wie zergings unter allen den gehenden Leuten
und im Bangen des langen Jahrs.

Wagen umrollten uns fremd, vorübergezogen,
Häuser umstanden uns stark, aber unwahr,—und keines
kannte uns je. *Was* war wirklich im All?

Nichts. Nur die Bälle. Ihre herrlichen Bogen.
Auch nicht die Kinder . . . Aber manchmal trat eines,
ach ein vergehendes, unter den fallenden Ball.

(In memoriam Egon von Rilke)

II, 8

You playmates of mine in the scattered parks of the city,
small friends from a childhood of long ago:
how we found and liked one another, hesitantly,
and, like the lamb with the talking scroll,

spoke with our silence. When we were filled with joy
it belonged to no one: it was simply there.
And how it dissolved among all the adults who passed by
and in the fears of the endless year.

Wheels rolled past us, we stood and stared at the carriages;
houses surrounded us, solid but untrue—and none
of them ever knew us. *What* in that world was real?

Nothing. Only the balls. Their magnificent arches.
Not even the children . . . But sometimes one,
oh a vanishing one, stepped under the plummeting ball.

(In memoriam Egon von Rilke)

II, 13

Sei allem Abschied voran, als wäre er hinter
dir, wie der Winter, der eben geht.
Denn unter Wintern ist einer so endlos Winter,
daß, überwinternd, dein Herz überhaupt übersteht.

Sei immer tot in Eurydike—, singender steige,
preisender steige zurück in den reinen Bezug.
Hier, unter Schwindenden, sei, im Reiche der Neige,
sei ein klingendes Glas, das sich im Klang schon zerschlug.

Sei—und wisse zugleich des Nicht-Seins Bedingung,
den unendlichen Grund deiner innigen Schwingung,
daß du sie völlig vollziehst dieses einzige Mal.

Zu dem gebrauchten sowohl, wie zum dumpfen und stummen
Vorrat der vollen Natur, den unsäglichen Summen,
zähle dich jubelnd hinzu und vernichte die Zahl.

II, 13

Be ahead of all parting, as though it already were
behind you, like the winter that has just gone by.
For among these winters there is one so endlessly winter
that only by wintering through it will your heart survive.

Be forever dead in Eurydice—more gladly arise
into the seamless life proclaimed in your song.
Here, in the realm of decline, among momentary days,
be the crystal cup that shattered even as it rang.

Be—and yet know the great void where all things begin,
the infinite source of our inmost vibration,
so that, this once, you may give it your perfect assent.

To all that is used-up, and to all the muffled and dumb
creatures in the world's full reserve, the unsayable sums,
joyfully add your*self,* and cancel the count.

II, 14

Siehe die Blumen, diese dem Irdischen treuen,
denen wir Schicksal vom Rande des Schicksals leihn,—
aber wer weiß es! Wenn sie ihr Welken bereuen,
ist es an uns, ihre Reue zu sein.

Alles will schweben. Da gehn wir umher wie Beschwerer,
legen auf alles uns selbst, vom Gewichte entzückt;
o was sind wir den Dingen für zehrende Lehrer,
weil ihnen ewige Kindheit glückt.

Nähme sie einer ins innige Schlafen und schliefe
tief mit den Dingen—: o wie käme er leicht,
anders zum anderen Tag, aus der gemeinsamen Tiefe.

Oder er bliebe vielleicht; und sie blühten und priesen
ihn, den Bekehrten, der nun den Ihrigen gleicht,
allen den stillen Geschwistern im Winde der Wiesen.

II, 14

Look at the flowers, so faithful to what is earthly,
to whom we lend fate from the very border of fate.
And if they are sad about how they must wither and die,
perhaps it is our vocation to be their regret.

All Things want to fly. Only *we* are weighed down by desire,
caught in ourselves and enthralled with our heaviness.
Oh what consuming, negative teachers we are
for them, while eternal childhood fills them with grace.

If someone were to fall into intimate slumber, and slept
deeply with Things—: how easily he would come
to a different day, out of the mutual depth.

Or perhaps he would stay there; and they would blossom and praise
their newest convert, who now is like one of them,
all those silent companions in the wind of the meadows.

II, 23

Rufe mich zu jener deiner Stunden,
die dir unaufhörlich widersteht:
flehend nah wie das Gesicht von Hunden,
aber immer wieder weggedreht,

wenn du meinst, sie endlich zu erfassen.
So Entzognes ist am meisten dein.
Wir sind frei. Wir wurden dort entlassen,
wo wir meinten, erst begrüßt zu sein.

Bang verlangen wir nach einem Halte,
wir zu Jungen manchmal für das Alte
und zu alt für das, was niemals war.

Wir, gerecht nur, wo wir dennoch preisen,
weil wir, ach, der Ast sind und das Eisen
und das Süße reifender Gefahr.

II, 23

Call me to the one among your moments
that stands before you ineluctably:
intimate as a dog's imploring glance
but, again, forever, turned away

when you think you are holding it at last.
What seems so far from you is most your own.
We are already free, and were dismissed
where we thought we soon would be at home.

Anxious, we keep longing for a foothold—
we, at times too young for what is old
and too old for what has never been;

doing justice only where we praise,
because we are the branch, the iron blade,
and sweet danger, ripening from within.

II, 24

O diese Lust, immer neu, aus gelockertem Lehm!
Niemand beinah hat den frühesten Wagern geholfen.
Städte entstanden trotzdem an beseligten Golfen,
Wasser und Öl füllten die Krüge trotzdem.

Götter, wir planen sie erst in erkühnten Entwürfen,
die uns das mürrische Schicksal wieder zerstört.
Aber sie sind die Unsterblichen. Sehet, wir dürfen
jenen erhorchen, der uns am Ende erhört.

Wir, ein Geschlecht durch Jahrtausende: Mütter und Väter,
immer erfüllter von dem künftigen Kind,
daß es uns einst, übersteigend, erschüttere, später.

Wir, wir unendlich Gewagten, was haben wir Zeit!
Und nur der schweigsame Tod, der weiß, was wir sind
und was er immer gewinnt, wenn er uns leiht.

II, 24

Oh the delight, ever new, out of loosened soil!
The ones who first dared were almost without any help.
Nonetheless, at fortunate harbors, cities sprang up,
and pitchers were nonetheless filled with water and oil.

Gods: we project them first in the boldest of sketches,
which sullen Fate keeps crumpling and tossing away.
But for all that, the gods are immortal. Surely we may
hear out the one who, in the end, will hear *us*.

We, one generation through thousands of lifetimes: women
and men, who are more and more filled with the child we will bear,
so that through it we may someday be shattered and overtaken.

We, the endlessly dared—how far we have come!
And only taciturn Death can know what we are
and how he must always profit when he lends us time.

II, 28

O komm und geh. Du, fast noch Kind, ergänze
für einen Augenblick die Tanzfigur
zum reinen Sternbild einer jener Tänze,
darin wir die dumpf ordnende Natur

vergänglich übertreffen. Denn sie regte
sich völlig hörend nur, da Orpheus sang.
Du warst noch die von damals her Bewegte
und leicht befremdet, wenn ein Baum sich lang

besann, mit dir nach dem Gehör zu gehn.
Du wußtest noch die Stelle, wo die Leier
sich tönend hob—; die unerhörte Mitte.

Für sie versuchtest du die schönen Schritte
und hofftest, einmal zu der heilen Feier
des Freundes Gang und Antlitz hinzudrehn.

II, 28

Oh come and go. You, almost still a child—
for just a moment fill out the dance-figure
into the constellation of those bold
dances in which dull, obsessive Nature

is fleetingly surpassed. For she was stirred
to total hearing just when Orpheus sang.
You were still moved by those primeval words
and a bit surprised if any tree took long

to step with you into the listening ear.
You knew the place where once the lyre arose
resounding: the unheard, unheard-of center.

For *its* sake you tried out your lovely motion
and hoped that you would one day turn your friend's
body toward the perfect celebration.

II, 29

Stiller Freund der vielen Fernen, fühle,
wie dein Atem noch den Raum vermehrt.
Im Gebälk der finstern Glockenstühle
laß dich läuten. Das, was an dir zehrt,

wird ein Starkes über dieser Nahrung.
Geh in der Verwandlung aus und ein.
Was ist deine leidendste Erfahrung?
Ist dir Trinken bitter, werde Wein.

Sei in dieser Nacht aus Übermaß
Zauberkraft am Kreuzweg deiner Sinne,
ihrer seltsamen Begegnung Sinn.

Und wenn dich das Irdische vergaß,
zu der stillen Erde sag: Ich rinne.
Zu dem raschen Wasser sprich: Ich bin.

II, 29

Silent friend of many distances, feel
how your breath enlarges all of space.
Let your presence ring out like a bell
into the night. What feeds upon your face

grows mighty from the nourishment thus offered.
Move through transformation, out and in.
What is the deepest loss that you have suffered?
If drinking is bitter, change yourself to wine.

In this immeasurable darkness, be the power
that rounds your senses in their magic ring,
the sense of their mysterious encounter.

And if the earthly no longer knows your name,
whisper to the silent earth: I'm flowing.
To the flashing water say: I am.

UNCOLLECTED POEMS

1923–1926

IMAGINÄRER LEBENSLAUF

Erst eine Kindheit, grenzenlos und ohne
Verzicht und Ziel. O unbewußte Lust.
Auf einmal Schrecken, Schranke, Schule, Frohne
und Absturz in Versuchung und Verlust.

Trotz. Der Gebogene wird selber Bieger
und rächt an anderen, daß er erlag.
Geliebt, gefürchtet, Retter, Ringer, Sieger
und Überwinder, Schlag auf Schlag.

Und dann allein im Weiten, Leichten, Kalten.
Doch tief in der errichteten Gestalt
ein Atemholen nach dem Ersten, Alten . . .

Da stürzte Gott aus seinem Hinterhalt.

IMAGINARY CAREER

At first a childhood, limitless and free
of any goals. Ah sweet unconsciousness.
Then sudden terror, schoolrooms, slavery,
the plunge into temptation and deep loss.

Defiance. The child bent becomes the bender,
inflicts on others what he once went through.
Loved, feared, rescuer, wrestler, victor,
he takes his vengeance, blow by blow.

And now in vast, cold, empty space, alone.
Yet hidden deep within the grown-up heart,
a longing for the first world, the ancient one . . .

Then, from His place of ambush, God leapt out.

Da dich das geflügelte Entzücken
über manchen frühen Abgrund trug,
baue jetzt der unerhörten Brücken
kühn berechenbaren Bug.

Wunder ist nicht nur im unerklärten
Überstehen der Gefahr;
erst in einer klaren reingewährten
Leistung wird das Wunder wunderbar.

Mitzuwirken ist nicht Überhebung
an dem unbeschreiblichen Bezug,
immer inniger wird die Verwebung,
nur Getragensein ist nicht genug.

Deine ausgeübten Kräfte spanne,
bis sie reichen, zwischen zwein
Widersprüchen . . . Denn im Manne
will der Gott beraten sein.

[As once the wingèd energy of delight]

As once the wingèd energy of delight
carried you over childhood's dark abysses,
now beyond your own life build the great
arch of unimagined bridges.

Wonders happen if we can succeed
in passing through the harshest danger;
but only in a bright and purely granted
achievement can we realize the wonder.

To work *with* Things in the indescribable
relationship is not too hard for us;
the pattern grows more intricate and subtle,
and being swept along is not enough.

Take your practiced powers and stretch them out
until they span the chasm between two
contradictions . . . For the god
wants to know himself in you.

Durch den sich Vögel werfen, ist nicht der
vertraute Raum, der die Gestalt dir steigert.
(Im Freien, dorten, bist du dir verweigert
und schwindest weiter ohne Wiederkehr.)

Raum greift aus uns und übersetzt die Dinge:
daß dir das Dasein eines Baums gelinge,
wirf Innenraum um ihn, aus jenem Raum,
der in dir west. Umgieb ihn mit Verhaltung.
Er grenzt sich nicht. Erst in der Eingestaltung
in dein Verzichten wird er wirklich Baum.

[What birds plunge through is not the intimate space]

What birds plunge through is not the intimate space
in which you see all forms intensified.
(Out in the Open, you would be denied
your self, would disappear into that vastness.)

Space reaches *from* us and construes the world:
to know a tree, in its true element,
throw inner space around it, from that pure
abundance in you. Surround it with restraint.
It has no limits. Not till it is held
in your renouncing is it truly there.

DAUER DER KINDHEIT
(Für E.M.)

Lange Nachmittage der Kindheit. . . . , immer noch nicht
Leben; immer noch Wachstum,
das in den Knien zieht—, wehrlose Wartezeit.
Und zwischen dem, was man sein wird, vielleicht,
und diesem randlosen Dasein—: Tode,
unzählige. Liebe umkreist, die besitzende,
das immer heimlich verratene Kind
und verspricht es der Zukunft; nicht seiner.

Nachmittage, da es allein blieb, von einem Spiegel zum andern
starrend; anfragend beim Rätsel des eigenen
Namens: Wer? Wer?—Aber die Andern
kehren nachhause und überwältigens.
Was ihm das Fenster, was ihm der Weg,
was ihm der dumpfe Geruch einer Lade
gestern vertraut hat: sie übertönens, vereitelns.
Wieder wird es ein Ihriges.
Ranken werfen sich so manchmal aus dichteren
Büschen heraus, wie sich sein Wunsch auswirft
aus dem Gewirr der Familie, schwankend in Klarheit.
Aber sie stumpfen ihm täglich den Blick an ihren gewohnteren
Wänden, jenen, den Aufblick, der den Hunden begegnet
und höhere Blumen
immer noch fast gegenüber hat.

Oh wie weit ists von diesem
überwachten Geschöpf zu allem, was einmal
sein Wunder sein wird, oder sein Untergang.
Seine unmündige
Kraft lernt List zwischen den Fallen.

Und das Gestirn seiner künftigen Liebe
geht doch schon längst unter den Sternen,
gültig. Welches Erschrecken
wird ihm das Herz einmal reißen dorthin,
daß es abkommt vom Weg seiner Flucht
und gerät in Gehorsam und heiteren Einfluß?

DURATION OF CHILDHOOD

(For E.M.)

Long afternoons of childhood. . . . , not yet really
life; still only growing-time
that drags at the knees—, time of defenseless waiting.
And between what we will perhaps become
and this edgeless existence—: deaths,
uncountable. Love, the possessive, surrounds
the child forever betrayed in secret
and promises him to the future; which is not his own.

Afternoons that he spent by himself, staring
from mirror to mirror; puzzling himself with the riddle
of his own name: Who? Who?—But the others
come home again, overwhelm him.
What the window or path
or the mouldy smell of a drawer
confided to him yesterday: they drown it out and destroy it.
Once more he belongs to them.
As tendrils sometimes fling themselves out from the thicker
bushes, his desire will fling itself out
from the tangle of family and hang there, swaying in the light.
But daily they blunt his glance upon their inhabited
walls—that wide innocent glance which lets dogs in
and holds the tall flowers,
still almost face to face.

Oh how far it is
from this watched-over creature to everything that will someday
be his wonder or his destruction.
His immature strength
learns cunning among the traps.

But the constellation
of his future love has long
been moving among the stars. What terror
will tear his heart out of the track of its fleeing
to place it in perfect submission, under the calm
influence of the heavens?

Welt war in dem Antlitz der Geliebten—,
aber plötzlich ist sie ausgegossen:
Welt ist draußen, Welt ist nicht zu fassen.

Warum trank ich nicht, da ich es aufhob,
aus dem vollen, dem geliebten Antlitz
Welt, die nah war, duftend meinem Munde?

Ach, ich trank. Wie trank ich unerschöpflich.
Doch auch ich war angefüllt mit zuviel
Welt, und trinkend ging ich selber über.

[World was in the face of the beloved]

World was in the face of the beloved—,
but suddenly it poured out and was gone:
world is outside, world can not be grasped.

Why didn't I, from the full, beloved face
as I raised it to my lips, why didn't I drink
world, so near that I could almost taste it?

Ah, I drank. Insatiably I drank.
But I was filled up also, with too much
world, and, drinking, I myself ran over.

HANDINNERES

Innres der Hand. Sohle, die nicht mehr geht
als auf Gefühl. Die sich nach oben hält
und im Spiegel
himmlische Straßen empfängt, die selber
wandelnden.
Die gelernt hat, auf Wasser zu gehn,
wenn sie schöpft,
die auf den Brunnen geht,
aller Wege Verwandlerin.
Die auftritt in anderen Händen,
die ihresgleichen
zur Landschaft macht:
wandert und ankommt in ihnen,
sie anfüllt mit Ankunft.

PALM

Interior of the hand. Sole that has come to walk
only on feelings. That faces upward
and in its mirror
receives heavenly roads, which travel
along themselves.
That has learned to walk upon water
when it scoops,
that walks upon wells,
transfiguring every path.
That steps into other hands,
changes those that are like it
into a landscape:
wanders and arrives within them,
fills them with arrival.

SCHWERKRAFT

Mitte, wie du aus allen
dich ziehst, auch noch aus Fliegenden dich
wiedergewinnst, Mitte, du Stärkste.

Stehender: wie ein Trank den Durst
durchstürzt ihn die Schwerkraft.

Doch aus dem Schlafenden fällt,
wie aus lagernder Wolke,
reichlicher Regen der Schwere.

GRAVITY

Center, how from all beings
you pull yourself, even from those that fly
winning yourself back, irresistible center.

He who stands: as a drink through thirst
gravity plunges down through him.

But from the sleeper falls
(as though from a motionless cloud)
the abundant rain of the heavy.

Ô LACRIMOSA

(Trilogie, zu einer künftigen Musik von Ernst Křenek)

I

Oh Tränenvolle, die, verhaltner Himmel,
über der Landschaft ihres Schmerzes schwer wird.
Und wenn sie weint, so weht ein weicher Schauer
schräglichen Regens an des Herzens Sandschicht.

Oh Tränenschwere. Waage aller Tränen!
Die sich nicht Himmel fühlte, da sie klar war,
und Himmel sein muß um der Wolken willen.

Wie wird es deutlich und wie nah, dein Schmerzland,
unter des strengen Himmels Einheit. Wie ein
in seinem Liegen langsam waches Antlitz,
das waagrecht denkt, Welttiefe gegenüber.

II

Nichts als ein Atemzug ist das Leere, und jenes
grüne Gefülltsein der schönen
Bäume: ein Atemzug!
Wir, die Angeatmeten noch,
heute noch Angeatmeten, zählen
diese, der Erde, langsame Atmung,
deren Eile wir sind.

III

Aber die Winter! Oh diese heimliche
Einkehr der Erde. Da um die Toten
in dem reinen Rückfall der Säfte
Kühnheit sich sammelt,
künftiger Frühlinge Kühnheit.
Wo das Erdenken geschieht
unter der Starre; wo das von den großen

O LACRIMOSA

(trilogy for future music of Ernst Křenek)

I

Oh tear-filled figure who, like a sky held back,
grows heavy above the landscape of her sorrow.
And when she weeps, the gentle raindrops fall,
slanting upon the sand-bed of her heart.

Oh heavy with weeping. Scale to weigh all tears.
Who felt herself not sky, since she was shining
and sky exists only for clouds to form in.

How clear it is, how close, your land of sorrow,
beneath the stern sky's oneness. Like a face
that lies there, slowly waking up and thinking
horizontally, into endless depths.

II

It is nothing but a breath, the void.
And that green fulfillment
of blossoming trees: a breath.
We, who are still the breathed-upon,
today still the breathed-upon, count
this slow breathing of earth,
whose hurry we are.

III

Ah, but the winters! The earth's mysterious
turning-within. Where around the dead
in the pure receding of sap,
boldness is gathered,
the boldness of future springtimes.
Where imagination occurs
beneath what is rigid; where all the green

Sommern abgetragene Grün
wieder zum neuen
Einfall wird und zum Spiegel des Vorgefühls;
wo die Farbe der Blumen
jenes Verweilen unserer Augen vergißt.

worn thin by the vast summers
again turns into a new
insight and the mirror of intuition;
where the flowers' color
wholly forgets that lingering of our eyes.

Jetzt wär es Zeit, daß Götter träten aus
bewohnten Dingen . . .
Und daß sie jede Wand in meinem Haus
umschlügen. Neue Seite. Nur der Wind,
den solches Blatt im Wenden würfe, reichte hin,
die Luft, wie eine Scholle, umzuschaufeln:
ein neues Atemfeld. Oh Götter, Götter!
Ihr Oftgekommnen, Schläfer in den Dingen,
die heiter aufstehn, die sich an den Brunnen,
die wir vermuten, Hals und Antlitz waschen
und die ihr Ausgeruhtsein leicht hinzutun
zu dem, was voll scheint, unserm vollen Leben.
Noch einmal sei es euer Morgen, Götter.
Wir wiederholen. Ihr allein seid Ursprung.
Die Welt steht auf mit euch, und Anfang glänzt
an allen Bruchstelln unseres Mißlingens . . .

[Now it is time that gods came walking out]

Now it is time that gods came walking out
of lived-in Things . . .
Time that they came and knocked down every wall
inside my house. New page. Only the wind
from such a turning could be strong enough
to toss the air as a shovel tosses dirt:
a fresh-turned field of breath. O gods, gods!
who used to come so often and are still
asleep in the Things around us, who serenely
rise and at wells that we can only guess at
splash icy water on your necks and faces,
and lightly add your restedness to what seems
already filled to bursting: our full lives.
Once again let it be your morning, gods.
We keep repeating. You alone are source.
With you the world arises, and your dawn
gleams on each crack and crevice of our failure . . .

Rose, oh reiner Widerspruch, Lust,
Niemandes Schlaf zu sein unter soviel
Lidern.

[Rose, oh pure contradiction]

Rose, oh pure contradiction, joy
of being No-one's sleep under so many
lids.

IDOL

Gott oder Göttin des Katzenschlafs,
kostende Gottheit, die in dem dunkeln
Mund reife Augen-Beeren zerdrückt,
süßgewordnen Schauns Traubensaft,
ewiges Licht in der Krypta des Gaumens.
Schlaf-Lied nicht,—Gong! Gong!
Was die anderen Götter beschwört,
entläßt diesen verlisteten Gott
an seine einwärts fallende Macht.

IDOL

God or goddess of the sleep of cats,
savoring godhead that in the dark
vat of the mouth crushes eye-berries, ripe,
into the sweet-grown nectar of vision,
eternal light in the palate's crypt.
Not a lullaby,—Gong! Gong!
What casts a spell over other gods
lets this most cunning god escape
into his ever-receding power.

GONG

Nicht mehr für Ohren . . . : Klang,
der, wie ein tieferes Ohr,
uns, scheinbar Hörende, hört.
Umkehr der Räume. Entwurf
innerer Welten im Frein . . . ,
Tempel vor ihrer Geburt,
Lösung, gesättigt mit schwer
löslichen Göttern . . . : Gong!

Summe des Schweigenden, das
sich zu sich selber bekennt,
brausende Einkehr in sich
dessen, das an sich verstummt,
Dauer, aus Ablauf gepreßt,
um-gegossener Stern . . . : Gong!

Du, die man niemals vergißt,
die sich gebar im Verlust,
nichtmehr begriffenes Fest,
Wein an unsichtbarem Mund,
Sturm in der Säule, die trägt,
Wanderers Sturz in den Weg,
unser, an Alles, Verrat . . . : Gong!

GONG

No longer for ears . . . : sound
which, like a deeper ear,
hears *us,* who only seem
to be hearing. Reversal of spaces.
Projection of innermost worlds
into the Open . . . , temple
before their birth, solution
saturated with gods
that are almost insoluble . . . : Gong!

Sum of all silence, which
acknowledges itself to itself,
thunderous turning-within
of what is struck dumb in itself,
duration pressed from time passing,
star re-liquefied . . . : Gong!

You whom one never forgets,
who gave birth to herself in loss,
festival no longer grasped,
wine on invisible lips,
storm in the pillar that upholds,
wanderer's plunge on the path,
our treason, to everything . . . : Gong!

À Monique:
un petit recueillement de ma gratitude

L'Heure du Thé

Buvant dans cette tasse sur laquelle, dans une langue inconnue, sont peut-être inscrits des signes de bénédiction et de bonheur, je la tiens dans cette main pleine de lignes à son tour que je ne saurais expliquer. Sont-elles d'accord ces deux écritures, et puisqu'elles sont seules entre elles et toujours secrètes sous la coupole de mon regard, vont-elles dialoguer à leur façon et se concilier, ces deux textes millénaires qu'un geste de buveur rapproche?

Chapelle Rustique

Comme la maison est calme: écoute! Mais, là-haut, dans la blanche chapelle, d'où vient ce surcroît de silence?—De tous ceux qui depuis plus d'un siècle y sont entrés pour ne pas être dehors, et qui, en s'agenouillant, se sont effrayés de leur bruit? De cet argent qui, en tombant dans le tronc, a perdu sa voix et qui n'aura qu'un petit bruissement de grillon quand il sera recueilli? Ou de cette douce absence de Sainte-Anne, patronne du sanctuaire, qui n'ose pas approcher, pour ne pas abîmer cette pure distance que suppose un appel?

»Farfallettina«

Toute agitée elle arrive vers la lampe, et son vertige lui donne un dernier répit confus avant d'être brûlée. Elle s'est abattue sur le vert tapis de la table, et sur ce fond avantageux s'étale pour un instant (pour une durée à elle que nous ne saurions mesurer) le luxe de son inconcevable splendeur. On dirait, en trop petit, une dame qui avait une panne en se rendant au Théâtre. Elle n'y arrivera point. Et d'ailleurs où est le Théâtre pour de si frêles spectateurs? . . . Ses ailes dont on aperçoit les minuscules baguettes d'or remuent comme un double éventail devant nulle figure; et, entre elles, ce corps mince, bilboquet où sont retombés deux yeux en boule d'émeraude . . .

C'est en toi, ma belle, que Dieu s'est épuisé. Il te lance à la flamme pour regagner un peu de sa force. (Comme un enfant qui casse sa tirelire.)

[FOUR SKETCHES]

To Monique:
a small reflection of my gratitude

Teatime

Drinking from this cup inscribed with signs in an unknown language, perhaps a message of blessing and joy, I hold it in this hand full of its own indecipherable lines. Do the two messages agree? And since they are alone with each other and forever hidden beneath the dome of my gaze, will they talk to each other in their own way and be reconciled, these two ancient texts brought together by the gesture of a man drinking tea?

Rustic Chapel

How calm the house is: listen! But up there, in the white chapel, where does that greater silence come from?—From all those who, for more than a century, have come in so as not to be out in the cold and, kneeling down, have been frightened at their own noise? From the money that lost its voice falling into the collection box and will speak in just a small cricket-chirp when it is taken out? Or from the sweet absence of Saint Anne, the sanctuary's patron, who doesn't dare to come closer, lest she damage that pure distance which a call implies?

"Farfallettina"

Shaking all over, she arrives near the lamp, and her dizziness grants her one last vague reprieve before she goes up in flames. She has fallen onto the green tablecloth, and upon that advantageous background she stretches out for a moment (for a unit of her own time which we have no way of measuring) the profusion of her inconceivable splendor. She looks like a miniature lady who is having a heart attack on the way to the theater. She will never arrive. Besides, where is there a theater for such fragile spectators? . . . Her wings, with their tiny golden threads, are moving like a double fan in front of no face; and between them is this thin body, a bilboquet onto which two eyes like emerald balls have fallen back . . .

It is in you, my dear, that God has exhausted himself. He tosses you into the fire so that he can recover a bit of his strength. (Like a little boy breaking into his piggy bank.)

Le Mangeur de Mandarines

Oh quelle prévoyance! Ce lapin entre les fruits. Pense! trente sept petits noyaux dans un seul exemplaire prêts à tomber un peu partout et à faire progéniture. Il a fallu que nous corrigions ça. Elle eût été capable de peupler la terre cette petite Mandarine entêtée qui porte une robe si large comme si elle devait encore grandir. Mal habillée en somme; plus occupée de multiplication que de mode. Montre-lui la grenade dans son armure de cuir de Cordoue: elle éclate d'avenir, se retient, dédaigne. . . . Et laissant entrevoir sa lignée possible, elle l'étouffe dans un berceau de pourpre. La terre lui semble trop évasive pour faire avec elle un pacte d'abondance.

The Tangerine-eater

Oh what foresight! This rabbit of the fruit-world! Imagine: thirty-seven little pits in a single specimen, ready to fall every-which-way and create offspring. We had to correct that. She could have populated the whole earth—this little headstrong Tangerine, wearing a dress too big for herself, as if she intended to keep on growing. In short: badly dressed; more concerned with reproduction than with style. Show her the pomegranate, in her armor of Cordova leather: *she* is bursting with future, holds herself back, condescends. . . . And, letting us catch just a glimpse of her possible progeny, she smothers them in a dark-red cradle. She thinks earth is too evasive to sign a pact of abundance.

ELEGIE

an Marina Zwetajewa-Efron

O die Verluste ins All, Marina, die stürzenden Sterne!
Wir vermehren es nicht, wohin wir uns werfen, zu welchem
Sterne hinzu! Im Ganzen ist immer schon alles gezählt.
So auch, wer fällt, vermindert die heilige Zahl nicht.
Jeder verzichtende Sturz stürzt in den Ursprung und heilt.
Wäre denn alles ein Spiel, Wechsel des Gleichen, Verschiebung,
nirgends ein Name und kaum irgendwo heimisch Gewinn?
Wellen, Marina, wir Meer! Tiefen, Marina, wir Himmel.
Erde, Marina, wir Erde, wir tausendmal Frühling, wie Lerchen,
die ein ausbrechendes Lied in die Unsichtbarkeit wirft.
Wir beginnens als Jubel, schon übertrifft es uns völlig;
plötzlich, unser Gewicht dreht zur Klage abwärts den Sang.
Aber auch so: Klage? Wäre sie nicht: jüngerer Jubel nach unten.
Auch die unteren Götter wollen gelobt sein, Marina.
So unschuldig sind Götter, sie warten auf Lob wie die Schüler.
Loben, du Liebe, laß uns verschwenden mit Lob.
Nichts gehört uns. Wir legen ein wenig die Hand um die Hälse
ungebrochener Blumen. Ich sah es am Nil in Kôm-Ombo.
So, Marina, die Spende, selber verzichtend, opfern die Könige.
Wie die Engel gehen und die Türen bezeichnen jener zu Rettenden,
also rühren wir dieses und dies, scheinbar Zärtliche, an.
Ach wie weit schon Entrückte, ach, wie Zerstreute, Marina,
auch noch beim innigsten Vorwand. Zeichengeber, sonst nichts.
Dieses leise Geschäft, wo es der Unsrigen einer
nicht mehr erträgt und sich zum Zugriff entschließt,
rächt sich und tötet. Denn daß es tödliche Macht hat,
merkten wir alle an seiner Verhaltung und Zartheit
und an der seltsamen Kraft, die uns aus Lebenden zu
Überlebenden macht. Nicht-Sein. Weißt du's, wie oft
trug uns ein blinder Befehl durch den eisigen Vorraum
neuer Geburt. . . . Trug: *uns*? Einen Körper aus Augen
unter zahllosen Lidern sich weigernd. Trug das in uns
niedergeworfene Herz eines ganzen Geschlechts. An ein Zugvogelziel
trug er die Gruppe, das Bild unserer schwebenden Wandlung.
Liebende dürften, Marina, dürfen soviel nicht

ELEGY

to Marina Tsvetayeva-Efron

Oh the losses into the All, Marina, the stars that are falling!
We can't make it larger, wherever we fling ourselves, to whatever
star we may go! In the Whole, all things are already numbered.
So when anyone falls, the perfect sum is not lessened.
Whoever lets go in his fall, dives into the source and is healed.
Is all of life then a game, a meaningless fluctuation
of sameness, nowhere a name, nowhere a lasting achievement?
Waves, Marina, we are ocean! Depths, Marina, we are sky.
Earth, Marina, we are earth, a thousand times April, like larks
that a song bursting out of them flings into invisible heights.
We begin it as joy, and already it wholly exceeds us;
suddenly the force of our weight bends the song down to lament.
Yet isn't lament really a younger, descending joy?
Even the gods below want to be praised, Marina.
So innocent are gods, they listen for praise like children.
Praising, my dearest—let us be lavish with praise.
Nothing really belongs to us. We put our hands lightly around
the necks of unbroken flowers. I saw it on the Nile, in Kom Ombo.
Just so, Marina, the kings offer up the gifts they renounce.
As angels draw marks as a signal on the doors of those to be saved,
we, though we seem to be tender, stop and touch this or that.
Ah, how remote already, how inattentive, Marina,
even in our innermost pretense. Signalers: nothing more.
This silent commerce, when life is no longer willing
to endure one of our kind, when it seizes him in its grip,
avenges itself, kills. For the fact that its strength *can* kill
was plain to us all from its delicacy and restraint
and from the curious power that transforms us from living beings
into survivors. Non-being. Do you remember how often
a blind command would carry us through the icy
waiting-room of new birth? . . . Us?—a body of eyes
under numberless lids, refusing. Carried the down-
thrown heart in our breast, the heart of a whole generation.
To a goal as welcome as the South is for migrating birds,
it carried the soaring image and plan of our transformation.
Lovers were not, Marina, *are* not permitted to know

von dem Untergang wissen. Müssen wie neu sein.
Erst ihr Grab is alt, erst ihr Grab besinnt sich, verdunkelt
unter dem schluchzenden Baum, besinnt sich auf Jeher.
Erst ihr Grab bricht ein; sie selber sind biegsam wie Ruten;
was übermäßig sie biegt, ründet sie reichlich zum Kranz.
Wie sie verwehen im Maiwind! Von der Mitte des Immer,
drin du atmest und ahnst, schließt sie der Augenblick aus.
(O wie begreif ich dich, weibliche Blüte am gleichen
unvergänglichen Strauch. Wie streu ich mich stark in die Nachtluft,
die dich nächstens bestreift.) Frühe erlernten die Götter
Hälften zu heucheln. Wir in das Kreisen bezogen
füllten zum Ganzen uns an wie die Scheibe des Monds.
Auch in abnehmender Frist, auch in den Wochen der Wendung
niemand verhülfe uns je wieder zum Vollsein, als der
einsame eigene Gang über der schlaflosen Landschaft.

destruction so deeply. Must be as if they were new.
Only their grave is old, only *it* ponders and darkens
under the sobbing tree, remembering all that has been.
Only their grave collapses; *they* are supple as reeds;
what bends them too far, rounds them into rich garlands.
How they blow about in the May wind! From the midst of the Ever,
in which you breathe and surmise, the moment has shut them out.
(Oh how I understand you, female flower on the same
imperishable stalk. How wildly I scatter myself into the night air
that in a moment will touch you.) The gods long ago
learned to dissemble halves. We, drawn into the cycle,
filled ourselves out to the whole, like the disk of the moon.
Even in the time of waning, in the weeks of our gradual change,
nothing could ever again help us to fulfillment, except
our own solitary course over the sleepless landscape.

Für Erika, zum Feste der Rühmung

Taube, die draußen blieb,   außer dem Taubenschlag,
wieder in Kreis und Haus,   einig der Nacht, dem Tag,
weiß sie die Heimlichkeit,   wenn sich der Einbezug
fremdester Schrecken schmiegt   in den gefühlten Flug.

Unter den Tauben, die   allergeschonteste,
niemals gefährdetste,   kennt nicht die Zärtlichkeit;
wiedererholtes Herz   ist das bewohnteste:
freier durch Widerruf   freut sich die Fähigkeit.

Über dem Nirgendssein   spannt sich das Überall!
Ach der geworfene,   ach der gewagte Ball,
füllt er die Hände nicht   anders mit Wiederkehr:
rein um sein Heimgewicht   ist er mehr.

[Dove that ventured outside]

To Erika, for the festival of praise

Dove that ventured outside,   flying far from the dovecote:
housed and protected again,   one with the day, the night,
knows what serenity is,   for she has felt her wings
pass through all distance and fear   in the course of her wanderings.

The doves that remained at home,   never exposed to loss,
innocent and secure,   cannot know tenderness;
only the won-back heart   can ever be satisfied: free,
through all it has given up,   to rejoice in its mastery.

Being arches itself   over the vast abyss.
Ah the ball that we dared,   that we hurled into infinite space,
doesn't it fill our hands   differently with its return:
heavier by the weight   of where it has been.

NOTES

Translating poems into equivalent formal patterns is to some extent a matter of luck, or grace, and this is especially true of rhymed poems. Rilke called rhyme "a goddess of secret and ancient coincidences" and said that "she is very capricious; one cannot summon or foresee her; she comes as happiness comes, hands filled with an achievement that is already in flower." Some of my favorite Rilke poems never got beyond a rough draft, because that sweet goddess refused to make even the briefest appearance. Otherwise I would have included: from *The Book of Pictures*, the tender and funny "Annunciation," in which the angel Gabriel is so moved by Mary's ripening beauty that he forgets what he was sent to announce; from *New Poems*, "Woman in Love" ("Die Liebende"), a deeply awed, Brahmsian love song to the night; and from *The Sonnets to Orpheus*, I 6, 9, 10, 12, 19; II 1, 12, 16, and 18.

I have included the selections from *The Notebooks of Malte Laurids Brigge* not to discourage readers from experiencing the novel in its entirety, but to show the power of these excerpts as prose-poems. With their density of texture, their metaphorical richness, and the strength and subtlety of their rhythms, they don't seem out of place among Rilke's greatest verse.

The German text in the preceding pages is that of the standard edition (*Sämtliche Werke* [SW], Frankfurt am Main: Insel Verlag, 1955–1966), except for two lines in the Fifth Elegy, where I have followed the Thurn und Taxis manuscript and the first edition.

Letters excerpted and translated in these notes can be found in the following collections (except where otherwise noted):

Briefe aus den Jahren 1902–1906. Leipzig: Insel Verlag, 1930.

Briefe aus den Jahren 1907–1914. Leipzig: Insel Verlag, 1933.

Briefe aus Muzot, 1921–1926. Leipzig: Insel Verlag, 1937.

Briefe. Wiesbaden: Insel Verlag, 1950.

Rainer Maria Rilke und Marie von Thurn und Taxis: Briefwechsel. Zürich/ Wiesbaden: Niehans & Rokitansky Verlag und Insel Verlag, 1951.

Rainer Maria Rilke/Lou Andreas-Salomé: Briefwechsel. Wiesbaden: Insel Verlag, 1952.

Rainer Maria Rilke/Katharina Kippenberg: Briefwechsel. Wiesbaden: Insel Verlag, 1954.

Briefwechsel mit Benvenuta. Eßlingen: Bechtle Verlag, 1954.

Briefe an Sidonie Nádherný von Borutin. Frankfurt am Main: Insel Verlag, 1973.

Briefe an Nanny Wunderly-Volkart. Frankfurt am Main: Insel Verlag, 1977.

FROM THE BOOK OF HOURS (1905)

I began with Things, which were the true confidants of my lonely childhood, and it was already a great achievement that, without any outside help, I managed to get as far as animals. But then Russia opened itself to me and granted me the brotherliness and the darkness of God, in whom alone there is community. That was what I *named* him then, the God who had broken in upon me, and for a long time I lived in the antechamber of his name, on my knees. Now, you would hardly ever hear me name him; there is an indescribable discretion between us, and where nearness and penetration once were, new distances stretch forth, as in the atom, which the new science conceives of as a universe in miniature. The comprehensible slips away, is transformed; instead of possession one learns relationship [*statt des Besitzes lernt man den Bezug*], and there arises a namelessness that must begin once more in our relations with God if we are to be complete and without evasion. The experience of feeling him recedes behind an infinite delight in everything that can be felt; all attributes are taken away from God, who is no longer sayable, and fall back into creation, into love and death. It is perhaps only this that again and again took place in certain passages in the Book of Hours, this ascent of God out of the breathing heart—so that the sky was covered with him—, and his falling to earth as rain. But saying even that is already too much.

(To Ilse Jahr, February 22, 1923)

[I am, O Anxious One. Don't you hear my voice] (Berlin-Schmargendorf, September 24, 1899)

[I find you, Lord, in all Things and in all] (Berlin-Schmargendorf, September 24, 1899)

FROM THE BOOK OF PICTURES (First edition, 1902; second edition, 1906)

Lament (Berlin-Schmargendorf, October 21, 1900)

Autumn Day (Paris, September 21, 1902)

Evening (Undated: 1902/1906; perhaps Sweden, autumn 1904)

The Blindman's Song (Paris, June 7, 1906)

This and the following three songs are part of a ten-poem cycle called *The Voices*.

To want to improve the situation of another human being presupposes an insight into his circumstances such as not even a poet has toward a character he himself has created. How much less insight is there in the so infinitely excluded helper, whose scatteredness becomes complete with his gift. Wanting to change or improve someone's situation means offering him, in exchange for difficulties in which he is practiced and experienced, other difficulties that will find him perhaps even more bewildered. If at any time I was able to pour out into the mold of my heart the imaginary voices of the dwarf or the beggar, the metal of this cast was not obtained from any wish that the dwarf or the beggar might have a less difficult time. On the contrary: only through a praising of their incomparable fate could the poet, with his full attention suddenly given to them, be true and fundamental, and there is nothing that he would have to fear and refuse so much as a corrected world in which the dwarfs are stretched out and the beggars enriched. The God of completeness sees to it that these varieties do not cease, and it would be a most superficial attitude to consider the poet's joy in this suffering multiplicity as an esthetic pretense.

(To Hermann Pongs, October 21, 1924)

The Drunkard's Song (Paris, June 7/12, 1906)

The Idiot's Song (Paris, June 7, 1906)

The Dwarf's Song (Paris, June 7, 1906)

FROM NEW POEMS (First Part, 1907; Second Part, 1908)

Do the *New Poems* still seem so impersonal to you? You see, in order to speak about what happened to me, what I needed was not so much an instrument of emotion, but rather: clay. Involuntarily I undertook to make use of "lyric poetry" in order to *form* not feelings but *things I had felt*; every one of life's events had to find a place in this forming, independently of the suffering or pleasure it had at first brought me. This formation would have been worthless if it hadn't gone as far as the *trans*-formation of every accidental detail; it had to arrive at the essence.

(To "une amie," February 3, 1923)

The Panther (Paris, 1903, or possibly late in 1902)

In addition to the panther in the Jardin des Plantes, Rilke was probably remembering a small Greek statue of a panther (or tiger).

In his studio in the rue de l'Université, Rodin has a tiny plaster cast of a tiger (antique) which he values very highly: C'est beau, c'est tout [It's beautiful, it's everything], he says of it. And from this little plaster copy I have seen what he means, what antiquity is and what links him to it. There is in this animal the same kind of aliveness in the modeling; on this little Thing (it is no higher than my hand is wide, and no longer than my hand is) there are a hundred thousand places, as if it were something really huge—a hundred thousand places that are all alive, active, and different. All this just in plaster! And the representation of the prowling stride is intensified to the highest degree, the powerful downward tread of the broad paws, and simultaneously that caution in which all strength is wrapped, that noiselessness.

(To Clara Rilke, September 27, 1902)

In Rodin's studio there is a cast of a panther, of Greek workmanship, hardly as big as a hand (the original is in the medallion collection of the Bibliothèque Nationale in Paris). If you look from the front under its body into the space formed by the four powerful soft paws, you seem to be looking into the depths of an Indian stone temple; so huge and all-inclusive does this work become.

(*Auguste Rodin*, 1902, SW 5, 173)

The Gazelle (Paris, July 17, 1907)

Yesterday I spent the whole morning in the Jardin des Plantes, looking at the gazelles. Gazella Dorcas, Linnaeus. There are a pair of them and also a single female. They were lying a few feet apart, chewing their cuds, resting, gazing. As women gaze out of pictures, they were gazing out of something, with a soundless, final turn of the head. And when a horse whinnied, the single one listened, and I saw the radiance from ears and horns around her slender head. . . . I saw the single one stand up, for a moment; she lay right down again; but while she was stretching and testing herself, I could see the magnificent workmanship of those legs (they are like rifles from which leaps are fired). I just couldn't tear myself away, they were so beautiful.

(To Clara Rilke, June 13, 1907)

l. 6, *songs of love:* Possibly a reference to the Song of Solomon, which, in the translation that Rilke used, frequently compares the beloved to a gazelle.

The Swan (Meudon, winter 1905/1906)

The Grownup (Paris, July 19, 1907)

There is an insightful study of this poem in Geoffrey H. Hartman's *The Unmediated Vision* (New Haven: Yale University Press, 1954).

l. 4, *the Ark of God:* The ark of the tabernacle, Exodus 25.

Going Blind (Paris, late June 1906)

Before Summer Rain (Paris, early July 1906)

Written after a visit to the Château de Chantilly.

l. 6, *Saint Jerome* (ca. 347–ca. 420): One of the four great Doctors of the Western Church, noted for his asceticism and pugnacity. Rilke may have been thinking of the Dürer engraving, dated 1514.

The Last Evening (Paris, June 1906)

Dedication, *Frau Nonna:* Rilke's friend Julie Freifrau von Nordeck zur Rabenau, whose first husband was killed in the battle of Königgrätz, July 3, 1866, at the age of thirty-one.

l. 14, *shako:* "A military cap in the shape of a truncated cone, with a peak and either a plume or a ball or 'pompom.' " (OED)

Portrait of My Father as a Young Man (Paris, June 27, 1906)

This poem, written three months after Josef Rilke's death, describes

the fine colored daguerrotype of my father that was taken when he was seventeen, just before his departure on the [Austrian army's] Italian campaign. Those first, naive photographs could be so movingly real—this one gives you the impression that you are looking at him through his mother's eyes, seeing the beautiful young face in its solemn, barely smiling presentiment of bravery and danger. In my childhood I must have seen it once among my father's papers; later it seemed as though it was missing for years—useless to ask where it had gone. Then, after he died, I found it among the possessions he had left behind, framed like a miniature in antique red velvet, intact—and I realized how unutterably it had taken form in my heart.

(To Magda von Hattingberg, February 11, 1914)

Self-Portrait, 1906 (Probably Paris, spring 1906)

Spanish Dancer (Paris, June 1906)

Tombs of the Hetaerae (Rome, early in 1904)

Hetaerae: Courtesans.

Orpheus. Eurydice. Hermes (Rome, early in 1904)

According to Ovid: After Eurydice, Orpheus' wife, died of a snakebite, the poet descended to the land of shadows to retrieve her, and held the whole underworld spellbound by the beauty of his song.

> Neither the dark queen
> nor the lord who rules the underworld could deny
> what he in his song had asked for, and they called
> Eurydice. She was there among the shades
> just recently arrived, and now walked toward them,
> slowly, the wound still fresh upon her ankle.
> Orpheus took her, with the one condition:
> if he should turn to look at her before
> they had passed the dismal valleys of Avernus,
> the gift would be revoked.
>
> They climbed the path
> through the deep silence, wrapped in total darkness.
> They had almost reached the rim of the upper world
> when he, afraid that she might slip, impatient
> to see her bright, beloved face, looked back:
> and in an instant, she began to fade,
> reaching out, struggling desperately to hold on
> to him, or to be held; but her hands could grasp
> nothing but thin air. She didn't blame
> her appalled husband for this second death
> (how could she blame such love?) and, calling out
> a last *Farewell!*, which he could barely hear,
> she vanished.

(Ovid, *Metamorphoses* X, 46 ff.)

Hermes: The messenger of the gods and the guide (*psychopompos*) who took the souls of the dead to the underworld.

l. 15, *in the blue cloak:* In Homer, dark blue is the color of mourning.

Alcestis (Capri, between February 7 and 10, 1907)

Several years after King Admetus' marriage, Death arrived to announce that Admetus had been condemned to die immediately, and could be saved only if someone else was willing to be taken in his stead. Only Alcestis, his wife, volunteered. Later, Hercules was so moved by Admetus' mourning that he pursued Death, snatched Alcestis away from him, and brought her back to Admetus. (This myth is the theme of the tragicomic *Alcestis* by Euripides.)

l. 1, *the messenger:* Hermes (the poem was originally entitled "Admetus. Alcestis. Hermes").

l. 72, *she:* The goddess Artemis, who was offended because Admetus had forgotten the customary prenuptial sacrifice to her.

Archaic Torso of Apollo (Paris, early summer 1908)

The inspiration for this sonnet, which is the first poem in *New Poems, Second Part,* was the early-fifth-century B.C. *Torso of a Youth from Miletus* in the Salle Archaïque of the Louvre.

The incomparable value of these rediscovered Things lies in the fact that you can look at them as if they were completely unknown. No one knows what their intention is and (at least for the unscientific) no subject matter is attached to them, no irrelevant voice interrupts the silence of their concentrated reality, and their duration is without retrospect or fear. The masters from whom they originate are nothing; no misunderstood fame colors their pure forms; no history casts a shadow over their naked clarity—: they *are.* That is all. This is how I see ancient art. The little tiger at Rodin's is like that, and the many fragments and broken pieces in the museums (which you pass by many times without paying attention, until one day one of them reveals itself to you, and shines like a first star . . .)

(To Lou Andreas-Salomé, August 15, 1903)

The companion piece, "Early Apollo," is the first poem in *New Poems* (Part One):

> . . . so ist in seinem Haupte
> nichts was verhindern könnte, daß der Glanz
>
> aller Gedichte uns fast tödlich träfe;
> denn noch kein Schatten ist in seinem Schaun,
> zu kühl für Lorbeer sind noch seine Schläfe
> und später erst wird aus den Augenbraun . . .

> . . . so, in his head,
> nothing can stop the radiance of all
>
> poems from nearly burning us to death;
> for there is still no shadow in his gaze,
> his forehead is too cool for a laurel-wreath,
> and not for another century will his eyebrows
>
> blossom . . .

Washing the Corpse (Paris, summer 1908)

Black Cat (Paris, summer 1908)

The Flamingos (Paris, autumn 1907, or Capri, spring 1908)

l. 1, *Fragonard:* Jean-Honoré Fragonard (pronounced Fragon*ar*), 1732–1806, French painter.

l. 8, *Phryne* (fourth century B.C.): Greek courtesan, famous for her beauty.

Buddha in Glory (Paris, summer 1908)

This is the final poem in *New Poems, Second Part.*

> Soon after supper I retire, and am in my little house by 8:30 at the latest. Then I have in front of me the vast blossoming starry night, and below, in front of the window, the gravel walk goes up a little hill on which, in fanatic taciturnity, a statue of the Buddha rests, distributing, with silent discretion, the unutterable self-containedness of his gesture beneath all the skies of the day and night. C'est le centre du monde [He is the center of the world], I said to Rodin.
>
> (To Clara Rilke, September 20, 1905)

Cf. the two earlier poems called "Buddha" in the first part of *New Poems* ("As though he were listening. Silence: something far" and "From far away the awe-struck pilgrim feels").

FROM REQUIEM (1909)

Requiem for a Friend (Paris, October 31–November 2, 1908)

Written in memory of Paula Modersohn-Becker (1876–1907). See Introduction, pp. xxix ff.

The fate that I tried to tell of and to lament in the Requiem is perhaps the essential conflict of the artist: the opposition and contradiction between objective and personal enjoyment of the world. It is no less conclusively demonstrated in a man who is an artist by necessity; but in a woman who has committed herself to the infinite transpositions of the artist's existence the pain and danger of this choice become inconceivably visible. Since she is physical far into her soul and is designed for bearing children of flesh and blood, something like a complete transformation of all her organs must take place if she is to attain a true fruitfulness of soul.

The birth processes which, in a purely spiritual way, the male artist enjoys, suffers, and survives, may, in a woman who is capable of giving birth to a work of art, broaden and be exalted into something that is of the utmost spirituality. But these processes undergo just a gradual intensification, and still remain, in unlimited ramifications, within the realm of the physical. (So that, exaggerating, one could say that even what is most spiritual in woman is still body: body become sublime.) Therefore, for her, any relapse into a more primitive and narrow kind of suffering, enjoying, and bringing forth is an overfilling of her organs with the blood that has been augmented for another, greater circulation.

Long ago I had a presentiment of this fate; but I experienced it in all its intensity when it actually brushed against me: when it stood in front of me, so huge and close that I could not shut my eyes.

(To Hugo Heller, June 12, 1909; in *Berliner Tageblatt,* November 29, 1929)

l. 5, *return:*

. . . his body became indescribably touching to him and of no further use than to be purely and cautiously present in, just as a ghost [*Revenant*], already dwelling elsewhere, sadly enters the realm that was tenderly laid aside, in order to belong once again, even if inattentively, to this once so indispensable world.

("An Experience," 1913, SW 6, 1038)

ll. 49 f., *a country / you never saw:* Rilke was probably thinking of Egypt here. Both he and Paula Becker were deeply impressed by the Egyptian sculptures in the Louvre. (H. W. Petzet, *Das Bildnis des Dichters: Paula Modersohn-Becker und Rainer Maria Rilke*, Frankfurt am Main: Insel Verlag, 1976, pp. 49 f.)

l. 80, *your naked body:* This probably refers to the wonderful *Self-Portrait on her Fifth Anniversary* (1906), where Paula Becker is wearing her amber necklace and is naked to the hips. There are two other self-portraits from 1906, half-length, in which she appears naked, wearing the amber necklace, and with pink flowers in her hands and hair. (Those interested should consult Gillian Perry, *Paula Modersohn-Becker*, New York: Harper & Row, 1979, which contains twenty-five color plates and ninety-three duotone illustrations.)

l. 83, *and didn't say: I am that; no: this is:* In one of his great letters on Cézanne, Rilke wrote:

> You notice better each time you look at these paintings how necessary it was to go beyond even love. It is of course natural to love each one of these Things if you have made them. But if you show that, you make them less well; you *judge* them instead of *saying* them. You cease to be impartial; and what is best of all, the love, remains outside the work, does not enter it, is left untransformed beside it. That is how mood-painting arose (which is in no way better than realism). They painted: I love this; instead of painting: here it is. In the latter, everyone must then look carefully to see whether I have loved it. That is not shown at all, and many people would even say that there is no love in it. So utterly has it been consumed in the act of making. This consuming of love in anonymous work, out of which such pure Things arise—perhaps no one has so completely succeeded in doing that as this old man.
>
> (To Clara Rilke, October 13, 1907)

ll. 85 f., *of such true / poverty:*

> Any kind of work delighted him: he worked even during meals, he read, he drew. He drew as he walked along the street, and quite early in the morning he drew the sleepy animals in the Jardin des Plantes. And when pleasure did not tempt him to work, poverty drove him to it. Poverty, without which his life would be unthinkable. He never forgets that it included him with the animals and flowers, without possessions among all those who are without possessions, and who have only God to depend on.
>
> (*Auguste Rodin,* 1907, SW 5, 228)

l. 117, *someone:* Otto Modersohn.

ll. 129 ff., *the objective world expanded . . . :* Paula's pregnancy.

l. 223, *Nikē:*

> I have seen such beautiful things in the Louvre. . . . The Nikē of Samothrace, the goddess of victory on the ship's hull, with the wonderful movement and the vast sea-wind in her clothes, is a miracle and seems like a whole world.
>
> (To Clara Rilke, September 26, 1902)

l. 232, *the freedom of a love:*

> For one human being to love another human being: that is perhaps the most difficult task that has been given to us, the ultimate, the final problem and proof, the work for which all other work is merely preparation. . . . Love does not at first mean merging, surrendering, and uniting with another person . . . Rather, it

is a high inducement for the individual to ripen, to become something in himself, to become world, to become world in himself for another's sake. . . . We are only just now beginning to consider the relation of one individual to a second individual objectively and without prejudice, and our attempts to live such relationships have no model before them. And yet in the changes brought about by time there are already many things that can help our timid novitiate.

The girl and the woman, in their new, individual unfolding, will only in passing be imitators of male behavior and misbehavior and repeaters of male professions. After the uncertainty of such transitions, it will become obvious that women were going through the abundance and variation of those (often ridiculous) disguises just so that they could purify their own essential nature and wash out the deforming influences of the other sex. . . . This humanity of woman, carried in her womb through all her suffering and humiliation, will come to light when she has stripped off the conventions of mere femaleness in the transformations of her outward status, and those men who do not yet feel it approaching will be surprised and struck by it. Someday . . . there will be girls and women whose name will no longer mean the mere opposite of the male, but something in itself, something that makes one think not of any complement and limit, but only of life and reality: the female human being.

This advance will (at first much against the will of the outdistanced men) transform the love experience, which is now filled with error, will change it from the ground up, and reshape it into a relation of one human being to another, no longer of man to woman. And this more human love (which will fulfill itself with infinite consideration and gentleness, and kindness and clarity in binding and releasing) will resemble what we are now preparing painfully and with great struggle: the love that consists in this—that two solitudes protect and border and greet each other.

(To Franz Xaver Kappus, May 14, 1904)

l. 235, *letting each other go:* In describing his admiration for the "incomparable" Leonora Christina Ulfeldt, daughter of King Christian IV of Denmark, who, because her husband had been accused of high treason, was imprisoned in the Blue Tower in Copenhagen from 1663 until 1685, Rilke wrote:

It seems to me that you could predict her conduct in prison if you knew of a certain little scene that was enacted just before her arrest in England. At this critical moment it happened that a young officer who was sent to her misunderstood his orders and demanded that she take off all the jewelry she was wearing and hand it over to him. Although this ought to have startled her (since she was not yet aware that she was in any danger) and thrown her into the utmost alarm, nevertheless, after a moment's consideration, she takes off all her jewels—the earrings, the necklaces, the brooches, the bracelets, the rings—and puts them into the officer's hands. The young man brings these treasures to his superior, who, at first terrified, then enraged, at this imprudence, which threatens to upset the whole undertaking, orders him, curtly and in the coarsest language, to return and give everything back to the Countess, and to beg her forgiveness, in any way he can think of, for his unauthorized blunder. What happened now is unforgettable. After considering for a moment, not longer than that first moment was, Countess Ulfeldt gestures for the bewildered officer to follow her, walks over to the mirror, and there takes the magnificent necklaces and brooches and rings from his hands, as if from the hands of a servant, and puts them on, with the greatest attentiveness and serenity, one after another.

Tell me, dear friend, do you know any other story in which it is so sublimely evident how we ought to behave toward the vicissitudes of life? This went through and through me: this same repose vis-à-vis giving up and keeping, this repose that is so filled with power. This should truly be taken to heart: it is perhaps nothing more than what individual saints have done, who, because they have lost what they love or were reminded of the continual possibility of loss, threw off all possessions and condemned the very desire for possession (: for that may be an enormous, hardly surpassable achievement—.) But this is more human, more patient, more adequate. *That* gesture of renunciation is magnificent, thrilling,—but it is not without arrogance, which is again cancelled only because it, in its own way, already belongs to heaven. But this silent, composed keeping and letting go, on the contrary, is full of moderation, is still earthly, through and through, and yet is already so great as to be incomprehensible.

(To Sidonie Nádherný von Borutin, February 4, 1912)

l. 245, *fame*:

Rodin was solitary before he was famous. And fame, when it arrived, made him perhaps even more solitary. For fame is, after all, only the sum of all the misunderstandings that gather around a new name.

(*Auguste Rodin,* 1902, SW 5, 141)

ll. 264 f., *an ancient enmity / between our daily life and the great work*:

The modest domestic circumstances of Tolstoy, the lack of comfort in Rodin's rooms—it all points to the same thing: that one must make up one's mind: either this or that. Either happiness or art. On doit trouver le bonheur dans son art [one must find happiness in one's art]: that too, more or less, is what Rodin said. And it is all so clear, so clear. The great artists have all let their lives become overgrown like an old path and have borne everything in their art. Their lives have become atrophied, like an organ they no longer use.

(To Clara Rilke, September 5, 1902)

Someday people will understand what made this great artist so great: the fact that he was a worker, who desired nothing but to enter, completely and with all his powers, into the humble and austere reality of his art. In this there was a certain renunciation of life. But precisely by such patience did he win life: for the world offered itself to his art.

(Auguste Rodin, 1902, SW 5, 201)

FROM THE NOTEBOOKS OF MALTE LAURIDS BRIGGE (1910; begun in Rome, February 8, 1904; written mostly during 1908/1909; finished in Leipzig, January 27, 1910)

The speaker in these passages is Malte Laurids Brigge, a twenty-eight-year-old Danish writer living in Paris.

[The Bird-feeders]

ll. 32f. *painted figurehead:*

The so-called galleon-figures: carved and painted statues from the bow of a ship. The sailors in Denmark sometimes set up these wooden statues, which have survived from old sailing-ships, in their gardens, where they look quite strange.
(To Witold Hulewicz, November 10, 1925)

[Ibsen]

l. 34, *and now you were among the alembics:*

where the most secret chemistry of life takes place, its transformations and precipitations.

(Ibid.)

l. 40, *You couldn't wait:*

Life, *our* present life, is hardly capable of being presented on stage, since it has wholly withdrawn into the invisible, the inner, communicating itself to us only through "august rumors." The dramatist, however, couldn't wait for it to become showable; he had to inflict violence upon it, this not yet producible life; and for that reason too his work, like a wand too strongly bent back, sprang from his hands and was as though it had never been done.

(Ibid.)

l. 67, *go away from the window:*

Ibsen spent his last days beside his window, observing with curiosity the people who passed by and in a way confusing these real people with the characters he might have created.

(Ibid.)

The Temptation of the Saint

l. 1, *those strange pictures:* The reference is to the paintings of Pieter Bruegel the Elder or of Hieronymus Bosch.

The Prodigal Son

Cf. Luke 15:11–32.

l. 23, *Tortuga:* Island off northwest Haiti. In the seventeenth century it was a base for the French and English pirates who ravaged the Caribbean.

l. 23, *Campeche:* Port in southeastern Mexico, frequently raided by pirates during the seventeenth century.

l. 24, *Vera Cruz:* The chief port of entry of Mexico. It was looted by pirates in 1653 and 1712.

l. 26, *Deodatus of Gozon:* A fourteenth-century member of the Order of the Knights of St. John of Jerusalem (Knights of Malta). Because so many had lost their lives trying to kill the famous dragon of Rhodes, the Grand Master of the Order had forbidden all knights even to approach its cave. Deodatus went ahead and killed the dragon, but because of his disobedience he was stripped of his knighthood. Later he was pardoned, and in 1346 he himself became Grand Master.

l. 103, *Les Baux:*

Magnificent landscape in Provence, a land of shepherds, even today still imprinted with the remains of the castles built by the princes of Les Baux, a noble family of prodigious bravery, famous in the 14th and 15th centuries for the splendor and strength of its men and the beauty of its women. As far as the princes of Les Baux are concerned, one might well say that a petrified time outlasts this family. Its existence is, as it were, petrified in the harsh, silver-gray landscape into which the unheard-of castles have crumbled. This landscape, near Arles, is an unforgettable drama of Nature: a hill, ruins, and village, abandoned, entirely turned to rock again with all its houses and fragments of houses. Far around, pasture: hence the shepherd is evoked: here, at the theater of Orange, and on the Acropolis, moving with his herds, mild and timeless, like a cloud, across the still-excited places of a great dilapidation. Like most Provençal families, the princes of Les Baux were superstitious gentlemen. Their rise had been immense, their good fortune measureless, their wealth beyond compare. The daughters of this family walked about like goddesses and nymphs, the men were turbulent demigods. From their battles they brought back not only treasures and slaves, but the most unbelievable crowns; they called themselves, by the way, "Emperors of Jerusalem." But in their coat-of-arms sat the worm of contradiction: to those who believe in the power of the number seven, "sixteen" appears the most dangerous counter-number, and the lords of Les Baux bore in their coat-of-arms the 16-rayed star (the star that led the three kings from the East and the shepherds to the manger in Bethlehem: for they believed that the family originated from the holy king Balthazar). The "good fortune" of this family was a struggle of the holy number "7" (they possessed cities, villages, and convents always in sevens) against the "16" rays of their coat-of-arms. And the seven succumbed.

(To Witold Hulewicz, November 10, 1925)

l. 108, *Alyscamps:* The ancient cemetery near Arles, with its uncovered sarcophagi.

ll. 139 f., *"sa patience de supporter une âme":* "his patience in enduring a soul."

This comes, I think, from Saint Theresa (of Avila).

(To Witold Hulewicz, November 10, 1925)

UNCOLLECTED POEMS, 1913–1918

The Spanish Trilogy (Ronda, between January 6 and 14, 1913)

ll. 41 f., *the distant call of birds / already deep inside him:*

Later, he remembered certain moments in which the power of *this* moment was already contained, as in a seed. He thought of the hour in that other southern garden (Capri) when the call of a bird did not, so to speak, break off at the edge of his body, but was simultaneously outside and in his innermost being, uniting both into one uninterrupted space in which, mysteriously protected, only one single place of purest, deepest consciousness remained. On that occasion he had closed his eyes, so that he might not be confused, in so generous an experience, by the outline of his body, and the Infinite passed into him from all sides, so intimately that he believed he could feel the stars which had in the meantime appeared, gently reposing within his breast.

("An Experience," 1913, SW 6, 1040)

l. 54, *the daily task of the shepherd:*

What I most took part in when I was in Ronda was the life of the shepherds on the great stony hillsides with the picturesque stone-oaks, each of them filling up with darkness the way a cloud's shadow moves over the fields. The morning departure, when after their night's rest the shepherds walk out carrying their long staffs on their shoulders; their quiet, lingering, contemplative outdoor presence, through which, in all its breadth, the greatness of the day pours down; and the evenings when they unrecognizably, with the twilight, climb up out of the valley in the air echoing with their flocks, and, above, on the valley's rim, again darkly gather themselves into the simplest of forms; and that they still use the long slings woven of bast, just like the one which David put his stone into, and with an exactly aimed throw, frighten back a straying animal into the mass of the flock; and that the air knows the color and weave of their thick clothing and treats it as it treats the other tempered presences of Nature; in short, that there are people there who are placed out in the overflowing fullness which we are only sometimes aware of, when we step out of the world of human relationships or when we look up from a book: how such a figure is and endures and, almost godlike, walks on, unhurried, over the hurrying events in which we spend our lives: all this could be counted among the pure experiences which could teach us the days and nights and everything that is most elemental.

(To Katharina Kippenberg, March 27, 1913)

Ariel (Ronda, early in 1913)

(*after reading Shakespeare's* Tempest): Rilke had just read the play for the first time.

l. 1, *you had set him free:* Cf. *The Tempest,* I.ii.250 ff.

l. 12, *to give up all your magic:* Cf. *The Tempest,* V.i.50 ff.

I know now that psychoanalysis would make sense for me only if I were really serious about the strange possibility of *no longer writing,* which during the completion of *Malte* I often dangled in front of my nose as a kind of relief. Then one might let one's devils be exorcised, since in daily life they are truly just disturbing and painful. And if it happened that the angels left too, one would have to understand this as a further simplification and tell oneself that in the new profession (which?), there would certainly be no use for them.

(To Lou Andreas-Salomé, January 24, 1912)

[Straining so hard against the strength of night] (Paris, late February, 1913)

The Vast Night (Paris, January 1914)

[You who never arrived] (Paris, winter 1913/1914)

Turning-point (Paris, June 20, 1914)

> Lou, dear, here is a strange poem, written this morning, which I am sending you right away because I involuntarily called it "Turning-point," because it describes *the* turning-point which no doubt must come if I am to stay alive.
>
> (To Lou Andreas-Salomé, June 20, 1914)

Epigraph, *sacrifice:* Rilke had defined sacrifice as "the boundless resolve, no longer limitable in any direction, to achieve one's purest inner possibility." (To Magda von Hattingberg, February 17, 1914)

Epigraph, *Kassner:* Rudolf Kassner (1873–1959), Austrian writer. The Eighth Elegy is dedicated to him.

l. 1, *For a long time he attained it in looking:*

> I love in-seeing. Can you imagine with me how glorious it is to in-see a dog, for example, as you pass it—by *in-see* I don't mean to look *through,* which is only a kind of human gymnastic that lets you immediately come out again on the other side of the dog, regarding it merely, so to speak, as a window upon the human world lying behind it: not that; what I mean is to let yourself precisely into the dog's center, the point from which it begins to be a dog, the place in it where God, as it were, would have sat down for a moment when the dog was finished, in order to watch it during its first embarrassments and inspirations and to nod that it was good, that nothing was lacking, that it couldn't have been better made. For a while you can endure being inside the dog; you just have to be alert and jump out in time, before its environment has completely enclosed you, since otherwise you would simply remain the dog in the dog and be lost for everything else. Though you may laugh, dear confidante, if I tell you *where* my very greatest feeling, my world-feeling, my earthly bliss was, I must confess to you: it was, again and again, here and there, in such in-seeing—in the indescribably swift, deep, timeless moments of this godlike in-seeing.
>
> (To Magda von Hattingberg, February 17, 1914)

Lament (Paris, early July 1914)

'We Must Die Because We Have Known Them' (Paris, July 1914)

Ptah-hotep: A high official under the pharaoh Asosi, during the Fifth Dynasty (ca. 2600 B.C.).

To Hölderlin (Irschenhausen, September 1914)

Hölderlin: Johann Christian Friedrich Hölderlin (1770–1843), one of the greatest German poets.

> During the past few months I have been reading your edition of Hölderlin with extraordinary feeling and devotion. His influence upon me is great and generous, as only the influence of the richest and inwardly mightiest can be. . . . I cannot tell you how deeply these poems are affecting me and with what inexpressible clarity they stand before me.
>
> (To Norbert von Hellingrath, July 24, 29, 1914)

l. 20, *for years that you no longer counted:* Hölderlin went incurably insane in 1806.

[Exposed on the cliffs of the heart] (Irschenhausen, September 20, 1914)

Death (Munich, November 9, 1915)

> Rilke told me how this poem arose. He was walking, alone as always, in a Munich park. All at once he seemed to see a hand before his eyes; on its level back a cup was standing. He saw this quite distinctly, and the verses describing it formed by themselves. He didn't quite know what to make of this, and went home still hazy about the meaning of what had been begun. As in a dream he continued the poem to its conclusion—and understood. And suddenly the last three lines were there, in strongest contrast to the preceding ones. As for the shooting star, he had seen it in Toledo. One night he had been walking across the bridge and suddenly a glorious meteor had plunged across the sky, from the zenith down to the dark horizon, and vanished.—That was death, in all its wonder.
>
> (Princess Marie von Thurn und Taxis-Hohenlohe, *Erinnerungen an Rainer Maria Rilke,* München-Berlin-Zürich: R. Oldenbourg, 1932, pp. 80 f.)

l. 1, *There stands death:*

> Tolstoy's enormous experience of Nature (I know hardly anyone who had so passionately entered inside Nature) made him astonishingly able to think and write out of a sense of the whole, out of a feeling for life which was permeated by the finest particles of death, a sense that death was contained everywhere in life, like a peculiar spice in life's powerful flavor. But that was precisely why this man could be so deeply, so frantically terrified when he realized that somewhere there was pure death, the bottle full of death or the hideous cup with the handle broken off and the meaningless inscription "Faith, love, hope," out of which people were forced to drink a bitterness of undiluted death.
>
> (To Lotte Hepner, November 8, 1915)

l. 17, *O shooting star:*

> At the end of the poem "Death," the moment is evoked (I was standing at night on the wonderful bridge of Toledo) when a star, falling through cosmic space in a tensed slow arc, simultaneously (how should I say this?) fell through my inner

space: the body's dividing outline was no longer there. And whereas this happened then through my eyes, once at an earlier time (in Capri) the same unity had been granted me through my hearing.

(To Adelheid von der Marwitz, January 14, 1919)

To Music (Munich, January 11–12, 1918)

Written in the guestbook of Frau Hanna Wolff, after a concert at her house.

DUINO ELEGIES (1923)

The Elegies take their name from Duino Castle, on the Adriatic Sea, where Rilke spent the winter of 1911/1912 as a guest of his friend Princess Marie von Thurn und Taxis-Hohenlohe (1855–1934); they are dedicated to her in gratitude, as having belonged to her from the beginning.

Rilke later told me how these Elegies arose. He had felt no premonition of what was being prepared deep inside him; though there may be a hint of it in a letter he wrote: "The nightingale is approaching—" Had he perhaps felt what was to come? But once again it fell silent. A great sadness came over him; he began to think that this winter too would be without result.

Then, one morning, he received a troublesome business letter. He wanted to take care of it quickly, and had to deal with numbers and other such tedious matters. Outside, a violent north wind was blowing, but the sun shone and the water gleamed as if covered with silver. Rilke climbed down to the bastions which, jutting out to the east and west, were connected to the foot of the castle by a narrow path along the cliffs, which abruptly drop off, for about two hundred feet, into the sea. Rilke walked back and forth, completely absorbed in the problem of how to answer the letter. Then, all at once, in the midst of his thoughts, he stopped; it seemed that from the raging storm a voice had called to him: "Who, if I cried out, would hear me among the angels' hierarchies?"

He stood still, listening. "What is that?" he whispered. "What is coming?"

Taking out the notebook that he always carried with him, he wrote down these words, together with a few lines that formed by themselves without his intervention. He knew that the god had spoken.

Very calmly he climbed back up to his room, set his notebook aside, and answered the difficult letter.

By the evening the whole First Elegy had been written.

(Princess Marie von Thurn und Taxis-Hohenlohe,
Erinnerungen an Rainer Maria Rilke, pp. 40 f.)

The Second Elegy was written shortly afterward, along with a number of fragments, the Third and most of the Sixth a year later, and the Fourth in 1915. Then, after years of excruciating patience, the other Elegies came through during a few days in February 1922.

> My dear friend,
> late, and though I can barely manage to hold the pen, after several days of huge obedience in the spirit—, you must be told, today, right now, before I try to sleep:
> I have climbed the mountain!
> At last! The Elegies are here, they exist. . . .
> So.
> Dear friend, now I can breathe again and, calmly, go on to something manageable. For this was larger than life—during these days and nights I have howled as I did that time in Duino—but, even after that struggle there, I didn't know that *such* a storm out of mind and heart could come over a person! That one has endured it! that one has endured.
> Enough. They are here.
> I went out into the cold moonlight and stroked the little tower of Muzot as if it were a large animal—the ancient walls that granted this to me.
>
> (To Anton Kippenberg, February 9, 1922)

A year before his death, Rilke wrote to his Polish translator:

> Affirmation of *life-AND-death* turns out to be one in the Elegies. . . . We of the here-and-now are not for a moment satisfied in the world of time, nor are we bound in it; we are continually overflowing toward those who preceded us, toward our origin, and toward those who seemingly come after us. In that vast "open" world, all beings *are*—one cannot say "contemporaneous," for the very fact that time has ceased determines that they all *are*. Everywhere transience is plunging into the depths of Being. . . . It is our task to imprint this temporary, perishable earth into ourselves so deeply, so painfully and passionately, that its essence can rise again, "invisibly," inside us. We are the bees of the invisible. We wildly collect the honey of the visible, to store it in the great golden hive of the invisible. The Elegies show us at this work, the work of the continual conversion of the beloved visible and tangible world into the invisible vibrations and agitation of our own nature . . . Elegies and Sonnets support each other constantly—, and I consider it an infinite grace that, with the same breath, I was permitted to fill both these sails: the little rust-colored sail of the Sonnets and the Elegies' gigantic white canvas.
>
> (To Witold Hulewicz, November 13, 1925)

The First Elegy (Duino, between January 12 and 16, 1912)

ll. 1 f., *among the angels' / hierarchies:*

The angel of the Elegies is that creature in whom the transformation of the visible into the invisible, which we are accomplishing, already appears in its completion . . . ; that being who guarantees the recognition of a higher level of reality in the invisible.—Therefore "terrifying" for us, because we, its lovers and transformers, still cling to the visible.

(To Witold Hulewicz, November 13, 1925)

"There is really *everything* in the ancient churches, no shrinking from anything, as there is in the newer ones, where only the 'good' examples appear. Here you see also what is bad and evil and horrible; what is deformed and suffering, what is ugly, what is unjust—and you could say that all this is somehow loved for God's sake. Here is the angel, who doesn't exist, and the devil, who doesn't exist; and the human being, who does exist, stands between them, and (I can't help saying it) their unreality makes him more real to me."

("The Young Workman's Letter," February 12–15, 1922, SW 6, 1120 f.)

l. 5, *the beginning of terror:*

More and more in my life and in my work I am guided by the effort to correct our old repressions, which have removed and gradually estranged from us the mysteries out of whose abundance our lives might become truly infinite. It is true that these mysteries are dreadful, and people have always drawn away from them. But where can we find anything sweet and glorious that would never wear *this* mask, the mask of the dreadful? Life—and we know nothing else—, isn't life itself dreadful? But as soon as we acknowledge its dreadfulness (not as opponents: what kind of match could we be for it?), but somehow with a confidence that this very dreadfulness may be something completely *ours,* though something that is just now too great, too vast, too incomprehensible for our learning hearts—: as soon as we accept life's most terrifying dreadfulness, at the risk of perishing from it (i.e., from our own Too-much!)—: then an intuition of blessedness will open up for us and, at this cost, will be ours. Whoever does not, sometime or other, give his full consent, his full and *joyous* consent, to the dreadfulness of life, can never take possession of the unutterable abundance and power of our existence; can only walk on its edge, and one day, when the judgment is given, will have been neither alive nor dead. To show the *identity* of dreadfulness and bliss, these two faces on the same divine head, indeed this one *single* face, which just presents itself this way or that, according to our distance from it or the state of mind in which we perceive it—: this is the true significance and purpose of the Elegies and the Sonnets to Orpheus.

(To Countess Margot Sizzo-Noris-Crouy, April 12, 1923)

l. 13, *our interpreted world:*

> *Wir* machen mit Worten und Fingerzeigen
> uns allmählich die Welt zu eigen,
> vielleicht ihren schwächsten, gefährlichsten Teil.

We, with words and pointing fingers, / gradually make the world our own— / (though) perhaps its weakest, most precarious part.

(Sonnets to Orpheus I, 16)

l. 36, *women in love:*

Certainly I have no window on human beings. They yield themselves to me only insofar as they take on words within me, and during these last few years they have been communicating with me almost entirely through two forms, upon which I base my inferences about human beings in general. What speaks to me of humanity —immensely, with a calm authority that fills my hearing with space—is the phenomenon of those who have died young and, even more absolutely, purely, inexhaustibly: *the woman in love.* In these two figures humanity gets mixed into my heart whether I want it to or not. They step forward on my stage with the clarity of the marionette (which is an exterior entrusted with conviction) and, at the same time, as completed types, which nothing can go beyond, so that the definitive natural-history of their souls could now be written.

As for the woman in love (I am not thinking of Saint Theresa or such magnificence of that sort): she yields herself to my observation much more distinctly, purely, i.e., undilutedly and (so to speak) unappliedly in the situation of Gaspara Stampa, Louize Labé, certain Venetian courtesans, and, above all, Marianna Alcoforado, that incomparable creature, in whose eight heavy letters woman's love is for the first time charted from point to point, without display, without exaggeration or mitigation, drawn as if by the hand of a sibyl. And there —my God—there it becomes evident that, as a result of the irresistible logic of woman's heart, this line was finished, perfected, not to be continued any further in the earthly realm, and could be prolonged only toward the divine, into infinity.

(To Annette Kolb, January 23, 1912)

l. 46, *Gaspara Stampa* (1523–1554): An Italian noblewoman who wrote of her unhappy love for Count Collaltino di Collalto in a series of some two hundred sonnets.

l. 63, *those who died young:*

In Padua, where one sees the tombstones of many young men who died there (while they were students at the famous university), in Bologna, in Venice, in

Rome, everywhere, I stood as a pupil of death: stood before death's boundless knowledge and let myself be educated. You must also remember how they lie resting in the churches of Genoa and Verona, those youthful forms, not envious of our coming and going, fulfilled within themselves, as if in their death-spasms they had for the first time bitten into the fruit of life, and were now, forever, savoring its unfathomable sweetness.

(To Magda von Hattingberg, February 16, 1914)

l. 67, *Santa Maria Formosa:* A church in Venice, which Rilke had visited in 1911. The reference is to one of the commemorative tablets, inscribed with Latin verses, on the church walls—probably the one that reads (in translation): "I lived for others while life lasted; now, after death, / I have not perished, but in cold marble I live for myself. / I was Willem Hellemans. Flanders mourns me, / Adria sighs for me, poverty calls me. / Died October 16, 1593."

l. 86, *through both realms:*

Death is the *side of life* that is turned away from us and not illuminated. We must try to achieve the greatest possible consciousness of our existence, which is at home in *both these unlimited realms,* and *inexhaustibly nourished by both.* The true form of life extends through *both* regions, the blood of the mightiest circulation pulses through *both:* there *is neither a this-world nor an other-world, but only the great unity,* in which the "angels," those beings who surpass us, are at home.

(To Witold Hulewicz, November 13, 1925)

l. 93, *the lament for Linus:* This ritual lament is mentioned in the *Iliad,* as part of a scene that Hephaestus fashioned on the shield of Achilles:

Girls and young men, with carefree hearts and innocent laughter,
were carrying the honey-sweet grapes, piled up in wicker baskets;
in their midst, a boy performed the ancient music of yearning,
plucking his clear-toned lyre and singing the lament for Linus
with his lovely voice, while the others moved to the powerful rhythm,
their feet pounding in the dance, leaping and shouting for joy.

(*Iliad* 18, 567 ff.)

According to one myth, Linus was a poet who died young and was mourned by Apollo, his father. Other versions state that he was the greatest poet of all time and was killed by Apollo in a jealous rage; or that he invented music and was the teacher of Orpheus.

The Second Elegy (Duino, late January–early February, 1912)

l. 3, *Tobias:* A young man in the apocryphal Book of Tobit. The story portrays, in passing, the easy, casual contact between a human being and an angel: "And when he went to look for a man to accompany him to Rages, he found Raphael, who was an angel. But Tobias did not know that. . . . And when Tobias had prepared everything necessary for the journey, his father Tobit said, 'Go with this man, and may God prosper your journey, and may the angel of God go with you.' So they both departed, and the young man's dog went along with them."

Tobit 5:4, 16 (in the Codex Vaticanus)

l. 12, *pollen of the flowering godhead:*

What is shown so beautifully in the world of plants—how they make no secret of their secret, as if they knew that it would always be safe—is exactly what I experienced in front of the sculptures in Egypt and what I have always experienced, ever since, in front of Egyptian Things: this exposure of a secret that is so thoroughly secret, through and through, in every place, that there is no need to hide it. And perhaps everything phallic (as I *fore*-thought in the temple of Karnak, for I couldn't yet think it) is just a setting-forth of the human hidden secret in the sense of the open secret of Nature. I can't remember the smile of the Egyptian gods without thinking of the word "pollen."

(To Lou Andreas-Salomé, February 20, 1914)

ll. 16 f., mirrors, *which scoop up the beauty* . . . :

The case of the Portuguese nun is so wonderfully pure because she doesn't fling the streams of her emotion on into the imaginary, but rather, with infinite strength, conducts this magnificent feeling back into herself: enduring *it,* and nothing else. She grows old in the convent, very old; she doesn't become a saint, or even a good nun. It is repugnant to her exquisite tact to apply to God what, from the very beginning, had never been intended for him, and what the Comte de Chamilly could disdain. And yet it was almost impossible to stop the heroic onrush of this love before its final leap: almost impossible, with such a powerful emotion pulsing in her innermost being, not to become a saint. If she—that measurelessly glorious creature—had yielded for even a moment, she would have plunged into God like a stone into the sea. And if it had pleased God to attempt with her what he continually does with the angels, casting all their radiance back into them—: I am certain that, immediately, just as she was, in that sad convent, she would have become an angel, in her deepest self.

(To Annette Kolb, January 23, 1912)

l. 20, *like a perfume:* The reference in the original text is to ambergris or incense burning on a hot coal. (Ernst Zinn, editor's note, SW 1, 792)

ll. 56–59, *you touch so blissfully because . . . / you feel pure duration:* In a letter to Princess Marie about her translation of this Elegy into Italian, Rilke wrote, "I am concerned about this passage, which is so dear to me," and after quoting it, he continued:

> This is meant quite literally: that the place where the lover puts his hand is thereby withheld from passing away, from aging, from all the near-disintegration that is always occurring in our integral nature—that simply beneath his hand, this place *lasts, is.* It must be possible, just as literally, to make this clear in Italian; in any paraphrase it is simply lost. Don't you agree? And I think of these lines with a special joy in having been able to write them.
>
> (To Princess Marie von Thurn und Taxis-Hohenlohe, December 16, 1913)

l. 66, *Weren't you astonished:* This is said to the lovers.

ll. 66 f., *the caution of human gestures / on Attic gravestones:*

> Once, in Naples I think, in front of some ancient gravestone, it flashed through me that I should never touch people with stronger gestures than the ones depicted there. And I really think that sometimes I get so far as to express the whole impulse of my heart, without loss or destiny, by gently placing my hand on someone's shoulder. Wouldn't that, Lou, wouldn't that be the only progress conceivable within the "restraint" that you ask me to remember?
>
> (To Lou Andreas-Salomé, January 10, 1912)

> One of his most definite emotions was to marvel at Greek gravestones of the earliest period: how, upon them, the mutual touching, the resting of hand in hand, the coming of hand to shoulder, was so completely unpossessive. Indeed, it seemed as if in these lingering gestures (which no longer operated in the realm of fate) there was no trace of sadness about a future parting, since the hands were not troubled by any fear of ending or any presentiment of change, since nothing approached them but the long, pure solitude in which they were conscious of themselves as the images of two distant Things that gently come together in the unprovable inner depths of a mirror.
>
> (Notebook entry, early November 1910; quoted in
> F.W. Wodtke, *Rilke und Klopstock,* Kiel diss., 1948, p. 28)

The Third Elegy (The beginning—probably the whole first section—: Duino, January/February 1912; continued and completed in Paris, late autumn 1913)

ll. 26 ff., *Mother,* you *made him small . . . :*

> O night without objects. Dim, outward-facing window; doors that were carefully shut; arrangements from long ago, transmitted, believed in, never quite understood. Silence on the staircase, silence from adjoining rooms, silence high up on the

ceiling. O mother: you who are without an equal, who stood before all this silence, long ago in childhood. Who took it upon yourself to say: Don't be afraid; I'm here. Who in the night had the courage to *be* this silence for the child who was frightened, who was dying of fear. You strike a match, and already the noise is you. And you hold the lamp in front of you and say: I'm here; don't be afraid. And you put it down, slowly, and there is no doubt: you are there, you are the light around the familiar, intimate Things, which are there without afterthought, good and simple and sure. And when something moves restlessly in the wall, or creaks on the floor: you just smile, smile transparently against a bright background into the terrified face that looks at you, searching, as if you knew the secret of every half-sound, and everything were agreed and understood between you. Does any power equal your power among the lords of the earth? Look: kings lie and stare, and the teller of tales cannot distract them. Though they lie in the blissful arms of their favorite mistress, horror creeps over them and makes them palsied and impotent. But you come and keep the monstrosity behind you and are entirely in front of it; not like a curtain it can lift up here or there. No: as if you had caught up with it as soon as the child cried out for you. As if you had arrived far ahead of anything that might still happen, and had behind you only your hurrying-in, your eternal path, the flight of your love.

(*The Notebooks of Malte Laurids Brigge,* SW 6, 777 f.)

l. 82, *some confident daily task:*

In the long, complicated solitude in which *Malte* was written, I felt perfectly certain that the strength with which I paid for him originated to a great extent from certain evenings on Capri when nothing happened except that I sat near two elderly women and a girl and watched their needlework, and sometimes at the end was given an apple that one of them had peeled.

(To Lou Andreas-Salomé, January 10, 1912)

The Fourth Elegy (Munich, November 22–23, 1915)

l. 27, *It at least is full:* This passage was influenced by Heinrich von Kleist's short essay–dialogue "On the Marionette Theater" (1810), which Rilke called "a masterpiece that again and again fills me with astonishment" (To Princess Marie, December 13, 1913). Kleist's character Herr C., in comparing the marionette and the human dancer, says that the marionette has two advantages:

First of all, a negative one: that it would never behave affectedly. . . . In addition, these puppets have the advantage that they are antigravitational. They know nothing of the inertia of matter, that quality which is most resistant to the dance: because the force that lifts them into the air is greater than the force that binds them to the earth. . . . Puppets need the ground only in order to touch it lightly, like elves, and reanimate the swing of their limbs through this momentary stop. We humans need it to rest on so that we can recover from the exertion of the dance. This moment of rest is clearly no dance in itself; the best we can do with it is to make it as inconspicuous as possible.

l. 35, *the boy with the immovable brown eye:* Rilke's cousin, who died at the age of seven. See note to Sonnets to Orpheus II, 8, p. 338.

Beside this lady sat the small son of a female cousin, a boy about as old as I, but smaller and more delicate. His pale, slender neck rose out of a pleated ruff and disappeared beneath a long chin. His lips were thin and closed tightly, his nostrils trembled a bit, and only one of his beautiful dark-brown eyes was movable. It sometimes glanced peacefully and sadly in my direction, while the other eye remained pointed toward the same corner, as if it had been sold and was no longer being taken into account.

(The Notebooks of Malte Laurids Brigge, SW 6, 732)

*l. 59, *Angel and puppet:* In Kleist's essay the narrator goes on to say that

no matter how cleverly he might present his paradoxes, he would never make me believe that a mechanical marionette could contain more grace than there is in the structure of the human body.

Herr C. replied that, in fact, it is impossible for a human being to be anywhere near as graceful as a marionette. Only a god can equal inanimate matter in this respect. Here is the point where the two ends of the circular world meet.

I was more and more astonished, and didn't know what I should say to such extraordinary assertions.

It seemed, he said, as he took a pinch of snuff, that I hadn't read the third chapter of the Book of Genesis with sufficient attention; and if a man wasn't familiar with that first period of all human development, one could hardly expect to converse with him about later periods, and certainly not about the final ones.

I told him that I was well aware what disorders consciousness produces in the natural grace of a human being. [Here follow two anecdotes: the first about a young man who by becoming aware of his physical beauty loses it; the second about a pet bear who can easily parry the thrusts of the most accomplished swordsman.]

"Now, my dear fellow," said Herr C., "you are in possession of everything you need in order to understand the point I am making. We see that in the world of Nature, the dimmer and weaker intellect grows, the more radiantly and imperiously grace emerges. But just as a section drawn through two lines, considered from one given point, after passing through infinity, suddenly arrives on the other side of that point; or as the image in a concave mirror, after vanishing into infinity, suddenly reappears right in front of us: so grace too returns when knowledge has, as it were, gone through an infinity. Grace appears most purely in that human form in which consciousness is either nonexistent or infinite, i.e., in the marionette or in the god."

"Does that mean," I said, a bit bewildered, "that we must eat again of the Tree of Knowledge in order to fall back into the state of innocence?"

"Certainly," he answered. "That is the last chapter in the history of the world."

There is a complete translation of the essay in TLS, October 20, 1978.

l. 77, *a pure event:*

Extensive as the "external" world is, with all its sidereal distances it hardly bears comparison with the dimensions, the *depth-dimensions,* of our inner being, which does not even need the spaciousness of the universe to be, in itself, almost unlimited. . . . It seems to me more and more as though our ordinary consciousness inhabited the apex of a pyramid whose base in us (and, as it were, beneath us) broadens out to such an extent that the farther we are able to let ourselves down into it, the more completely do we appear to be included in the realities of earthly and, in the widest sense, *worldly,* existence, which are not dependent on time and space. From my earliest youth I have felt the intuition (and have also, as far as I could, lived by it) that at some deeper cross-section of this pyramid of consciousness, mere *being* could become an event, the inviolable presence and simultaneity of everything that we, on the upper, "normal," apex of self-consciousness, are permitted to experience only as entropy.

(To Nora Purtscher-Wydenbruck, August 11, 1924)

The Fifth Elegy (Muzot, February 14, 1922)

This Elegy, the last one to be written, replaced "Antistrophes."

I had intended to make a copy of the other three Elegies for you today, since it is already Sunday again. But now—imagine!—in a radiant afterstorm, another Elegy has been added, the "Saltimbanques" ["Acrobats"]. It is the most wonderful completion; only now does the circle of the Elegies seem to me truly closed. It is not added on as the Eleventh, but will be inserted (as the Fifth) before the "Hero-Elegy." Besides, the piece that previously stood there seemed to me, because of its different kind of structure, to be unjustified in that place, though beautiful as a poem. The new Elegy will replace it (and how!), and the supplanted poem will appear in the section of "Fragmentary Pieces" which, as a second part of the book of Elegies, will contain everything that is contemporaneous with them, all the poems that time, so to speak, destroyed before they could be born, or cut off in their development to such an extent that the broken edges show.—And so now the "Saltimbanques" too exist, who even from my very first year in Paris affected me so absolutely and have haunted me ever since.

(To Lou Andreas-Salomé, February 19, 1922)

Dedication, *Frau Hertha Koenig:* The owner of Picasso's large (84" × 90 $\frac{3}{8}$") 1905 painting *La Famille des Saltimbanques,* which she had bought in December 1914. The painting made such a deep impression on Rilke that he wrote to Frau Koenig asking if he could stay in her Munich home while she was away for the summer of 1915, so that he could live beneath the great work, "which gives me the courage for this request." The request was granted, and Rilke spent four months with the "glorious Picasso."

The other source for the Fifth Elegy is Rilke's experience, over a number of years, with a troupe of Parisian circus people.

In front of the Luxembourg Gardens, near the Panthéon, Père Rollin and his troupe have spread themselves out again. The same carpet is lying there, the same coats, thick winter overcoats, taken off and piled on top of a chair, leaving just enough room for the little boy, the old man's grandson, to come and sit down now and then during breaks. He still needs to, he is still just a beginner, and those headlong leaps out of high somersaults down onto the ground make his feet ache. He has a large face that can contain a great many tears, but sometimes they stand in his widened eyes almost out to the edge. Then he has to carry his head cautiously, like a too-full cup. It's not that he is sad, not at all; he wouldn't even notice it if he were; it is simply the pain that is crying, and he has to let it cry. In time it gets easier and finally it goes away. Father has long since forgotten what it was like, and Grandfather—oh it has been sixty years since he forgot, otherwise he wouldn't be so famous. But look, Père Rollin, who is so famous at all the fairs, doesn't "work" anymore. He doesn't lift the huge weights anymore, and though he was once the most eloquent of all, he says nothing now. He has been transferred to beating the drum. Touchingly patient, he stands with his too-far-gone athlete's face, its features now sagging into one another, as if a weight had been hung on each of them and had stretched it out. Dressed simply, a sky-blue knitted tie around his colossal neck, he has retired at the peak of his glory, in this coat, into this modest position upon which, so to speak, no glitter ever falls. But anyone among these young people who has ever seen him, knows that in those sleeves the famous muscles lie hidden whose slightest touch used to bring the weights leaping up into the air. The young people have clear memories of such a masterful performance, and they whisper a few words to their neighbors, show them where to look, and then the old man feels their eyes on him, and stands pensive, undefined, and respectful. That strength is still there, young people, he says to himself; it's not so available as it used to be, that's all; it has descended into the roots; it's still there somewhere, all of it. And it is really far too great for just beating a drum. He lays into it, and beats it much too often. Then his son-in-law has to whistle over to him and make a warning sign just when he is in the middle of one of his tirades. The old man stops, frightened; he tries to excuse himself with his heavy shoulders, and stands ceremoniously on his other leg. But already he has to be whistled at again. "Diable. Père! Père Rollin!" He has already hit the drum again and is hardly aware he has done it. He could go on drumming forever, they mustn't think he will get tired. But there, his daughter is speaking to him; quick-witted and strong, and with more brains than any of the others. She is the one who holds things together, it's a joy to see her in action. The son-in-law works well, no one can deny that, and he likes his work, it's a part of him. But she has it in her blood; you can see that. This is something she was born to. She's ready now: "Musique," she shouts. And the old man drums away like fourteen drummers. "Père Rollin, hey, Père Rollin," calls one of the spectators, and steps right up, recognizing him. But the old man only incidentally nods in response; it is a point of honor, his drumming, and he takes it seriously.

(July 14, 1907; SW 6, 1137 ff.)

l. 14, *the large capital D:* The five standing figures in Picasso's painting seem to be arranged in the shape of a D.

l. 17, *King Augustus the Strong* (1670–1733): King of Poland and elector of Saxony. To entertain his guests at the dinner table, he would, with one hand, crush together a thick pewter plate.

l. 64, *"Subrisio Saltat.":* "Acrobats' smile." During the printing of the Elegies, Rilke explained this in a note on the proof sheets:

> As if it were the label on a druggist's urn; abbreviation of *Subrisio Saltat(orum).* The labels on these receptacles almost always appear in abbreviated form.
>
> (Ernst Zinn, "Mitteilungen zu R. M. Rilkes Ausge-
> wählten Werken," in *Dichtung und Volkstum* 40, p. 132)

l. 92, *Madame Lamort:* Madame Death.

The Sixth Elegy (Begun at Duino, February/March 1912; lines 1–31: Ronda, January/February 1913; lines 42–44: Paris, late autumn 1913; lines 32–41: Muzot, February 9, 1922)

l. 8, *Like the god stepping into the swan:* Cf. "Leda" (*New Poems*).

l. 20, *Karnak:* Rilke spent two months in Egypt early in 1911 and was deeply moved by the incomprehensible temple-world of Karnak, which I saw the very first evening, and again yesterday, under a moon just beginning to wane: saw, saw, saw—my God, you pull yourself together and with all your might you try to believe your two focused eyes—and yet it begins above them, reaches out everywhere above and beyond them (only a god can cultivate such a field of vision) . . .

(To Clara Rilke, January 18, 1911)

In *the team of galloping horses* (l. 19) Rilke is referring to the battle scenes carved on the huge pillars in the Temple of Amun, which depict the pharaoh-generals in their conquering chariots.

l. 31, *Samson:* Judges 13:2, 24; 16:25 ff.

The Seventh Elegy (Muzot, February 7, 1922; lines 87–end: February 26, 1922)

ll. 2 ff., *you would cry out as purely as a bird:*

The bird is a creature that has a very special feeling of trust in the external world, as if she knew that she is one with its deepest mystery. That is why she sings in it as if she were singing within her own depths; that is why we so easily receive a birdcall into our own depths; we seem to be translating it without residue into our emotion; indeed, it can for a moment turn the whole world into inner space, because we feel that the bird does not distinguish between her heart and the world's.

(To Lou Andreas-Salomé, February 20, 1914)

l. 7, *the silent lover:*

> Learn, inner man, to look on your inner woman,
> the one attained from a thousand
> natures . . .

("Turning-point")

l. 36, *Don't think that fate is more than the density of childhood:*

What we call fate does not come to us from outside: it goes forth from within us.

(To Franz Xaver Kappus, August 12, 1904)

l. 37, *how often you outdistanced the man you loved:*

Woman has something of her very own, something suffered, accomplished, perfected. Man, who always had the excuse of being busy with more important matters, and who (let us say it frankly) was not at all adequately prepared for love, has not since antiquity (except for the saints) truly entered into love. The Trouba-

dours knew very well how little they could risk, and Dante, in whom the need
became great, only skirted around love with the huge arc of his gigantically evasive
poem. Everything else is, in this sense, derivative and second-rate. . . . You see,
after this very salutary interval I am expecting man, the man of the "new heartbeat," who for the time being is getting nowhere, to take upon himself, for the
next few thousand years, his own development into the lover—a long, difficult,
and, for him, completely new development. As for the woman—withdrawn into
the beautiful contour she has made for herself, she will probably find the composure to wait for this slow lover of hers, without getting bored and without too
much irony, and, when he arrives, to welcome him.

(To Annette Kolb, January 23, 1912)

l. 71, *in your endless vision:*

For the angel of the Elegies, all the towers and palaces of the past are existent
because they have long been invisible, and the still-standing towers and bridges of
our reality are *already* invisible, although still (for us) physically lasting. . . . All
the worlds in the universe are plunging into the invisible as into their next-deeper
reality; *a few stars intensify immediately and pass away in the infinite consciousness of
the angels—, others are entrusted to beings who slowly and laboriously transform them,
in whose terrors and delights they attain their next invisible realization. We,* let it be
emphasized once more, *we, in the sense of the Elegies, are these transformers of the
earth; our entire existence, the flights and plunges of our love, everything, qualifies us
for this task* (beside which there is, essentially, no other).

(To Witold Hulewicz, November 13, 1925)

l. 73, *Pillars:*

. . . a calyx column stands there, alone, a survivor, and you can't encompass it,
so far out beyond your life does it reach; only together with the night can you
somehow take it in, perceiving it with the stars, as a whole, and then for a second
it becomes human—a human experience.

(To Clara Rilke, January 18, 1911)

l. 73, *pylons:* "The monumental gateway to an Egyptian temple, usually
formed by two truncated pyramidal towers connected by a lower architec-
tural member containing the gate." (OED)

l. 73, *the Sphinx:* See note to the Tenth Elegy, ll. 73 ff., p. 333.

l. 84, *a woman in love—, oh alone at night by her window:* Cf. "Woman in Love"
(*New Poems*).

l. 87, *filled with departure:*

I sometimes wonder whether longing can't radiate out from someone so power-fully, like a storm, that nothing can come to him from the opposite direction. Perhaps William Blake has somewhere drawn that—?

(To Princess Marie von Thurn und Taxis-Hohenlohe, May 14, 1912)

The Eighth Elegy (Muzot, February 7/8, 1922)

Dedication, *Rudolf Kassner:* See note to "Turning-point," p. 313.

l. 2, *into the Open:*

You must understand the concept of the "Open," which I have tried to propose in this Elegy, as follows: The animal's degree of consciousness is such that it comes into the world without at every moment setting the world over against itself (as we do). The animal is *in* the world; we stand *in front of* the world because of the peculiar turn and heightening which our consciousness has taken. So by the "Open" it is not sky or air or space that is meant; they, too, for the human being who observes and judges, are "objects" and thus "opaque" and closed. The animal or the flower presumably *is* all that, without accounting for itself, and therefore has before itself and above itself that indescribably open freedom which has its (extremely fleeting) equivalents for us perhaps only in the first moments of love, when we see our own vastness in the person we love, and in the ecstatic surrender to God.

(To Lev P. Struve, February 25, 1926, in Maurice Betz,
Rilke in Frankreich: Erinnerungen—Briefe—Dokumente,
Wien / Leipzig / Zürich: Herbert Reichner Verlag, 1937)

ll. 2 f., *Only* our *eyes are turned / backward:* In describing his experience of "reaching the other side of Nature," Rilke uses the mirror image of this metaphor:

In general, he was able to notice how all objects yielded themselves to him more distantly and, at the same time, somehow more truly; this might have been due to his own vision, which was no longer directed forward and diluted in empty space; he was looking, as if over his shoulder, *backward* at Things, and their now completed existence took on a bold, sweet aftertaste, as though everything had been spiced with a trace of the blossom of parting.

("An Experience," 1913, SW 6, 1039)

l. 13, *fountain:* Here, as well as in the Ninth Elegy, l. 33, and Sonnets to Orpheus I, 8, l. 2, this is meant in its older sense of "a spring or source of water issuing from the earth and collecting in a basin, natural or artificial; also, the head-spring or source of a stream or river." (OED)

l. 53 ff., *Oh bliss of the* tiny *creature . . . :*

That a multitude of creatures which come from externally exposed seeds have *that* as their maternal body, that vast sensitive freedom—how much at home they must feel in it all their lives; in fact they do nothing but leap for joy in their mother's womb, like little John the Baptist; for this same space has both conceived them and brought them forth, and they never leave its security.

Until in the bird everything becomes a little more uneasy and cautious. The nest that Nature has given him is already a small maternal womb, which he only covers instead of wholly containing it. And suddenly, as if it were no longer safe enough outside, the wonderful maturing flees wholly into the darkness of the creature and emerges into the world only at a later turning-point, experiencing it as a second world and never entirely weaned from the conditions of the earlier, more intimate one.

(Rivalry between mother and world—)

(Notebook entry, February 20, 1914; SW 6, 1074 f.)

The Ninth Elegy (Lines 1–6a and 77–79: Duino, March 1912; the rest: Muzot, February 9, 1922)

l. 5, *escaping from fate:* Cf. Sonnets to Orpheus II, 12:

Und die verwandelte Daphne
will, seit sie lorbeern fühlt, daß du dich wandelst in Wind.

And the transfigured Daphne,
feeling herself become laurel, wants you to change into wind.

l. 7, *happiness:*

The reality of any joy in the world is indescribable; only in joy does creation take place (happiness, on the contrary, is only a promising, intelligible constellation of things already there); joy is a marvelous increasing of what exists, a pure addition out of nothingness. How superficially must happiness engage us, after all, if it can leave us time to think and worry about how long it will last. Joy is a moment, unobligated, timeless from the beginning, not to be held but also not to be truly lost again, since under its impact our being is changed chemically, so to speak, and does not only, as may be the case with happiness, savor and enjoy itself in a new mixture.

(To Ilse Erdmann, January 31, 1914)

ll. 9 f., *the heart, which / would exist in the laurel too:*

Hardly had she cried her breathless prayer
when a numbness seized her body; her soft breasts
were sealed in bark, her hair turned into leaves,
her arms into branches; her feet, which had been so quick,
plunged into earth and rooted her to the spot.
Only her shining grace was left. Apollo
still loved her; he reached out his hand to touch
the laurel trunk, and under the rough bark
could feel her heart still throbbing . . .

(Ovid, *Metamorphoses* I, 548 ff.)

ll. 32 ff., *house, / bridge . . . :*

Even for our grandparents a "house," a "well," a familiar tower, their very clothes, their coat, was infinitely more, infinitely more intimate; almost everything was a vessel in which they found what is human and added to the supply of what is human.

(To Witold Hulewicz, November 13, 1925)

l. 59, *the rope-maker in Rome or the potter along the Nile:*

I often wonder whether things unemphasized in themselves haven't exerted the most profound influence on my development and my work: the encounter with a dog; the hours I spent in Rome watching a rope-maker, who in his craft repeated one of the oldest gestures in the world—as did the potter in a little village on the Nile; standing beside his wheel was indescribably and in a most mysterious sense fruitful for me. . . .

(To Alfred Schaer, February 26, 1924)

l. 77, *our intimate companion, Death:*

We should not be afraid that our strength is insufficient to endure any experience of death, even the closest and most terrifying. Death is not *beyond* our strength; it is the measuring-line at the vessel's brim: we are *full* whenever we reach it— and being full means (for us) being heavy.—I am not saying that we should *love* death; but we should love life so generously, so without calculation and selection, that we involuntarily come to include, and to love, death too (life's averted half); this is in fact what always happens in the great turmoils of love, which cannot be held back or defined. Only because we exclude death, when it suddenly enters our thoughts, has it become more and more of a stranger to us; and because we have kept it a stranger, it has become our enemy. It is conceivable that it is infinitely closer to us than life itself—. What do we know of it?!

Prejudiced as we are against death, we do not manage to release it from all its distorted images. It is a *friend,* our deepest friend, perhaps the only one who can never be misled by our attitudes and vacillations—and this, you must understand, *not* in the sentimental-romantic sense of life's opposite, a denial of life: but our friend precisely when we most passionately, most vehemently, assent to being here, to living and working on earth, to Nature, to love. Life simultaneously says Yes and No. Death (I implore you to believe this!) is the true Yes-sayer. It says *only* Yes. In the presence of eternity.

(To Countess Margot Sizzo-Noris-Crouy, January 6, 1923)

The Tenth Elegy (Lines 1–12: Duino, January/February 1912; continued in Paris, late autumn 1913; new conclusion, lines 13–end: Muzot, February 11, 1922)

Lou, dear Lou, finally:

At this moment, Saturday, the eleventh of February, at 6 o'clock, I am putting down my pen after completing the last Elegy, the Tenth. The one (even then it was intended as the last one) whose first lines were already written in Duino: "Someday, emerging at last from the violent insight, / let me sing out jubilation and praise to assenting angels. . . ." What there was of it I once read to you; but only the first twelve lines have remained, all the rest is new and: yes, very, very glorious!—Imagine! I have been allowed to survive until this. Through everything. Miracle. Grace.

(To Lou Andreas-Salomé, February 11, 1922)

l. 20, *market of solace:*

I reproach all modern religions for having provided their believers with consolations and glossings-over of death, instead of giving them the means of coming to an understanding with it. With it and with its full, unmasked cruelty: this cruelty is so immense that it is precisely with *it* that the circle closes: it leads back into a mildness which is greater, purer, and more perfectly clear (all consolation is muddy!) than we have ever, even on the sweetest spring day, imagined mildness to be.

(To Countess Margot Sizzo-Noris-Crouy, January 6, 1923)

l. 21, *the church:*

The Christian experience enters less and less into consideration; the primordial God outweighs it infinitely. The idea that we are sinful and need to be redeemed as a prerequisite for God is more and more repugnant to a heart that has comprehended the earth. Sin is the most wonderfully roundabout path to God—but why should *they* go wandering who have never left him? The strong, inwardly quivering bridge of the Mediator has meaning only where the abyss between God and us is admitted—; but this very abyss is full of the darkness of God; and where someone experiences it, let him climb down and howl away inside it (that is more necessary than crossing it). Not until we can make even the abyss our dwelling-place will the paradise that we have sent on ahead of us turn around and will everything deeply and fervently of the here-and-now, which the Church embezzled for the Beyond, come back to us; then all the angels will decide, singing praises, in favor of the earth!

(To Ilse Jahr, February 22, 1923)

l. 62, *the vast landscape of Lament:*

The land of Lament, through which the elder Lament guides the dead youth, is *not* to be *identified* with Egypt, but is only, as it were, a reflection of the Nile-land in the desert clarity of the consciousness of the dead.

(To Witold Hulewicz, November 13, 1925)

ll. 73–88, *But as night approaches . . . / . . . the indescribable outline:*

Go look at the Head of Amenophis the Fourth in the Egyptian Museum in Berlin; feel, in this face, what it means to be opposite the infinite world and, within such a limited surface, through the intensified arrangement of a few features, to form a weight that can balance the whole universe. Couldn't one turn away from a starry night to find the same law blossoming in this face, the same grandeur, depth, inconceivableness? By looking at such Things I learned to see; and when, later, in Egypt, many of them stood before me, in their extreme individuality, insight into them poured over me in such waves that I lay for almost a whole night beneath the great Sphinx, as though I had been vomited out in front of it by my whole life.

You must realize that it is difficult to be alone there; it has become a public square; the most irrelevant foreigners are dragged in *en masse.* But I had skipped dinner; even the Arabs were sitting at a distance, around their fire; one of them noticed me, but I got away by buying two oranges from him; and then the darkness hid me. I had waited for nightfall out in the desert, then I came in slowly, the Sphinx at my back, figuring that the moon must already be rising (for there was a full moon) behind the nearest pyramid, which was glowing intensely in the sunset. And when at last I had come around it, not only was the moon already far up in the sky, but it was pouring out such a stream of brightness over the endless landscape that I had to dim its light with my hand, in order to find my way among the heaps of rubble and the excavations. I found a place to sit down on a slope near the Sphinx, opposite that gigantic form, and I lay there, wrapped in my coat, frightened, unspeakably taking part. I don't know whether my existence ever emerged so completely into consciousness as during those night hours when it lost

all value: for what was it in comparison with all that? The dimension in which
it moved had passed into darkness; everything that is world and existence was
happening on a higher plane, where a star and a god lingered in silent confrontation. You too can undoubtedly remember experiencing how the view of a landscape, of the sea, of the great star-flooded night inspires us with the sense of
connections and agreements beyond our understanding. It was precisely this that
I experienced, to the highest degree; here there arose an image built on the pattern
of the heavens; upon which thousands of years had had no effect aside from a little
contemptible decay; and most incredible of all was that this Thing had human
features (the fervently recognizable features of a human face) and that, in such an
exalted position, these features were enough. Ah, my dear— I said to myself, "This,
this, which we alternately thrust into fate and hold in our own hands: it must be
capable of some great significance if even in such surroundings its form can persist."
This face had taken on the customs of the universe; single parts of its gaze and
smile were damaged, but the rising and setting of the heavens had mirrored into
it emotions that had endured. From time to time I closed my eyes and, though
my heart was pounding, I reproached myself for not experiencing this deeply
enough; wasn't it necessary to reach places in my astonishment where I had never
been before? I said to myself, "Imagine, you could have been carried here blind-
folded and been set down on a slope in the deep, barely-stirring coolness—you
wouldn't have known where you were and you would have opened your eyes—"
And when I really did open them, dear God: it took quite a long time for them
to endure it, to take in this immense being, to achieve the mouth, the cheek, the
forehead, upon which moonlight and moonshadows passed from expression to
expression. How many times already had my eyes attempted this full cheek; it
rounded itself out so slowly that there seemed to be room up there for *more* places
than in our world. And then, as I gazed at it, I was suddenly, unexpectedly, taken
into its confidence, I received a knowledge of that cheek, experienced it in the
perfect emotion of its curve. For a few moments I didn't grasp what had happened.
Imagine: this: Behind the great projecting crown on the Sphinx's head, an owl had
flown up and had slowly, indescribably *audibly* in the pure depths of the night,
brushed the face with her faint flight: and now, upon my hearing, which had
grown very acute in the hours-long nocturnal silence, the outline of that cheek
was (as though by a miracle) inscribed.

(To Magda von Hattingberg, February 1, 1914)

l. 108, *hazel-trees:* Rilke had originally written "willows"; this was corrected
on the advice of a friend, who sent him a small handbook of trees and shrubs.

What a kind thought it was of yours to introduce me so clearly and thoroughly
to the elements of "catkinology" with your book and the explanatory letter; after
this there is no need for further or more exact information: I am convinced! So
(remarkably enough) there are no "hanging" willow catkins; and even if there

were some rare, tropical exception, I still would not be able to use it. The place in the poem that I wanted to check for factual accuracy stands or falls according to whether the reader can understand, with his *first* intuition, precisely this *falling* of the catkins; otherwise, the image loses all meaning. So the absolutely *typical* appearance of this inflorescence must be evoked—and I immediately realized from the very instructive illustrations in your little book that the shrub which, years ago, supplied me with the impression I have now used in my work must have been a hazelnut tree; whose branches are furnished most densely, *before* the leaves come out, with long, perpendicularly hanging catkins. So I know what I needed to know and have changed the text from "willow" to "hazel."

(To Elisabeth Aman-Volkart, June 1922)

APPENDIX to DUINO ELEGIES

[Fragment of an Elegy] (Duino, late January 1912)

Written between the First and Second Elegies.

[Original Version of the Tenth Elegy] (Lines 1–15: Duino, January / February 1912; continued in Paris, late in 1913)

Antistrophes (Lines 1–4: Venice, summer 1912; the rest: Muzot, February 9, 1922)

See note to the Fifth Elegy, p. 324.

Antistrophe: "The returning movement, from left to right, in Greek choruses and dances, answering to the previous movement of the strophe from right to left; hence, the lines of choral song recited during this movement." (OED)

from THE SONNETS TO ORPHEUS (1923)

These strange Sonnets were no intended or expected work; they appeared, often *many* in one day (the first part of the book was written in about three days), completely unexpectedly, in February of last year, when I was, moreover, about to gather myself for the continuation of those other poems—the great Duino Elegies. I could do nothing but submit, purely and obediently, to the dictation of this inner impulse; and I understood only little by little the relation of these verses to the figure of Vera Knoop, who died at the age of eighteen or nineteen, whom I hardly knew and saw only a few times in her life, when she was still a child, though with extraordinary attention and emotion. Without my arranging it this way (except for a few poems at the beginning of the second part, all the sonnets kept the chronological order of their appearance), it happened that only the next-to-last poems of both parts explicitly refer to Vera, address her, or evoke her figure.

This beautiful child, who had just begun to dance and attracted the attention of everyone who saw her, by the art of movement and transformation which was innate in her body and spirit,—unexpectedly declared to her mother that she no longer could or would dance (this happened just at the end of childhood). Her body changed, grew strangely heavy and massive, without losing its beautiful Slavic features; this was already the beginning of the mysterious glandular disease that later was to bring death so quickly. During the time that remained to her, Vera devoted herself to music; finally she only drew—as if the denied dance came forth from her ever more quietly, ever more discreetly.

(To Countess Margot Sizzo-Noris-Crouy, April 12, 1923)

Even to me, in the way they arose and imposed themselves on me, the Sonnets to Orpheus are perhaps the most mysterious, most enigmatic dictation I have ever endured and achieved; the whole first part was written down in a single breathless obedience, between the 2nd and 5th of February 1922, without one word being in doubt or having to be changed. And that at a time when I had braced myself for another great work and was already occupied with it. How can one help growing in reverence and endless gratitude, through such experiences in one's own existence.

(To Xaver von Moos, April 20, 1923)

I, 1 (Muzot, February 2/5, 1922)

l. 2, *Orpheus:* According to Greek mythology, the song of Orpheus was so enchantingly beautiful that the animals in the forest and even the rocks and trees gathered to listen.

During a visit to Sion (a town not far from Muzot), Rilke's friend Baladine Klossowska had discovered a postcard reproduction of Cima da Conegliano's pen-and-ink drawing (ca. 1500) of this scene: Orpheus sitting under a tree, playing a kind of viol, with a bird, a pair of deer, and a pair of rabbits intently listening. Madame Klossowska tacked the card to the wall opposite Rilke's desk and left it there on her departure from Muzot in November 1921.

I, 2 (Muzot, February 2/5, 1922)

l. 1, *almost a girl:* Cf. the end of "Turning-point":

> Look, inner man, at your inner girl.

The deepest experience of the creative artist is feminine, for it is an experience of conceiving and giving birth. The poet Obstfelder once wrote, speaking of the face of a stranger: "When he began to speak, it was as though a *woman* had taken a seat within him." It seems to me that every poet has had that experience in beginning to speak.

> (To a young woman, November 20, 1904)

I, 3 (Muzot, February 2/5, 1922)

ll. 3 f., *crossing / of heart-roads:* "The sanctuaries that stood at crossroads in classical antiquity were dedicated to sinister deities like Hecate, not to Apollo, the bright god of song." (Hermann Mörchen, *Rilkes Sonette an Orpheus*, Stuttgart: W. Kohlhammer Verlag, 1958, p. 66)

l. 13, *True singing:*

It is not only the *hearable* in music that is important (something can be pleasant to hear without being *true*). What is decisive for me, in all the arts, is not their outward appearance, not what is called the "beautiful"; but rather their deepest, most inner origin, the buried reality that calls forth this appearance.

> (To Princess Marie von Thurn und Taxis-Hohenlohe, November 17, 1912)

l. 14, *A gust inside the god. A wind:*

All in a few days, it was a nameless storm, a hurricane in the spirit (like that time at Duino), everything that was fiber and fabric in me cracked.

> (Ibid., February 11, 1922, just after the completion of the Elegies)

I, 5 (Muzot, February 2/5, 1922)

ll. 5 f., *When there is poetry, / it is Orpheus singing:*

Ultimately there is only *one* poet, that infinite one who makes himself felt, here and there through the ages, in a mind that can surrender to him.

> (To Nanny Wunderly-Volkart, July 29, 1920)

True art can issue only from a purely anonymous center.

> (To R.S., November 22, 1920)

I, 7 (Muzot, February 2/5, 1922)

I, 8 (Muzot, February 2/5, 1922)

I, 25 (Muzot, February 2/5, 1922)

Rilke's note: "To Vera." (In a copy of the Sonnets sent to Herr and Frau Leopold von Schlözer on May 30, 1923)
Vera Ouckama Knoop (1900–1919) was the young dancer to whom the whole cycle is dedicated. Her mother had recently sent Rilke a detailed, moving account of her illness and death.

II, 4 (Muzot, February 15/17, 1922)

Any "allusion," I am convinced, would contradict the indescribable *presence* of the poem. So in the unicorn no parallel with Christ is meant; rather, all love of the non-proven, the non-graspable, all belief in the value and reality of whatever our heart has through the centuries created and lifted up out of itself: that is what is praised in this creature. . . . The unicorn has ancient associations with virginity, which were continually honored during the Middle Ages. Therefore this sonnet states that, though it is nonexistent for the profane, it comes into being as soon as it appears in the "mirror" which the virgin holds up in front of it (see the tapestries of the 15th century) and "in her," as in a second mirror that is just as pure, just as mysterious.

(To Countess Margot Sizzo-Noris-Crouy, June 1, 1923)

II, 8 (Muzot, February 15/17, 1922)

l. 4, *the lamb with the talking scroll:* Rilke's note: "the lamb (in medieval paintings) which speaks only by means of a scroll with an inscription on it."

Dedication, *Egon von Rilke* (1873–1880): Youngest child of Rilke's father's brother.

I think of him often and keep returning to his image, which has remained indescribably moving to me. So much "childhood"—the sad and helpless side of childhood—is embodied for me in his form, in the ruff he wore, his little neck, his chin, his beautiful disfigured eyes. So I evoked him once more in connection with that eighth sonnet, which expresses transience, after he had already served, in the Notebooks of Malte Laurids Brigge, as the model for little Erik Brahe, who died in childhood.

(To Phia Rilke, January 24, 1924, in Carl Sieber, *René Rilke: Die Jugend Rainer Maria Rilkes*, Leipzig: Insel Verlag, 1932)

II, 13 (Muzot, February 15/17, 1922)

In a letter telling Vera's mother about the unexpected appearance of the second part of the Sonnets, Rilke wrote:

Today I am sending you only *one* of these sonnets, because, of the entire cycle, it is the one that is closest to me and ultimately the one that is the most valid.

(To Gertrud Ouckama Knoop, March 18, 1922)

The thirteenth sonnet of the second part is for me the most valid of all. It includes all the others, and it expresses *that* which, though it still far exceeds me, my purest, most final achievement would someday, in the midst of life, have to be.

(To Katharina Kippenberg, April 2, 1922)

l. 14, *cancel the count:*

Renunciation of love or fulfillment in love: *both* are wonderful and beyond compare only where the entire love-experience, with *all* its barely differentiable ecstasies, is allowed to occupy a central position: there (in the rapture of a few lovers or saints of *all* times and *all* religions) renunciation and completion are identical. Where the infinite *wholly* enters (whether as minus or plus), the ah so human number drops away, as the road that has now been completely traveled, —and what remains is the having arrived, *the being!*

(To Rudolf Bodländer, March 23, 1922)

II, 14 (Muzot, February 15/17, 1922)

II, 23 (Muzot, February 17/23, 1922)

Rilke's note: "To the reader."

l. 3, *a dog's imploring glance:*

Alas, I have not completely gotten over expecting the "nouvelle opération" to come from some human intervention; and yet, what's the use, since it is my lot to pass the human by, as it were, and arrive at the extreme limit, the edge of the earth, as recently in Cordova, when an ugly little bitch, in the last stage of pregnancy, came up to me. She was not a remarkable animal, was full of accidental puppies over whom no great fuss would be made; but since we were all alone, she came over to me, hard as it was for her, and raised her eyes enlarged by trouble and inwardness and sought my glance—and in her own there was truly everything that goes beyond the individual, to I don't know where, into the future or into the incomprehensible. The situation ended in her getting a lump of sugar from my coffee, but incidentally, oh so incidentally, we read Mass together, so to speak; in itself, the action was nothing but giving and receiving, yet the sense and the seriousness and our whole silent understanding was beyond all bounds.

(To Princess Marie von Thurn und Taxis-Hohenlohe, December 17, 1912)

II, 24 (Muzot, February 19/23, 1922)

l. 5, *Gods:*

Does it confuse you that I say God and gods and, for the sake of completeness, haunt you with these dogmatic words (as with a ghost), thinking that they will have some kind of meaning for you also? But grant, for a moment, that there is a realm beyond the senses. Let us agree that from his earliest beginnings man has created gods in whom just the deadly and menacing and destructive and terrifying elements in life were contained—its violence, its fury, its impersonal bewilderment —all tied together into one thick knot of malevolence: something alien to us, if you wish, but something which let us admit that we were aware of it, endured it, even acknowledged it for the sake of a sure, mysterious relationship and inclusion in it. For *we were this too;* only we didn't know what to do with this side of our experience; it was too large, too dangerous, too many-sided, it grew above and beyond us, into an excess of meaning; we found it impossible (what with the many demands of a life adapted to habit and achievement) to deal with these unwieldy and ungraspable forces; and so we agreed to place them outside us.—But since they were an overflow of our own being, its most powerful element, indeed were *too* powerful, were huge, violent, incomprehensible, often monstrous—: how could they not, concentrated in one place, exert an influence and ascendancy over us? And, remember, from the outside now. Couldn't the history of God be treated as an almost never-explored area of the human soul, one that has always been postponed, saved, and finally neglected . . . ?

And then, you see, the same thing happened with death. Experienced, yet not to be fully experienced by us in its reality, continually overshadowing us yet never truly acknowledged, forever violating and surpassing the meaning of life—it too was banished and expelled, so that it might not constantly interrupt us in the search for this meaning. Death, which is probably so close to us that the distance between it and the life-center inside us cannot be measured, now became something external, held farther away from us every day, a presence that lurked somewhere in the void, ready to pounce upon this person or that in its evil choice. More and more, the suspicion grew up against death that it was the contradiction, the adversary, the invisible opposite in the air, the force that makes all our joys wither, the perilous glass of our happiness, out of which we may be spilled at any moment. . . .

All this might still have made a kind of sense if we had been able to keep God and death at a distance, as mere ideas in the realm of the mind—: but Nature knew nothing of this banishment that we had somehow accomplished—when a tree blossoms, death as well as life blossoms in it, and the field is full of death, which from its reclining face sends forth a rich expression of life, and the animals move patiently from one to the other—and everywhere around us, death is at home, and it watches us out of the cracks in Things, and a rusty nail that sticks out of a plank somewhere, does nothing day and night except rejoice over death.

(To Lotte Hepner, November 8, 1915)

II, 28 (Muzot, February 19/23, 1922)

Rilke's note: "To Vera."

II, 29 (Muzot, February 19/23, 1922)

Rilke's note: "To a friend of Vera's."

l. 3, *like a bell:*

> With this bell tower the little island, in all its fervor, is attached to the past; the tower fixes the dates and dissolves them again, because ever since it was built it has been ringing out time and destiny over the lake, as though it included in itself the visibility of all the lives that have been surrendered here; as though again and again it were sending their transitoriness into space, invisibly, in the sonorous transformations of its notes.
>
> (To Countess Aline Dietrichstein, June 26, 1917)

l. 4, *What feeds upon your face:*

> O und die Nacht, die Nacht, wenn der Wind voller Weltraum
> uns am Angesicht zehrt— . . .
>
> *Oh and the night, the night, when the wind full of cosmic space*
> *Feeds upon our face—*
>
> (First Elegy, ll. 18 f.)

> Erkennst du mich, Luft, du, voll noch einst meiniger Orte?
>
> *Do you recognize me, Air, still full of places once mine?*
>
> (Sonnets to Orpheus II, 1, l. 12)

l. 10, *in their magic ring:*

> [The poet's] is a naive, aeolian soul, which is not ashamed to dwell where the senses intersect [*sich kreuzen*], and which lacks nothing, because these unfolded senses form a ring in which there are no gaps . . .
>
> ("The Books of a Woman in Love," 1907, SW 6, 1018)

UNCOLLECTED POEMS, 1923–1926

Imaginary Career (Schöneck, September 15, 1923)

[As once the wingèd energy of delight] (Muzot, mid-February 1924)

[What birds plunge through is not the intimate space] (Muzot, June 16, 1924)

Duration of Childhood (Ragaz, July 4 or 5, 1924)

Dedication, *E.M. :* Erika Mitterer. In May 1924, at the age of eighteen, she had sent Rilke two poems, initiating an extensive correspondence in verse, from which this poem and "Dove that ventured outside" are taken.

[World was in the face of the beloved] (Ragaz, mid-July 1924)

Palm (Muzot, around October 1, 1924)

Gravity (Muzot, October 5, 1924)

This "taking life heavily" that my books are filled with . . . means nothing (don't you agree?) but a taking according to true weight, and thus according to truth: an attempt to weigh Things by the carat of the heart, instead of by suspicion, happiness, or chance.

(To Rudolf Bodländer, March 13, 1922)

He who is solitary . . . can remember that all beauty in animals and plants is a silent, enduring form of love and yearning, and he can see animals, as he sees plants, patiently and willingly uniting and increasing and growing, not out of physical pleasure, not out of physical pain, but bowing to necessities that are greater than pleasure and pain, and more powerful than will and withstanding. If only human beings could more humbly receive this mystery—which the world is filled with, even in its smallest Things—, could bear it, endure it, more solemnly, feel how terribly heavy it is, instead of taking it lightly. If only they could be more reverent toward their own fruitfulness, which is essentially *one,* whether it is manifested as mental or physical . . .

(To Franz Xaver Kappus, July 16, 1903)

Women, in whom life lingers and dwells more immediately, more fruitfully, and more confidently, must surely have become riper and more human in their depths than light easygoing man, who is not pulled down beneath the surface of life by the weight of any bodily fruit . . .

(Ibid., May 14, 1904)

O Lacrimosa (Paris, May or June 1925)

O Lacrimosa: "O tearful [woman]." The epithet usually refers to Mary lamenting for Jesus at the foot of the cross.

Ernst Křenek (1900–   ): Austrian composer. His setting for this poem, for "high voice" with piano accompaniment, was published in 1926 as his opus 48.

You know that, in general, all attempts to surprise my verses with music have been unpleasant for me, since they are unrequested additions to something already complete in itself. It has rarely happened that I have written verses which seemed either suited for, or in need of, stirring up the musical element, out of a mutual center. With the little trilogy "O Lacrimosa" (which would like to pretend an imaginary Italian origin, in order to be still more anonymous than it already is—) something remarkable happened to me: this poem arose *for music*—, and then came the wish that sometime (sooner or later) it might be *your* music in which these impulses could find their fulfillment and their permanence.

(To Ernst Křenek, November 5, 1925)

[Now it is time that gods came walking out] (Muzot, mid-October 1925)

[Rose, oh pure contradiction] (In the testament of October 27, 1925)

At Rilke's request, these lines were carved on his gravestone in the churchyard of Raron.

Idol (First line: Paris, summer 1925; completed: Muzot, November, 1925)

Gong (Muzot, November 1925)

[Four Sketches] (Muzot, December 8, 1925)

The "little notebook with four prose-pieces" was sent to Monique Briod on December 10.

l. 8, *Rustic Chapel:* The small St. Anne chapel next to Muzot.

. . . the abandoned rustic chapel which I take care of; because of its decrepitude, no mass is read in it any longer, and so it is now given back to all the gods and is always filled with open simple homage.

(To Clara Rilke, April 23, 1923)

l. 17, *"Farfallettina":* Little butterfly.

l. 26, *bilboquet:* A wooden toy, consisting of a cord with a ball on one end and a stick on the other; the object of the game is to catch the ball on the spike-end of the stick.

Elegy (Muzot, June 8, 1926)

Dedication, *Marina Tsvetayeva* (1892–1941): One of the great modern Russian poets. She and Rilke never met in person, but they exchanged a number of intense letters during the spring and summer of 1926. Her long elegy, "Novo-godnee" ("For the New Year"), written early in 1927, describes the impact of Rilke's death on her.

l. 18, *Kom Ombo:* Probably a stop on Rilke's trip to Egypt in 1911.

l. 20, *marks as a signal on the doors:* Cf. Exodus 12:7, 13.

[Dove that ventured outside] (Ragaz, August 24, 1926)

Written to Erika Mitterer after she had undergone a serious operation.

> That a person who through the horrible obstructions of those years had felt himself split to the very depths of his soul, into a Once and an irreconcilable, dying Now: that such a person should experience the grace of perceiving how in yet more mysterious depths, beneath this torn-open split, the continuity of his work and of his spirit was being re-established—this seems to me more than just a private event. For with it, a measure is given for the inexhaustible stratification of our nature; and many people who, for one reason or another, believe that they have been torn apart, might draw special comfort from this example of continuability. (The thought occurs to me that this comfort too may somehow have entered into the achievement of the great Elegies, so that they express themselves more completely than they could have done without endangerment and rescue.)
>
> (To Arthur Fischer-Colbrie, December 18, 1925)

AFTERWORD

R.M.R. in memoriam

You honored what is heaviest. You knew
the pull of earth; and you were pulled apart
by the dark angel's voice that seemed as though
it called from somewhere outside your own heart.
You chose the tao of suffering, which led
past every common joy, past the humane
fulfillments, and delivered you instead
to cancer, in a Nessus'-shirt of pain.

Now, breathless, weightless, you can only fall
into yourself: the invisible, unheard
center that you sang. Ahead of all
parting, you might lean back against your chair
and see a sun-lit garden path. A bird
might whistle through you, in the cool morning air.

ACKNOWLEDGMENTS

I would like to thank Michael André Bernstein, Chana Bloch, Jonathan Galassi (my editor), W. S. Merwin, and Robert Pinsky for their many valuable comments. A letter from Ralph Freedman persuaded me to include the two sections of early poems. I had help with the German of several of the uncollected poems from Jutta Hahne, and with the French prose-poems from my brother, to whom this book is dedicated, with love.

During the months when I was studying the Elegies, I lived in close daily contact with Jacob Steiner's great line-by-line commentary, *Rilkes Duineser Elegien* (Bern/München: Francke Verlag, 1962), and found it an almost never-failing source of illumination.

Finally, I must acknowledge my debt to the work of J. B. Leishman, M. D. Herter Norton, and C. F. MacIntyre, and to the Young, Boney, Guerne, and Gaspar versions of the *Elegies,* the Poulin *Elegies and Sonnets,* the Betz *Cahiers de M. L. Brigge,* and miscellaneous translations by Randall Jarrell, Robert Lowell, Robert Bly, W. D. Snodgrass, and Rika Lesser.

And my greatest debt: to Vicki.

INDEX OF TITLES AND FIRST LINES
(German and French)

INDEX OF TITLES AND FIRST LINES
(English)

ABOUT THE AUTHOR

STEPHEN MITCHELL was born in Brooklyn, New York, in 1943, studied at Amherst and Yale, and now lives in Berkeley, California. His previous books include *Dropping Ashes on the Buddha: The Teaching of Zen Master Seung Sahn* (Grove Press, 1976); *Into the Whirlwind: A Translation of the Book of Job* (Doubleday, 1979); and *Points of Departure: Poems by Dan Pagis* (Jewish Publication Society of America, 1981).